MTTC 59 Special Education – Emotionally Impaired
Teacher Certification Exam

By: Sharon Wynne, M.S
Southern Connecticut State University

"And, while there's no reason yet to panic, I think it's only prudent that we make preparations to panic."

XAMonline, INC.
Boston

To obtain permission(s) to use the material from this work for any purpose including workshops or seminars, please submit a written request to:

XAMonline, Inc.
21 Orient Ave.
Melrose, MA 02176
Toll Free 1-800-509-4128
Email: info@xamonline.com
Web www.xamonline.com
Fax: 1-781-662-9268

Library of Congress Cataloging-in-Publication Data

Wynne, Sharon A. Special Education – Emotionally Impaired Teacher Certification / Sharon A. Wynne
ISBN 978-1-58197-973-2
1. Special Education – Emotionally Impaired   2. Study Guides.
3. MTTC   4. Teachers' Certification & Licensure.   5. Careers

Disclaimer:
The opinions expressed in this publication are the sole works of XAMonline and were created independently from the National Education Association, Educational Testing Service, or any State Department of Education, National Evaluation Systems or other testing affiliates.

Between the time of publication and printing, state specific standards as well as testing formats and website information may change that are not included in part or in whole within this product. Sample test questions are developed by XAMonline and reflect similar content as on real tests; however, they are not former tests. XAMonline assembles content that aligns with state standards but makes no claims nor guarantees teacher candidates a passing score. Numerical scores are determined by testing companies such as NES or ETS and then are compared with individual state standards. A passing score varies from state to state.

Printed in the United States of America   œ-1

MTTC: Special Education – Emotionally Impaired
ISBN: 978-1-58197-973-2

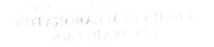

About the Test

The purpose of the Michigan Test for Teacher Certification (MTTC) is to identify educator candidates who have the knowledge, skills, and understanding an entry-level teacher needs in order to teach effectively in a Michigan classroom.

Test Format
The test is a criterion-referenced test with about 100 multiple choice questions that have four options as possible answers.

Subarea	Approximate Percentage of Questions on Test
Human Development and the Educational Implications of Emotional Impairments	21%
Evaluation, Assessment, and Individualized Education Programs (IEPs)	21%
Behavior Management	18%
Methodology and Instruction	22%
Program and Service Delivery	18%

Scoring
A scaled score of 220 represents a passing score.

Locations, Dates, and Fees
For current dates, locations, and fees please go to http://www.mttc.nesinc.com/

Table of Contents

Great Study and Testing Tips!

What to study in order to prepare for the subject assessments is the focus of this study guide but equally important is *how* you study.

You can increase your chances of truly mastering the information by taking some simple, but effective steps.

Study Tips:

1. <u>Some foods aid the learning process.</u> Foods such as milk, nuts, seeds, rice, and oats help your study efforts by releasing natural memory enhancers called CCKs (*cholecystokinin*) composed of *tryptophan*, *choline*, and *phenylalanine*. All of these chemicals enhance the neurotransmitters associated with memory. Before studying, try a light, protein-rich meal of eggs, turkey, and fish. All of these foods release the memory enhancing chemicals. The better the connections, the more you comprehend.

Likewise, before you take a test, stick to a light snack of energy boosting and relaxing foods. A glass of milk, a piece of fruit, or some peanuts all release various memory-boosting chemicals and help you to relax and focus on the subject at hand.

2. <u>Learn to take great notes.</u> A by-product of our modern culture is that we have grown accustomed to getting our information in short doses (i.e.,TV news sound bites or USA Today style newspaper articles).

Consequently, we've subconsciously trained ourselves to assimilate information better in <u>neat little packages</u>. If your notes are scrawled all over the paper, it fragments the flow of the information. Strive for clarity. Newspapers use a standard format to achieve clarity. Your notes can be much clearer through use of proper formatting. A very effective format is called the <u>*"Cornell Method."*</u>

Take a sheet of loose-leaf lined notebook paper and draw a line all the way down the paper about 1-2" from the left-hand edge.

Draw another line across the width of the paper about 1-2" up from the bottom. Repeat this process on the reverse side of the page.

Look at the highly effective result. You have ample room for notes, a left hand margin for special emphasis items or inserting supplementary data from the textbook, a large area at the bottom for a brief summary, and a little rectangular space for just about anything you want.

3. <u>Get the concept then the details.</u> Too often we focus on the details and don't gather an understanding of the concept. However, if you simply memorize only dates, places, or names, you may well miss the whole point of the subject. A key way to understand things is to put them in your own words. If you are working from a textbook, automatically summarize each paragraph in your mind. If you are outlining text, don't simply copy the author's words.

Rephrase them in your own words. You remember your own thoughts and words much better than someone else's, and subconsciously tend to associate the important details to the core concepts.

4. <u>Ask Why?</u> Pull apart written material paragraph by paragraph and don't forget the captions under the illustrations.

Example: If the heading is "Stream Erosion", flip it around to read "Why do streams erode?" Then answer the question.

If you train your mind to think in a series of questions and answers, not only will you learn more, but it also helps to lessen the test anxiety because you are used to answering questions.

5. <u>Read for reinforcement and future needs.</u> Even if you only have 10 minutes, put your notes or a book in your hand. Your mind is similar to a computer; you have to input data in order to have it processed. *By reading, you are creating the neural connections for future retrieval.* The more times you read something, the more you reinforce the learning of ideas.

Even if you don't fully understand something on the first pass, *your mind stores much of the material for later recall.*

6. <u>Relax to learn so go into exile.</u> Our bodies respond to an inner clock called biorhythms. Burning the midnight oil works well for some people, but not everyone.

If possible, set aside a particular place to study that is free of distractions. Shut off the television, cell phone, pager and exile your friends and family during your study period.

If you really are bothered by silence, try background music. Light classical music at a low volume has been shown to aid in concentration over other types of music.

Music that evokes pleasant emotions without lyrics are highly suggested. It relaxes you.

7. <u>Use arrows not highlighters.</u> At best, it's difficult to read a page full of yellow, pink, blue, and green streaks.
Try staring at a neon sign for a while and you'll soon see my point, the horde of colors obscure the message.

8. <u>Budget your study time</u>. Although you shouldn't ignore any of the material, *allocate your available study time in the same ratio that topics may appear on the test.*

Testing Tips:

1. <u>Get smart, play dumb.</u> **Don't read anything into the question.** Don't make an assumption that the test writer is looking for something else than what is asked. Stick to the question as written and don't read extra things into it.

2. <u>Read the question and all the choices *twice* before answering the</u> <u>question.</u> You may miss something by not carefully reading. Read and then re-reading both the question and the answer.

If you really don't have a clue as to the right answer, leave it blank on the first time through. Go on to the other questions, as they may provide a clue as to how to answer the skipped questions.

If later on you still can't answer the skipped questions . . . ***Guess.***
The only penalty for guessing is that you *might* get it wrong. Only one thing is certain, if you don't put anything down you will get it wrong!

3. <u>Turn the question into a statement.</u> Look at the way the questions are worded. The syntax of the question usually provides a clue. Does it seem more familiar as a statement rather than as a question? Does it sound strange?

By turning a question into a statement you may be able to spot an answer. If it sounds right it may also trigger memories of material you have read.

4. <u>Look for hidden clues.</u> It's actually very difficult to compose multiple-foil (choice) questions without giving away part of the answer in the options presented.

In most multiple-choice questions you can often readily eliminate one or two of the potential answers. This leaves you with only two real possibilities and automatically your odds go to fifty-fifty for very little work.

5. <u>Trust your instincts.</u> For every fact that you have read, you subconsciously retain something of that knowledge. On questions that you aren't really certain about, go with your basic instincts. **Your first impression on how to answer a question is usually correct.**

6. <u>Mark your answers directly on the test booklet.</u> Don't bother trying to fill in the optical scan sheet on the first pass through the test.

7. <u>Watch the clock</u>! You have a set amount of time to answer the questions. Don't get bogged down trying to answer a single question at the expense of 10 questions you can more readily answer.

COMPETENCY 1.0 HUMAN DEVELOPMENT AND THE EDUCATIONAL IMPLICATIONS OF EMOTIONAL IMPAIRMENTS

Skill 1.1 Demonstrate knowledge of human development and behavior.

Normality in child behavior is influenced by society's attitudes and cultural beliefs about what is normal for children (e.g., The motto for the Victorian era was "Children should be seen and not heard"). However, criteria for what is "normal" involves consideration of these questions:

- *Is the behavior age appropriate?* An occasional tantrum may be expected for a toddler, but is not typical for a high school student.
- *Is the behavior pathological in itself?* Drug or alcohol use would be harmful to children, regardless of how many engage in it.
- *How persistent is the problem?* A kindergarten student initially may be afraid to go to school. However, if the fear continued into first or second grade, then the problem would be considered persistent.
- *How severe is the behavior?* –Self-injurious, cruel, and extremely destructive behaviors, would be examples of behaviors that require intervention.
- *How often does the behavior occur?* –An occasional tantrum in a young child or a brief mood of depression in an adolescent would not be considered problematic. However, if the behaviors occur frequently, that behavior would not be characteristic of normal child development.
- *Do several problem behaviors occur as a group?* – Clusters of behaviors, especially severe behaviors that occur together, may be indicative of a serious problem such as schizophrenia.
- *Is the behavior sex-appropriate?* Cultural and societal attitudes towards gender change over time. While attitudes towards younger boys playing with dolls or girls preferring sports to dolls have relaxed, children eventually are expected as adults to conform to the expected behaviors for males and females.

Certain stages of child development have their own sets of problems, and it should be kept in mind that short-term undesirable behaviors can and will occur over these stages. Child development is also a continuum, and children may manifest these problem behaviors somewhat earlier or later than their peers.

Problem Behaviors Associated with Childhood Stages of Development

(See Gelfand et al., p. 120)

Toddler (1-3)	Preschool (3-5)	Elementary (6-10)	Early Adolescence	Adolescent (15-18)
Temper tantrums	Temper tantrums	Temper tantrums	Temper tantrums	--
Refuses to do things when asked	Refuses to do things when asked	--	--	--
Demands constant attention	Demands constant attention	--	--	--
Over activity	Over activity	Over activity	--	--
Specific fears	Specific fears	--	--	--
--	Oversensitivity	Oversensitivity	--	--
Inattentive	--	--	--	--
--	Lying	Lying	--	--
--	--	Jealousy	Jealousy	--
--	Negativism	--	--	--
--	--	School achievement problems	School achievement problems	School achievement problems
--	--	Excessive reserve	Excessive reserve	--
--	--	--	Moodiness	--
--	--	--	--	Substance abuse
--	--	--	--	Truancy or skipping school
--	--	--	--	Minor law violations (i.e., stealing, trespassing)
--	--	--	--	Sexual misconduct

Skill 1.2   Demonstrate knowledge of major theories of educational psychology as they relate to emotional impairments.

The teacher of special needs students must have a thorough understanding of the content matter that is taught from kindergarten through twelfth grade for two important reasons. First, she will be instructing students whose functioning abilities can span all grade levels, and second, she must be able to use specialized instruction in order to teach content in required subject areas. The actual content and sequence of concepts learners with special needs that must be taught are the same as those used with the regular student. However, special learning strategies, techniques, and approaches must be utilized. For instance, task sequences must be analyzed and broken down into a hierarchy of subskills for students with learning difficulties. Often it helps when the content is made meaningful to learners and when skills are taught in a firsthand, functional manner.

The content areas of reading such as vocabulary, decoding skills, comprehension, math like fact mastery, computational operations, reasoning, verbal problem solving, language arts, and social skills training are broad in scope. They entail a specific instructional sequence that all learners must follow and are basic to being able to succeed in other subject areas. However, being able to plan, predict, diagnose, and assess the instructional content appropriate for individual learners necessitates a full and complete understanding by the special educator of sequential skills hierarchies and the development of learners with special needs.

Jean Piaget recognized the importance of structuring thinking in order to learn. According to his theory, each person approaches the learning task with an existing cognitive structure or schemata. The learner adapts to the environment and structures new knowledge in two complimentary ways: assimilation and accommodation.

Assimilation: Learners incorporate new experiences into their already existing cognitive structure. New experiences provide practice and strengthen their existing cognitive structures. For example, a child learns that balls are objects, which can be grasped and thrown.

Accommodation: Learners focus on the new gestures of a learning task, thereby changing or modifying their cognitive structures. As the child grasps balls of differing sizes, textures, and firmness, he or she learns that balls are different, and that some objects that look like balls cannot be thrown. The cognitive stages outlined by Piaget are:

1. <u>Sensorimotor intelligence</u> - birth to 18 months. The child differentiates himself or herself from the rest of the world and learns object constancy.

2. <u>Preoperational thought, representational thinking</u> - 18 months to 4-5 years. Private symbols and representations precede language, which begins during this stage. Children are still unable to take another person's view of things.

3. <u>Preoperational thought, intuitional thinking -</u> 5 - 7 years. The child begins to understand conservation of amount, quantity, number, and weight. He/she can attend to more than one aspect of an object at one time and begins to understand the reversibility of some operations, though he or she cannot explain personal conclusions.

4. <u>Concrete operation</u> - 7 to 11 years. The child organizes his or her perceptions and symbols and becomes able to classify and categorize along several dimensions at the same time.

5. <u>Formal operations -</u> 12 years through adulthood. The learner can deal with abstractions, hypothetical situations, and logical thinking.

Jerome Bruner, like Jean Piaget, believed that knowledge developed in an evolutionary Sequence. Bruner suggested that knowledge is represented in three forms; enactive, iconic, and symbolic.

1. Knowledge is initially acquired at the enactive or concrete action level. It is demonstrated through action like throwing a ball or by direct manipulation such as bundling sticks in groups of ten.

2. The information that is digested and recorded at the enactive stage is recalled in a mental image or seen in a visual representation at the iconic level. Knowledge at this level has a visual or perceptual organization; it is communicated by pictures and forms. An example of iconic knowledge is the mental manipulation of images of concrete objects such as solving single verbal problems, picturing ones, tens, and hundreds units.

3. Finally, the information reaches the symbolic level through spoken words of written symbols. This type of knowledge represents information about concrete and semi concrete situations in a symbolic manner. "The use of symbols allows for easy problem-solving actions" (Thornton, Tucker, Dossey, & Bazik, 1983, p. 86). The highest and most formalized level is symbolic knowledge. An example would be the use of symbols in the form of numerals to calculate the answer to a specified mathematical operation.

Both Piaget and Bruner dealt with language as it related to cognitive growth. Bruner theorized that once children begin to acquire language, they use it further shape their thoughts. Piaget proposed that language is acquired as children take in or assimilate the language in the environment, and then modify it with their knowledge and ideas. What language is assimilated is directly influenced by each child's reasoning processes. Children's language becomes more sophisticated with age because they are able to understand more complex language, and thus modify it with more complex ideas. The primary educational implication for the developmental learning movement through theorized stages is its element of predictability. Some students move through developmental stages or levels at a slower or faster pace than others. What students learn depends on their existing cognitive structure, language development, and the experiences and knowledge that they bring to the learning situation. It is important that entry level skills be diagnosed, and that students be able to use the knowledge, experiences, and skills they already possess in learning situations.

Students with disabilities and who take medications often experience medication side effects that can impact their behavior and educational development. For example, teachers may perceive the child is unmotivated or drowsy, and not fully understand the cognitive effects that medications can have on a child. Some medications may impair concentration, which can lead to poor processing ability, lower alertness, and cause drowsiness and hyperactivity. Students who take several medications may have an increased risk of behavioral and cognitive side effects. The student's parents should let the school know when the student is beginning or changing medication so teachers can look out for possible side effects.

Antidepressants-There are three different classes of antidepressants that students can take. One type is called the selective serotonin-reuptake inhibitors (SSRIs). The SSRIs block certain receptors from absorbing serotonin. Over time, SSRIs may cause changes in brain chemistry. The side effects of SSRIs include dry mouth, insomnia or restless sleep, increased sweating, and nausea. It can also cause mood swings in people with bipolar disorders.

A second type of antidepressant that may be used is the tricyclic antidepressants. They are considered good for treating depression and obsessive-compulsive behavior. They cause similar side effects to the SSRIs and may also cause sedation, tremor, seizures, dry mouth, light sensitivity, and mood swings in people with bipolar disorders.

A third type of antidepressant is the monoamine oxidase inhibitors (MAOIs). They are not as widely used as the other two types because many have unpleasant and life-threatening interactions with many other drugs, including common over-the-counter medications. People taking MAOIs must also follow a special diet, because these medications interact with many foods. The list of foods to avoid includes chocolate, aged cheeses, and more.

Stimulants- often prescribed to help with attention deficit disorder and attention deficit hyperactivity disorder. The drugs can have side effects including agitation, restlessness, aggressive behavior, dizziness, insomnia, headache, and tremors.

Anti-Anxiety Medication-In severe cases of anxiety an anti-anxiety medication (tranquilizer) may be prescribed. Most tranquilizers have a potential for addiction and abuse. They tend to be sedating and can cause a variety of unpleasant side effects including blurred vision, confusion, sleepiness, and tremors.

If educators are aware of the types of medication that their students are taking, along with the myriad of side effects, they will be able to better respond if the side effects of the medication change their students behavior, response rate, and attention span.

Skill 1.3 **Demonstrate knowledge of the characteristics of students with special needs, the types of impairments or disabilities, and the ways in which various types of impairments or disabilities influence human development.**

Students with mild learning, intellectual, and behavior disabilities are identifiable by academic and social behaviors that deviate from those of their classmates. Characteristics common to students with these mild disabilities were identified by Henley, Ramsey, and Algozzine (1993). They are clustered under psychological, educational, and social characteristics as follows:

1. Psychological Characteristics
   - Mild disability undetected until beginning school years.
   - Cause of mild disability is difficult to detect.
   - Physical appearance the same as students in full time regular education.
   - Poor self-concept.

2. Educational Characteristics
   - Lack of interest in schoolwork.
   - Prefer concrete rather an abstract lessons.
   - Weak listening skills.
   - Low achievement.
   - Limited verbal and/or writing skills.
   - Right hemisphere preference in learning activities
   - Respond better to active rather than passive learning tasks.
   - Have areas of talent or ability that are overlooked by teachers.
   - Prefer to receive special help in regular classroom.
   - Higher dropout rate than regular education students.
   - Achieve in accordance with teacher expectations.
   - Require modifications in classroom instruction.
   - Are distractible.

3.   Social Characteristics
- Experience friction when interacting with others.
- Function better outside of school than in school.
- Need adult approval.
- Have difficulties finding and maintaining employment after school.
- Stereotyped by others.
- Behavior problems exhibited.

Generalities can be made about this population. First, students with mild intellectual disabilities, learning disabilities, and behavior disorders are the largest subgroup of students receiving special education services. The total group of students with mild intellectual, learning, and behavior disabilities comprise about half of the total special education population.

Second, they are served during their school-aged years. Mild disabilities are often unrecognized before and after school years.

Third, no nationally accepted criteria exist; therefore, the categories of mental retardation, learning disabilities, and behavior disorders are unreliable. Each state has developed its own criteria, and so a student may be eligible for special education service delivery in one state and not necessarily so in another. Regardless, while many students with mild disabilities receive special education services, there are some who are incorrectly identified as having a mild disability and others who have a mild disability are overlooked.

Last, students with mild disabilities are most likely to be placed in the regular classroom and in resource services. Effective collaboration between general and special education teachers is vital.

STATE CHARACTERISTICS THAT DIFFERENTIATE MILD FROM MODERATE AND SEVERE DISABILITIES

Common characteristics of students with mild intellectual, learning, and behavioral disabilities are listed in clusters in Competency/Skills 2. These clusters contain characteristics representative of psychological, educational, and social behaviors. The aforementioned characteristics and behaviors are discussed below, with comparisons given between mild and moderate to severe.

Mild Disabilities-The psychological cluster is characterized by items that refer to the fact the disability is difficult to detect. Typically, a mild disability remains undetected until the child begins school. The condition surfaces when learning demands are placed upon the individual and the person is unable to produce accordingly. The physical appearance of the student is the same as that of students in full-time regular education, and the causes of the mild disability are usually unknown. A poor self-concept often results.

Since the problem generally becomes apparent first in the educational setting, characteristics reflective of educational behaviors are common. The child is a low achiever and exhibits an obvious lack of interest in schoolwork. The preference for concrete rather than abstract lessons reflects his or her need for better understanding for what is being taught.

These students respond better to active rather than passive learning tasks. Teachers often observe weak listening skills and limited verbal and/or writing skills. These students may be distractible. Unfortunately, teachers sometimes overlook talents and abilities that many of these students possess. These students are often self-conscious in classroom instruction in order for learning to occur. They require modifications in classroom instruction in order for learning to occur. Due to the difficulties these students experience in school, they often have a higher dropout rate than regular education students.

Socially, students with mild disabilities sometimes experience friction when interacting with others and demonstrate problem behaviors in the classroom. They show a need for adult approval and are often stereotyped by others. During school years most function better outside of school than in school. However, following school years many experience difficulties finding and maintaining employment.

Moderate to Severe Disabilities-The characteristics given for the psychological cluster outlined for students with mild disabilities contrasts from those with more severe disabilities. In general, more severe disabilities are detected at birth and have known etiologies. Appearance is often different from those with mild, or no discernable, disabilities.

Educationally, those with moderate disabilities are generally able to acquire functional, consumer skills. Having a reduced class size and a structured learning schedule are helpful. Use of hands-on concrete learning materials and experiences are essential. Students with severe disabilities are usually taught adaptive skills to heighten functioning in latter years.

Socially, students with moderate disabilities function more in line with mental age than with chronological age. Many have one or a few friends, and are able to effectively participate in group activities. Those with severe disabilities are more limited in social participation.

IDENTIFY CHARACTERISTICS OF STUDENTS WITH LEARNING DISABLITIES

The individual with a specific learning disability exhibits a discrepancy between achievement and potential. Deficiencies can occur within a spectrum of skill areas. The youngster typically shows a low level of performance in one of several skill areas. Rarely is a uniform pattern of academic development demonstrated. The cause of delayed academic performance is not due to limited cognitive ability, sensory and physical impairments, emotional disturbances, or environmental deprivation. The child or youth with a disability is recognized by:

1. Hyperactivity: a rate of motor activity higher than normal.
2. Perceptual difficulties: visual, auditory, and haptic perceptual problems.
3. Perceptual-motor impairments: poor integration of visual and motor systems, often affecting fine motor coordination.
4. General coordination deficits: clumsiness in physical activities.
5. Disorders of memory and thinking: memory deficits, trouble with problem solving, concept formation, and association. Poor awareness of own metacognitive skills (learning strategies).
6. Disorders of attention: short attention span, distractibility, lack of selective attention, perseveration.
7. Emotional liability: frequent changes in mood, low tolerance or frustration, sensitive to others.
8. Impulsiveness: acts before considering consequences, poor impulse control, often followed by remorsefulness.
9. Academic problems in reading, math, writing, or spelling: significant discrepancies in ability levels.
10. Disorders in speech, hearing, and sight: high proportion of auditory and visual perceptual difficulties.
11. Equivocal neurological signs and electroencephalogram (EEG) irregularities, neurological abnormalities (soft signs), which may or may not be due to brain injury.
12. Social adjustment: frequently poor adjustment, low self-esteem, social isolation or reckless and uninhibited, learned helplessness, poor motivation, external focus of control, poor reaction to environmental changes.
13. Interpersonal problems: over-excitable in a group, better relations with limited number of peers, frequently poor judgment exhibited, often overly affectionate and clinging.
14. Problems in achievement: academic disability, poor graphics (wiring), disorganized, slow in finishing work.
15. Intraindividual discrepancies: uneven development between different areas on functioning.

IDENTIFY CHARACTERISTICS OF STUDENTS WITH INTELLECTUAL DISABILITIES

Mental retardation, called intellectual disabilities in some states, refers to significantly sub-average general intellectual functioning existing concurrently with impairments in adaptive behavior. Sub-average intellectual functioning is determined by scores of two or more standard deviations below the mean on a standardized test of intelligence. Students exhibiting mental handicaps typically show a flat profile in academic areas.

Adaptive behavior differs according to age and situation. For example, during infancy and early childhood sensor motor, self-help, communication, and socialization skills are considered important. During middle childhood and early adolescence abilities involving learning processes and interpersonal social skills are essential. During late adolescence and adulthood vocational skills, vocational abilities, and social responsibilities are important.

The general characteristics of individuals with intellectual disabilities are as follows:

1. IQ of 70 or below.
2. Limited cognitive ability, delayed academic achievement, particularly in language-related subjects.
3. Deficits in memory, which often relate to poor initial perception, or inability to apply stored information to relevant situations.
4. Impaired formulation of learning strategies.
5. Delayed language development with frequent speech defects.
6. Difficulty in attending to relevant aspects of stimuli, slowness in reaction time or in employing alternative strategies.
7. Short attention span in which student is easily distracted.
8. Delayed academic readiness, slower rate of learning.
9. Delayed social skills.
10. Poor motivation, dependency; reliance upon external focus of control.

Characteristics with regard to the degree of retardation fall into four categories.

1. Mild (IQ of 55 to 70)
    a) Delays in most areas (i.e., communication, motor, academics).
    b) Often not distinguished from "normal" children until school age.
    c) Can acquire both academic and vocational skills. Can become self-supporting.

2. Moderate (IQ of 35-40 to 50-55)
    a) Only fair motor development, clumsy.
    b) Poor social awareness.
    c) Can be taught to communicate.
    d) Can profit from training in social and vocational skills. Needs supervision, but can perform semiskilled labor as an adult.

3. Severe (IQ of 20-25 to 35-40)
    a) Poor motor development
    b) Minimal speech and communication.
    c) Minimal ability to profit from training in health and self-help skills. May contribute to self-maintenance under constant supervision as an adult.

4. Profound (IQ below 20-25)
    a) Gross retardation, both mental and sensor-motor.
    b) Little or no development of basic communication skills.
    c) Dependency on others to maintain basic life functions.
    d) Lifetime of complete supervision (i.e., institution, home, nursing home).

IDENTIFY CHARACTERISTICS OF STUDENTS WITH SPEECH/LANGUAGE IMPAIRMENTS

As a group, youngsters with speech and language impairments generally score below other children on measures of intelligence, achievement, and adaptive social skills. However, this is in part attributable to the fact that a large percentage of children with mental, physical, behavioral, and learning disabilities exhibit speech and language disorders secondary to their major disability.

Children with markedly deviant or delayed speech and language generally have concurrent difficulties with severe intellectual disabilities, chronic emotionally/behavioral disturbances, or acute hearing problems, and function at a delayed developmental level.

Children with speech impairments who have no observable organic defects perform slightly lower than average on tests of motor proficiency. Problems are most likely to occur in the areas of coordination, application of strength, and rhythm. Children with communication disorders tend to demonstrate less interaction with peers.

In addition to these general characteristics, children with cleft palates tend to be underachieving and to show more personality problems (e.g., shyness, inhibition, and social withdrawal) than normal children. Also, children who stutter severely exhibit much anxiety and have low self-esteem.

Speech Disorders-Children with speech disorders are characterized by one or more of the following:

1. Unintelligible speech, or speech that is difficult to understand, and articulation disorders (distortions, omissions, substitutions).
2. Speech-flow disorders (sequence, duration, rate, rhythm, fluency).
3. Unusual voice quality (nasality, breathiness, hoarseness), pitch, intensity, quality disorders.
4. Peculiar physical mannerisms when speaking.
5. Obvious emotional discomfort when trying to communicate (particularly stutterers and clutterers).
6. Damage to nerves or brain centers which control muscles used in speech (dysarthria).

Language Disorders-Language disorders are often considered just one category of speech disorder, but the problem is really a separate one with different origins and causes. Language-disordered children exhibit one or more of the following characteristics.

1. Difficulty in comprehending questions, commands, or statements (receptive language problems).
2. Inability to adequately express their own thoughts (expressive language problems).
3. Language that is below the level expected for the child's chronological age (delayed language).
4. Interrupted language development (dysphasia).
5. Qualitatively different language.
6. Total absence of language (aphasia).

IDENTIFY CHARACTERISTICS OF STUDENTS WITH HEARING IMPAIRMENTS

Similarly to other physical and sensory impairments, it is not the hearing impairment itself but how significant others respond to the hearing-impaired child that ultimately influences whether the child will show behavioral problems. The possibility of communicative isolation increases the need for social interaction. Acceptance is crucial. Adjustment, immaturity, and appearance of self-centeredness are not unusual social problems.

Educationally, hearing impaired individuals demonstrate a lower level of achievement than their hearing proficient peers. Speech and language development may be affected. Because most tests of intelligence rely heavily upon verbal skills, it is difficult to assess the true capacities of a deaf child. Generally, the use of nonverbal tests and/or sign language produces more scores in the normal range of intelligence. Those who do score in the range of mental retardation have other disabling conditions such as learning disabilities, visual impairment, and so forth.

The child with hearing handicaps may exhibit the following behavioral and physical symptoms.

1. Appearance of not paying attention.
2. Turns head or ear toward speaker.
3. Has difficulty following oral directions, and frequently loses place during oral reading.
4. Concentrates on speaker's face or mouth.
5. Exhibits acting-out behavior, and is stubborn, shy, withdrawn, or paranoid.
6. Reluctant to participate in oral activities.
7. Asks teacher or peers to repeat instructions and questions.
8. Best achievement accomplished in small groups.
9. Frequent speech defects, particularly misarticulation.
10. Disparity between expected and actual achievement.
11. Certain medical indications (frequent colds, earaches, sore throats, sinus congestions, chronic allergies, fluid running from the ears, mouth, and nose).
12. Complains of ringing or buzzing in the ears.

Table 1.3-1 Hearing Loss: Effects of Degree and Type

NORMAL RANGE (0-2- dB)

Areas of Concern	Effects
Problematic causes.	Slight fluctuating conductive loss.
Ability to hear speech without a hearing aid.	No difficulty with normal conversation.
Educational implications.	None specifically.
Extent of communicative handicaps.	None.
Auditory rehabilitative consideration.	Probably needs no treatment.

MILD LOSS (20-40) dB

Areas of Concern	Effects
Problematic causes.	Most likely conductive from otitis media, sensorineural loss may result from mild illness or disease.
Ability to hear speech without a hearing aid.	Is able to hear most speech except soft or whispered; hears vowels but may miss unvoiced consonants, often says "huh?" and may turn the television, radio, or stereo volume loud.
Educational implications.	Typically has difficulty hearing faint or distant speech, may experience problems in Integrated Language Arts subjects.
Extent of communicative handicaps.	Mild handicap; possible speech disorder or language delay, may omit final and voiceless consonants.
Auditory rehabilitative consideration.	Losses that are medically treatable need favorable classroom seating and other environmental accommodations, sensorineural problems may require hearing aid, speech reading, or auditory training.

MODERATE LOSS (40-60 dB)

Areas of Concern	Effects
Problematic causes.	Conductive losses result from ottitis media or a middle ear problem; sensorineural losses result from ear disease or illness.
Ability to hear speech without a hearing aid.	Hearing is a problem in most conversational settings, in groups, or in the presence of background noise; hears louder voiced consonants; turns television, radio, or stereo volume loud and has trouble hearing on the phone.
Educational implications.	Understands face-to-face conversational speech; may miss up to 50% of discussion in the classroom if voices are soft or speakers are not in line of vision.
Extent of communicative handicaps.	Possible difficulty with auditory learning, mild to moderate language delay, articulation problems with final and voiceless consonants, may not pay attention.
Auditory rehabilitative consideration.	Same as mild loss, may also need special class for the hearing impaired or special tutoring.

SEVERE LOSS (60-80 dB)

Areas of Concern	Effects
Problematic causes.	Most likely sensorineural, although mixed is possible; causes include rubella, meningitis, RH incompatibility, and heredity
Ability to hear speech without a hearing aid.	Can only hear very loud speech; cannot carry on a conversation without help; cannot use the telephone without amplification
Educational implications.	May be able to hear loud voices about one foot from ear and to identify some environmental sounds; speech and language may deteriorate
Extent of communicative handicaps.	Probable severe language and speech disorders; frequent learning disorders; may have no intelligible speech
Auditory rehabilitative consideration.	Same as in moderate loss; may need placement in school for the deaf

EMOTIONALLY IMPAIRED   15

PROFOUND LOSS (Greater than 80 dB)

Areas of Concern	Effects
Problematic causes.	Mostly sensorineural, may include mixed; rubella, meningitis, RH compatibility, heredity, and ear diseases are contributing factors
Ability to hear speech without a hearing aid.	Can hear only extremely loud shouts; cannot understand spoken language; cannot hear television, radio, or stereo; cannot use the telephone
Educational implications.	More aware of vibrations than tonal patterns; relies on vision as primary avenue for communication; speech and language may deteriorate further
Extent of communicative handicaps.	Severe and language deficits; no oral speech, or characteristic; "deaf-like" speech and voice
Auditory rehabilitative consideration.	Same as severe; will need placement in deaf-oral school or school for the deaf

Adapted from W.W. Green, "Hearing Disorders," Table 5-3, p. 208, in Berdine and Blackhurst, (eds.). An Introduction to Special Education, 2nd ed. Copyright 1985 by W.H. Berdine and A.E. Blackhurst. By permission of Little, Brown, and Company. Also adapted from Report of a Committee for a Comprehensive Plan for Hearing Impaired Children, Office of the Superintendent of Public Instruction. Title VI Elementary and Secondary Act and the Division of Services for Crippled Children May 1968.

INDENTIFY CHARACTERISTICS OF STUDENTS WITH VISUAL IMPAIRMENTS

As a group, visually impaired children tend to develop physically and to understand and use language similarly to their sighted peers. Only a few minor aspects of communication, such as the use of gestures, have been found to differ. Though it wouldn't be expected, blind children tend to use language, which reflects visual experiences, and thus exhibit verbalism or verbal reality. For example, to the word "grass" they are likely to respond with "visual" words such as "green" or "brown." It has been concluded that they learn many words and word meanings from their own use in the language rather than from personal experience.

Studies indicate students with visual impairments tend to have intelligence score distributions similar to those of normal children. But, the development of conceptual or cognitive abilities typically lags behind that of sighted peers. Perhaps the only accurate way of comparing intellectual abilities of sighted and sight-impaired children is by examining performance on skills where the visual disorder is not a factor. Typically, students with visual disabilities seem to exhibit a greater attention level than sighted children.

The social adjustment and self-concept development by children with visual handicaps tend to be influenced by association with significant others. Furthermore, restricted mobility and consequent limited experiences may cause passivity and dependency, resulting ultimately in learned helplessness.

The child with a visual problem often exhibits one or more of the following behaviors:

1. Rubs the eyes excessively.
2. Shuts or covers one eye; tilts the head or thrusts the head forward.
3. Shows sensitivity to light or glare; not able to see things at certain times of the day.
4. Squirms, blinks, frowns, and/or makes facial distortions while reading or doing other close work.
5. Complains of scratchy feeling, burning, or itching of the eyes.
6. Experiences difficulty with reading or other work requiring close visual contact; may experience headaches, dizziness, or nausea following close eye work.
7. Holds reading material too closely or too far away, or frequently changes the distance from near to far or from far to near.
8. Exhibits a tendency to lose place in sentence or on page.
9. Shows poor spacing in writing and has difficulty in staying on the line.
10. Often confuses letters of similar shape (e.g., o/a, c/e, n/m/h, f/t).
11. Frequently reverses letters, syllables, or words.
12. Experiences difficulty in seeing distant objects.
13. Tunes out material written on the chalkboard.

Medically, the visually impaired child often has one or more of the following physical indicators:

1. Red eyelids.
2. Recurring sty's or swollen lids.
3. Crust on lids among the lashes.
4. Thick discharges from the eyes.
5. Inflamed and watery eyes.
6. Crossed eyes, or eyes that do not appear to be straight.
7. Pupils of uneven size.
8. Eyes that move excessively (nystagmus).
9. Drooping eyelids.

IDENTIFY CHARACTERISTICS OF STUDENTS WITH PHYSICAL DISABILITIES AND OTHER HEALTH IMPAIRMENTS

Children with physical impairments possess a variety of disabling conditions. Although there are significant differences among these conditions, similarities also exist. Each condition usually affects one particular system of the body, such as the cardiopulmonary system (i.e., blood vessels, heart, and lungs) or the musculoskeletal system (i.e., spinal cord, brain nerves) etc. Some conditions develop during pregnancy, birth, or infancy because of known or unknown factors which may affect the fetus or newborn infant. Other conditions occur later due to injury (trauma), disease, or factors not fully understood.

In addition to motor disorders, individuals with physical disabilities may have multi-disabling conditions such as concomitant hearing impairments, visual impairments, perceptual disorders, speech defects, behavior disorders, mental handicaps, performance, and emotional responsiveness.

Some characteristics which may occur with individuals with physical disabilities and other health impairments are:

1. Lack of physical stamina, fatigue.
2. Chronic illness; poor endurance.
3. Deficient motor skills, normal movement may be prevented.
4. May cause physical limitations or impede motor development; a prosthesis or an orthosis may be required.
5. Mobility and exploration of one's environment may be limited.
6. Limited self-care abilities.
7. Progressive weakening and degeneration of muscles.
8. Frequent speech and language defects, communication may be prevented, echolatia orthosis may be present.
9. May experience pain and discomfort throughout the body.
10. May display emotional (psychological) problems which require treatment.
11. Social adjustments may be needed, may display maladaptive social behavior.
12. May necessitate long-term medical treatment.
13. May have embarrassing side effects from certain diseases or treatment.
14. May exhibit erratic or poor attendance patterns.

IDENTIFY CHARACTERISTICS OF STUDENTS WITH MULTIDISABILITIES

Children who have multiple disabilities are an extremely heterogeneous population. Their characteristics are determined by the type and severity of their combined disabilities, thus they differ in their sensory, motor, social, and cognitive abilities. Although any number of combinations of disabilities is possible, major dimensions typically include mental retardation, neurological impairments, emotional disturbance, or deafness and blindness.

Those whose impairments combine to form multiple disabilities often exhibit characteristics on a severe level. Low self-esteem and poor social skills often characterize this population. Youngsters with severe disabilities may possess profound language or perceptual-cognitive deprivations. Moreover, they may have extremely fragile physiological conditions. "It is important to understand that the problem of severe/profound disabilities...It is the extent of the disabilities that results in the child's classification, not the type of disabilities." (Blackhurst & Berdine, 1985, pp. 473-474).

Among the characteristics that can be present with youth with severely or profound multi-disabilities are:

1. Multiple disabilities.
2. Often not toilet trained.
3. Frequently non-ambulatory.
4. Aggressiveness toward others without provocation and antisocial behavior.
5. Markedly withdrawn, or unresponsive to others.
6. No attention to even the most pronounced social stimuli.
7. Self-mutilation i.e., head banging, biting, and scratching or cutting of self).
8. Rumination (i.e., self-induced vomiting, swallowing vomitus).
9. Self-stimulation (i.e., rocking, hand-flapping).
10. Intense temper tantrums of unknown origin.
11. Excessive, pointless imitation, or the total absence of the ability to imitate.
12. Inability to be controlled verbally.
13. Seizures.
14. Extremely brittle medical existence (i.e., life-threatening conditions such as congenital heart disease, respiratory difficulties, metabolic disorders, central nervous system disorders, and digestive malfunctions).

KNOW THE CHARACTERISTICS OF AUTISM

In 1981 the condition of autism was moved from the exceptionality category of the seriously emotionally disturbed to that of other health impaired by virtue of a change in language in the original definitions under Public Law 94-142 ("Education of Handicapped Children" Federal Register, 1977). With IDEA, in 1990 autism was made into a separate exceptionality category. Refer to Competency 13 for additional information on autism.

Autism is a severe language disorder which affects thinking, communication, and behavior (Smith & Luckasson, 1992). The condition occurs in about four out of 10,000 persons. It is characterized by dysfunctional interpersonal relationships, abnormal or no language, extreme withdrawal by some, self-stimulation and other ritualistic movements, and frequently self-injurious behaviors.

When autism was initially identified, it was thought to be a psychosocial problem caused by parents who were either cold and aloof or hostile to their children. Early on, autism was thought to be a form of mental illness. Some have even associated autism with mental retardation.

In IDEA, the 1990 EHA Amendment, autism was finally classified as a separate exceptionality category. In this federal regulation, autism is defined as a developmental disability that affects verbal and nonverbal communication. It is thought to be caused by a neurological or biochemical dysfunction. Cognitive deficits are present and the condition is generally evident before age three. These and other characteristics are such that educational performance is adversely affected.

Smith and Luckasson (1992, p. 227) list the following characteristics:

1. **Absent or distorted relationship with people** - Inability to relate to people except as objects, inability to express affection, or ability to build and maintain only distant, suspicious, or bizarre relationships.

2. **Extreme or peculiar problems in communications** - Absence of verbal language or language that is not functional, such as echolalia (parroting what one hears), misuse of pronouns (e.g., he for you and I for her), neologisms (made up, meaningless words or sentences), talk that bears little or no resemblance to reality.

3. **Self-stimulation** - repetitive, stereotyped behavior that seems to have no purpose other than providing sensory stimulation (this may take a wide variety of forms, such as swishing saliva, twirling objects, patting one's cheeks, flapping one's hands, staring, etc.).

4. **Self-injury** - repeated physical self-abuse, such as biting, scratching, or poking oneself, head banging, etc.

5. **Perceptual anomalies** - unusual responses or absence of responses to stimuli that seems to indicate sensory impairments or unusual sensitivity.

The term does not include children with characteristics of the exceptionality Serious Emotional Disturbance as it is defined in federal regulations. Treatment is closer to the categories of Emotional/Behavioral Disorders and Language/Communications Impairments. That is because behavioral interventions such as behavior modification and alternative communication devices like communication boards, typewriters, and computers are currently being used to shape behaviors that are more appropriate and to provide avenues for communication to occur.

KNOW THE CHARACTERISTICS OF TRAUMATIC BRAIN INJURY

Traumatic brain injury is occurring to more children and youth than ever before. Ironically, many of these injuries are preventable. Automobile accidents, falls, high fever, and child abuse are among the most frequent causes. Proper use of seat belts, adult supervision, preventive medical care, and parent education are possible ways to prevent many incidents. Traumatic brain injury too often results in brain damage, which can range from mild to profound and be temporary or permanent. The brain injury generally affects the individual physically, cognitively, emotionally, and socially (Hallahan & Kauffman, 1994).

According to the National Head Injury Foundation, there are approximately 500,000 cases of traumatic brain injury each year. Statistics report about 100,000 of those victims die, and another 100,000 are debilitated for life. Traumatic brain injury is the leading killer of persons under thirty-four years old, and the leading cause of the injury is motor vehicle accidents. Child abuse accounts for 64% of head injuries (Smith & Luckasson, 1992). This is unclear – 64% child abuse majority mv accidents...?

Like autism, traumatic brain injury became a separate exceptionality category under IDEA in 1990. Educational plans need to be concerned with cognitive, social/behavioral, and sensorimotor domains.

UNDERSTAND THE TRAITS OF ATTENTION DEFICIT DISORDER (ADD) AND HOW TO ACCOMMODATE STUDENTS WITH ADD IN THEIR LEARNING

Of the approximately forty-five million children in the United State under the age of eighteen, it has been conservatively estimated that three to six percent of them have an attention disorder. Attention deficit disorders are a physiological, neurological problem characterized by the inability to pay attention and impulsiveness. Some are overactive, typically referred to as hyperactive. They generate much energy and are frequently restless, fidgety, and easily distracted. Others may be under active or sluggish. Attention disorders occur two to four times more frequently in boys than girls. They occur in persons of all ability levels and in every socioeconomic group.

Attentional problems usually begin in early childhood or in the elementary school years. They often continue into adolescence and adulthood, and can last a lifetime. Each child or adolescent with an attention disorder manifests difficulties in an individual manner, although a core of behaviors indicative of attentional disorders has been identified.

In the fall of 1990, Congress inquired of the public whether to add Attention Deficit Disorders as a special education exceptionality category. Early 1991 it was decided not to do so for several reasons. First, many of these students were qualifying for the federally designated categories of Specific Learning Disabilities and Emotionally/Behaviorally Disordered. Second, there is no neurological test that will confirm the condition of ADD. Therefore, testing for the disorder might become an ambiguous endeavor.

Since that time, many of these students have been accommodated in the regular classroom without having been declared eligible for any exceptionality category. Legal experts have used the terminology "students with disabilities" stated in Public Law 93-112 (Rehabilitation Act of 1973), since Attention Deficit Disorders is not specifically named as a category in Public Law 94-142 (EHA), or its amendment Public Law 101-476 (IDEA). Special accommodations must be given the youngster in the regular classroom by the general education teacher if the school receives documented evidence that a student has the disorder and needs special accommodations in order to control behavior and learn (e.g., a letter from the physician treating the youngster).

To be diagnosed as having ADHD, a child, adolescent, or adult must demonstrate eight of the following symptoms and they must have occurred before the age of seven. The behavioral symptoms have been coded as to whether they are indicative of inattention, impulsivity, or hyperactivity.

CODE: **A=Inattention**   **B=Impulsivity**   **C=Hyperactivity**

C	1.	Often fidgets with hands or feet or squirms in seat.
C	2.	Has difficulty remaining seated when required to do so.
A	3.	Is easily distracted be extraneous stimuli.
B	4.	Has difficulty waiting turn in games or group situations.
B	5.	Often blurts out answers to questions before they have been completed.
A	6.	Has difficulty following through on instructions from others (not due to oppositional behavior or failure of comprehension), e.g., fails to finish tasks and chores.
A	7.	Has difficulty sustaining attention in tasks or play activities.
B	8.	Often shifts from one uncompleted activity to another.
C	9.	Has difficulty playing quietly.
C	10.	Often talks excessively.
B	11.	Often interrupts or intrudes on others, e.g., butts into other children's games.
A	12.	Often doesn't seem to listen to what is being said about him/her.
B	13.	Often loses things necessary for talks or activities at school, or at home like toys, pencils, books, assignments, etc.
C	14.	Often engages in physically dangerous activities without considering possible consequences (not for the purpose of thrill-seeking), e.g., runs into street without looking.

KNOW CHARACTERISTICS OF STUDENTS WITH SOCIAL MALADJUSTMENT

A student with social maladjustment is defined as one whose values and/or behaviors are in conflict with the school, home, or community (Brewton, Undated). Students with ordinary classroom behavior problems and social problems are not included in this category.

According to state and federal law, students with social maladjustment are ineligible for services in Emotional/Behavioral Disorders unless they have an emotional/behavioral disorder as well. Social maladjustment is not defined in the federal guidelines; however, this condition is considered independent of an emotionally based disability.

Youth who exhibit socially maladjusted behaviors are those who persistently refuse to meet what are considered minimum standards of conduct and whose behaviors and values are most often in conflict with society's standards. These students are disruptive and defy teachers. They intimidate and harass other students, and in general, refuse to respect the rights of others. They maintain a consistent pattern of aberrant and antisocial behavior without signs of guilt, remorse, or concern for the feelings of others. Their deviant behavior occurs largely from their tendency to place their own needs above those of others.

Though not in chronic distress, these students may demonstrate situational anxiety, depression, or agitation in response to certain isolated events, like when they are faced with serious consequences for their behavior. They are often motivated to continue their behavior by the approval they receive from a deviant group or gang. The immediate gratification of their behavior outweighs any consideration of long-term consequences. Typically, they are unable to benefit from previously experienced consequences, and exhibit any lack of motivation to change.

The following characteristics are listed on the Social Maladjustment Checklist by Brewton (undated).

1. Participates in activities of deviant clique or peer group.
2. Projects tough image.
3. Expresses feelings of being unfairly treated.
4. Blames others for difficulties.
5. Avoids displays of emotional vulnerability (denies soft, hurt or needful feelings).
6. Engages in early smoking.
7. Engages in early drinking.
8. Engages in substance abuse.
9. Displays precocious (early or excessive) sexual activity.
10. Shows poor frustration tolerance.
11. Shows little or no remorse for violating rules.
12. Exhibits temper outbursts when confronted with wrong-doing.
13. Exhibits reckless behavior, with frequent physical injuries.
14. Initiates fights.
15. Receives school suspensions.
16. Has experienced legal difficulties (delinquency).
17. Displays truancy.
18. Has run away from home.
19. Lies.
20. Participates in acts of vandalism.
21. Engages in theft.
22. Violates rules at home and at school.

Table 2-3 Differences Between Severely Emotionally Disturbed (SED) and Socially Maladjusted (SM)

SED	SM
Self-critical, unable to have fun	Little remorse, pleasure seeking
Fantasy, naïve, gullible	Street-wise
Consistently poor	More situationally dependent
Affective disorder	Character disorder
Hurts self or others as an end	Hurts others as a means to an end
Easily hurt	Acts tough; survivor
Tense; fearful	Appears relaxed; "cool"
Ignored or rejected	Accepted by sociocultural group
Law-abiding, younger, no real friends	Bad companions, same age or older
Seen as unable to comply	Seen as unwilling to comply
Inconsistent achievements,	Generally low achievement
Good attendance record,	Excessive absences
Appreciates help	Doesn't want help
Blames self	Blames others
Psychological	Sociological
Wants to trust, feels insecure	Dumb to trust others
Withdrawn, unhappy	Outgoing
Emotional support, likes structure,	Warmth; dislikes structure
Decrease in anxiety	Needs to increase anxiety
Overly complain	Non-complaint, hostile
Aware as problem exists	Denies problem
Inappropriate for age	Appropriate for age
Hyperactive; hypoactive	Normal, but acts out
Variable, labile	Relatively stable, even

Adapted from Clarizio, H.F., (1987). Differentiating emotionally impaired from socially maladjusted students. Psychology in the Schools, 24.

IDENTIFY CHARACTERISTICS OF STUDENTS WHO ARE GIFTED AND TALENTED

All categories of exceptional children list deficits in one or more developmental areas with the exception of the Gifted and Talented. This is the only area of exceptional children and youth which focuses upon a surplus of ability or talent. Though myths containing stereotypes of the gifted population have typically delineated undesirable characteristics (e.g., social ineptness, physical weakness, emotional instability), studies have shown superiority in these very domains.

In the physical realm, gifted children as a group are superior in physical development when compared with their age mates of average intelligence. A large number of gifted children demonstrate outstanding athletic ability and are superior competitors in a variety of sports.

Academically, gifted children are ahead of peers in school achievement. They display wide and varied interests. The gifted population tends to prepare for occupations that demand greater than average intellectual ability, creativity, and motivation, thus distinguishing themselves among their peers as adults.

In the emotional and social areas, gifted children tend to be happy and well liked by their peers. Studies report the majority to be emotionally stable, self-sufficient, and social leaders at school, and to perceive themselves in a positive manner. Creative achievements produced by gifted adults (e.g., artists, writers, musicians, scientists) have been made in spite of, not because of, emotional distress. Sometimes the gifted have been more susceptible to difficulties because of their high intellect. On the monument to Edgar Allen Poe at West Point, where he was an unsuccessful cadet, the inscription reads, "There is nothing in this world of great beauty without some strangeness in the making." This idea appears to have only occasional or situational validity and is not borne out by statistics.

A positive relationship exists between intellectual giftedness and talent. However, talented generally connotes specific abilities (e.g., musical, artistic) that may or may not correspond with an individual's attributes in overall intellectual or leadership skills. As within any area of exceptionality, there are individual differences and not every gifted person will fit the group description.

Characteristics of the gifted and talented population include the following:

1. Giftedness may not be detectable at birth, but becomes apparent at an early age.
2. Tend to demonstrate mental and physical superiority at an early age.
3. Are capable of high performance.
4. Are able as children to adapt to play with peers and to social relationship with adults.
5. Are taller, heavier, and stronger than their average age mates are.
6. Appear healthier and more energetic than other children their age; act in a well-adjusted manner.
7. Possess a strong vocabulary; demonstrate mature language skills.
8. May enjoy schoolwork; may be bored in school.
9. Learn to read easily, often teaching themselves before entering school.
10. Tend to be more advanced in reading than math, handwriting, or art.
11. Memorize easily and retain what is learned.
12. Show interest in abstract ideas.
13. Often display a keen curiosity, possess unusual knowledge and quick wit, and make associations readily.
14. Are critical of themselves and others.
15. Are self-sufficient, resourceful, and participate in a large number of extracurricular activities.
16. Possess self-confidence and perseverance.
17. Are frequently selected by peers as leaders.
18. Often display dominant, forceful, competitive types of behavior.
19. Sometimes have astounding and diversified talents (i.e., visual and performing arts, physical activities), show creative and/or productive thinking.
20. Come from all socioeconomic levels, even though a sizable correlation exists between intelligence quotient (IQ) and higher than average socioeconomic status; have good decision-making abilities.
21. Most become professionals and managers; may excel as educators.
22. Often respond to assignments in novel ways.

Skill 1.4 Demonstrate knowledge of types and characteristics of emotional impairments.

Children whose behavior deviates from society's standards for normal behavior for certain ages and stages of development are considered to have an emotional impairment. Behavioral expectations vary from setting to setting – for example, it is acceptable to yell on the football field, but not as the teacher is explaining a lesson to the class.

Different cultures have their standards of behavior, further complicating the question of what constitutes a behavioral problem. People also have their personal opinions and standards for what is tolerable and what is not. Some behavioral problems are openly expressed; others are inwardly directed and not very obvious. As a result of these factors, the terms behavioral disorders and emotional disturbance have become almost interchangeable.

While almost all children at times exhibit behaviors that are aggressive, withdrawn, or otherwise inappropriate, the IDEA definition of serious emotional disturbance focuses on behaviors that persist over time, are intense, and impairs a child's ability to function in society.

The behaviors must not be caused by temporary stressful situations or other causes (i.e., depression over the death of a grandparent, or anger over the parents' impending divorce). In order for a child to be considered seriously emotionally disturbed, he or she must exhibit one or more of the following characteristics over a **long period of time** and to a **marked degree** that **adversely affects** a child's educational performance.

- Inability to learn, that cannot be explained by intellectual, sensory, or health factors.

- Inability to maintain satisfactory interpersonal relationships.

- Inappropriate types of behaviors.

- General pervasive mood of unhappiness or depression.

- Physical symptoms or fears associated with personal or school problems.

- Schizophrenic children are covered under this definition, and social maladjustment by itself does not satisfy this definition unless it is accompanied by one of the other conditions of SED.

The diagnostic categories and definitions used to classify mental disorders come from the American Psychiatric Association's publication Diagnostic and Statistical Manual of Mental Disorders (DSM-IV), the handbook that is used by psychiatrists and psychologists. The DSM-IV is a multiaxial classification system consisting of dimensions (axes) coded along with the psychiatric diagnosis. The axes are:

- Axis I   Principal psychiatric diagnosis (e.g., overanxious disorder).

- Axis II   Developmental problems (e.g., developmental reading disorder).

- Axis III Physical disorders (e.g., allergies).

- Axis IV   Psychosocial stressors (e.g., divorce).

- Axis V   Rating of the highest level of adaptive functioning (includes intellectual and social). Rating is called Global Assessment Functioning (GAF) score.

While the DSM-IV diagnosis is one way of identifying a serious emotional disturbance, there are other ways of classifying the various forms that behavior disorders manifest themselves. The following tables summarize some of these classifications.

Externalizing Behaviors	Internalizing Behaviors
Aggressive behaviors expressed outwardly toward others	Withdrawing behaviors that are directed inward to oneself
Manifested as hyperactivity, persistent aggression, irritating behaviors that are impulsive and distractible.	Social withdrawal.
Examples: hitting, cursing, stealing, arson, cruelty to animals, hyperactivity.	Depression, fears, phobias, elective mutism, withdrawal, anorexia and bulimia.

Well-known instruments used to assess children's behavior have their own categories (scales) to classify behaviors. The following table illustrates the scales used in some of the widely used instruments.

Walker Problem Identification Checklist	Burks' Behavior Rating Scales (BBRS)	Devereux Behavior Rating Scale (adolescent)	Revised Behavior Problem Checklist (Quay & Peterson)
Acting out	Excessive self-blame	Unethical behavior	Major scales
Withdrawal	Excessive anxiety	Defiant-resistive	Conduct Disorder
Distractibility	Excessive withdrawal	Domineering-sadistic	Socialized aggression
Disturbed peer Relations	Excessive dependency	Heterosexual interest	Attention-problems-immaturity
Immaturity	Poor ego strength	Hyperactive expansive	Anxiety—withdrawal
	Poor physical strength	Poor emotional control	
	Poor coordination	Need approval, dependency	Minor scales
	Poor intellectuality	Emotional disturbance	Psychotic behavior
	Poor academics	Physical inferiority--timidity	Motor excess
	Poor attention	Schizoid withdrawal	
	Poor impulse control	Bizarre speech and cognition	
	Poor reality contact	Bizarre actions	
	Poor sense of identity		
	Excessive suffering		
	Poor anger control		
	Excessive sense of persecution		
	Excessive aggressiveness		
	Excessive resistance		
	Poor social conformity		

Disturbance may also be categorized in degrees: mild, moderate or severe. The degree of disturbance will affect the type and degree of interventions and services required by emotionally handicapped students. Degree of disturbance also must be considered when determining the least restrictive environment and the services named fro free, appropriate education for these students. An example of a set of criteria for determining the degree of disturbance is the one developed by P.L. Newcomer.

Degree of Disturbance

Criteria	Mild	Moderate	Severe
Precipitating events	Highly stressful	Moderately stressful	Not stressful
Destructiveness	Not destructive	Occasionally destructive	Usually destructive
Maturational appropriateness	Behavior typical for age	Some behavior untypical for age	Behavior too young or too old
Personal functioning	Cares for own needs	Usually cares for own needs	Unable to care for own needs
Social functioning	Usually able to relate to others	Usually unable to relate to others	Unable to relate to others
Reality index	Usually sees events as they are	Occasionally sees events as they are	Little contact with reality
Insight index	Aware of behavior	Usually aware of behavior	Usually not aware of behavior
Conscious control	Usually can control behavior	Occasionally can control behavior	Little control over behavior
Social responsiveness	Usually acts appropriately	Occasionally acts appropriately	Rarely acts appropriately

Source: Understanding and Teaching Emotionally Disturbed Children and Adolescents, (2nd ed., p. 139), by P.L. Newcomer, 1993, Austin, TX: Pro-De. Copyright 1993. Reprinted with permission.

IDENTIFY THE CHARACTERISTICS OF EMOTIONALLY HANDICAPPED CHILDREN

Children with emotional handicaps or behavioral disorders are not always easy to identify. It is, of course, easy to identify the acting-out child who is constantly fighting, who cannot stay on task for more than a few minutes, or who shouts obscenities when angry.

It is not always easy to identify the child who internalizes his or her problems, on the other hand, or may appear to be the "model" student, but suffers from depression, shyness, or fears. Unless the problem becomes severe enough to impact school performance, the internalizing child may go for long periods without being identified or served.

Studies of children with behavioral and emotional disorders share some general characteristics:

Lower academic performance: While it is true that some emotionally disturbed children have above average IQ scores, the majority are behind their peers in measures of intelligence and school achievement. Most score in the "slow learner" or "mildly mentally retarded" range on IQ tests, averaging about 90. Many have learning problems that exacerbate their acting out or "giving-up" behavior. As the child enters secondary school, the gap between his or her and non-handicapped peers widens until the child may be as many as 2 to 4 years behind in reading and/or math skills by high school. Children with severe degrees of impairment may be un-testable.

Social skills deficits: Students with deficits may be uncooperative, selfish in dealing with others, unaware of what to do in social situations, or ignorant of the consequences of their actions. This may be a combination of lack of prior training, lack of opportunities to interact, and dysfunctional value systems and beliefs learned from their family.

Classroom behaviors: Often, classroom behavior is highly disruptive to the classroom setting. Emotionally disturbed children are often out of their seat, running around the room, hitting, fighting, or disturbing their classmates, stealing or destroying property, defiant and noncompliant, and/or verbally disruptive. They do not follow directions and often do not complete assignments.

Aggressive behaviors: Aggressive children often fight or instigate their peers to strike back at them. Aggressiveness may also take the form of vandalism or destruction of property. Aggressive children also engage in verbal abuse.

Delinquency: As emotionally disturbed, acting-out children enter adolescence, they may become involved in socialized aggression (i.e.,gang membership) and delinquency. Delinquency is a legal term, rather than a medical, and describes truancy, and actions that would be criminal if they were committed by adults. Of course, not every delinquent is classified as emotionally disturbed, but children with behavioral and emotional disorders are especially at risk for becoming delinquent because of their problems at school (the primary place for socializing with peers), deficits in social skills that may make them unpopular at school, and/or dysfunctional homes.

Withdrawn behaviors: Children who manifest withdrawn behaviors may consistently act in an immature fashion or prefer younger children to play with. They may daydream or complain of being sick in order to "escape" to the clinic, cry, cling to the teacher, ignore other's attempt to interact, or suffer from fears or depression.

Schizophrenia and psychotic behaviors: Children may have bizarre delusions, hallucinations, incoherent thoughts, and disconnected thinking. Schizophrenia typically manifests itself between the ages of 15 and 45, and the younger the onset, the more severe the disorder. These behaviors usually require intensive treatment beyond the scope of the regular classroom setting.

Autism: This behavior appears very early in childhood. It is associated with brain damage and severe language impairment. Six common features of autism are:

- Apparent sensory deficit –The child may appear not to see or hear or react to a stimulus, then react in an extreme fashion to a seemingly insignificant stimulus.
- Severe affect isolation—The child does not respond to the usual signs of affection such as smiles and hugs.
- Self-stimulation – Stereotyped behavior takes the form of repeated or ritualistic actions that make no sense to others, such as hand flapping, rocking, staring at objects, humming the same sounds for hours at a time.
- Tantrums and self-injurious behavior (SIB) –Autistic children may bite themselves, pull their hair, bang their heads, or hit themselves. They can throw severe tantrums and direct aggression and destructive behavior toward others.
- Echolalia—also known as "parrot talk." The autistic child may repeat what is played on television, for example, or respond to others by repeating what was said to him. Alternatively, he may simply not speak at all.
- Severe deficits in behavior and self-care skills. Autistic children may behave like children much younger than themselves.

**Gender:** Many more boys than girls are identified as having emotional and behavioral problems, especially hyperactivity and attention deficit disorder, autism, childhood psychosis and problems with under-control (aggression, socialized aggression). Girls, on the other hand, have more problems with over-control (i.e., withdrawal and phobias). Boys are much more prevalent than girls in problems with mental retardation and language and learning disabilities.

**Age Characteristics**: When they enter adolescence, girls tend to experience affective or emotional disorders such as anorexia, depression, bulimia, and anxiety at twice the rate of boys, which mirrors the adult prevalence pattern.

**Family Characteristics:** Having a child with an emotional or behavioral disorder does not automatically mean that the family is dysfunctional. However, there are family factors that create or contribute to the development of behavior disorders and emotional disturbance, such as:
- Abuse and neglect.
- Lack of appropriate supervision.
- Lax, punitive, and/or lack of discipline.
- High rates of negative types of interaction among family members.
- Lack of parental concern and interest.
- Negative adult role models.
- Lack of proper health care and/or nutrition.
- Disruption in the family.

Skill 1.5   Analyze the effects of emotional impairments on human development and adult life roles.

See skill 1.1 for normal human development.

Prior to testing a student for an emotional disability, the special educator and parents will see student behaviors that are not typical. While every student is an individual, there is a point when behaviors cross over from an individual personality difference and what is considered socially, behaviorally, and emotionally outside the norm.

Certain stages of child development have their own sets of problems, and it should be kept in mind that short-term undesirable behaviors can and will occur over these stages. Child development is also a continuum, and children may manifest these problem behaviors somewhat earlier or later than their peers.

About 15-20% of the school-aged population between 6 and 17 years old receive special education services. The categories of learning disabilities and emotional disturbance are the most prevalent. Exceptional students are very much like their peers without disabilities. The main difference is that they have an intellectual, emotional, behavioral, or physical deficit that significantly interferes with their ability to benefit from education.

THE ETIOLOGY OF EMOTIONAL DISTURBANCE.

Medical Factors-Some emotional disturbances are the result of chemical imbalance or neurological dysfunction. Schizophrenia, bipolar disorders, and depression would fall into this category.

Medical in nature, these causes are not the result of the student's environment or family life unless caused by the maternal, prenatal use of a substance such as drugs or alcohol. An example of emotional disturbance that can be caused by maternal, prenatal alcohol consumption is fetal alcohol syndrome (FAS). According to the Centers for Disease Control and Prevention (2006, http://www.cdc.gov/ncbddd/fas/fasask.htm#character), children with FAS are at risk for psychiatric problems, criminal behavior, unemployment, and incomplete education.

Shared Psychotic Disorders are those in which an emotionally disturbed person influences the perceptions and reactions of an otherwise emotionally healthy individual. The previously healthy individual then becomes emotionally disturbed as well.

Abuse Whether abuse to the child or to a parent, the effect transcends the immediate situation to interaction with others in the home, school, and community. If the child with a disability is the one who is abused, he/she will be distrustful of others. He/she may also continue the cycle of behavior by acting out in abusive ways towards others.

If a parent of the child with a disability is being abused, the child may feel responsible. He may be actively trying to protect the abused parent. At the least, he will carry emotional and possibly psychological effects of living in a home where abuse happens.

A parent who is being abused will be less likely to be able to attend to the needs of the child with a disability. He or she may be secretive about the fact that the abuse even occurs. Unfortunately, having a child with a disability puts excessive strain on a marriage and abusive tendencies may be exaggerated.

Neglect If a child with a disability is neglected physically or emotionally, he or she may exhibit a number of behaviors. He or she will most likely be distrustful of adults in general, may horde classroom materials, snacks, etc. and at the very least will be unfocused on school work.

In the instances of abuse and neglect (or suspected instances), the special educator (as all educators) is a mandated reporter to the appropriate agency (such as DCFS – Division of Child and Family Services).

Substance Abuse If a child with a disability or a parent is involved in substance abuse, that abuse will have a negative effect in the areas of finances, health, productivity, and safety. It is important for the special education teacher to be aware of signs of substance abuse. He or she should be proactive in teaching drug awareness and should also know the appropriate school channels for getting help for the student, as well as community agencies that can help parents involved in substance abuse.

THE IMPLICATIONS EMOTIONAL DISTURBANCE PAST THE CHILDHOOD YEARS.

Emotional Disturbance in the Teen Years-Every adolescent progresses at varying rates in developing his/her ability to think in more complex ways. Each adolescent develops his/her own view of the world. Some adolescents may be able to apply logical operations to school work long before they are able to apply them to personal dilemmas. When emotional issues arise, they often interfere with an adolescent's ability to think in more complex ways. The ability to consider possibilities, as well as facts, may influence decision making, often in negative ways.

This is especially true in the case of an adolescent with an emotional disturbance. Already atypical responses to him/herself and others are heightened when the student is in the emotionally charge phase of adolescence.

Emotional Disturbance in Adulthood-The appearance of those with special needs in media such as television and movies generally are those who rise above their "label" as disabled, because of an extraordinary skill. This isn't clear to me. Perhaps more intro?

Most people in the community are portrayed as accepting the "disabled" person when that special skill is noted. In addition, those who continue to express revulsion or prejudice towards the person with a disability often express remorse when the special skill is noted or peer pressure becomes too intense. This portrayal often ignores those who appear normal by appearance with learning and emotional disabilities, who often feel and suffer from the prejudices.

The most significant group any individual faces is their peers. Pressure to appear normal and not "needy" in any area is still intense from early childhood to adulthood. During teen years when young people are beginning to "express their individuality," the very appearance of walking into a Special Education classroom often brings feelings of inadequacy, and labeling by peers that the student is "special." Being considered normal is the desire of all individuals with disabilities regardless of the age or disability. People with disabilities today, as many years ago, still measure their successes by how their achievements mask/hide their disabilities. This paragraph doesn't seem to be fit here.

Certainly an emotional disturbance can impact all areas of life in adulthood. The most difficult cultural/community outlook on those who are disabled comes in the adult work world where disabilities of persons can become highly evident often causing those with special needs difficulty in finding work and keeping their jobs. This is a particularly difficult place for those who have not learned to self advocate or accommodate for their area/s of special needs.

Family life -Family life can be inconsistent, abusive, and at the very least stressful. The emotionally disturbed adult may have difficulty with day-to-day responsibilities of home and parenting. Housekeeping, home maintenance, following a budget may be overwhelming.

Because he/she may have difficulty attaining or keeping a job, family finances can be impacted. The cost of needed medications can also present a financial hardship. The effect on children of the emotionally disturbed parent can be extensive. Some children may be neglected or abused verbally or physically.

Self-Advocacy Skills-Learning about one's self involves the identification of learning styles, strengths and weakness, interests, and preferences. For students with mild disabilities, developing an awareness of the accommodations they need will help them ask for necessary accommodations on a job and in postsecondary education. Students can also help identify alternative ways they can learn.

Self-advocacy involves the ability to effectively communicate one's own rights, needs, and desires and to take responsibility for making decisions that impact one's life.

There are many elements in developing self-advocacy skills in students who are involved in the transition process. Helping the student to identify future goals or desired outcomes in transition planning areas is a good place to start. Self-knowledge is critical for the student in determining the direction that transition planning will take.

The role of the teacher in promoting self-advocacy should include encouraging the student to participate in the IEP process as well as other key parts of their educational development. Self-advocacy issues and lessons are effective when they are incorporated into the student's daily life.

Teachers should listen to the student's problems and ask the student for input on possible changes that he/she may need. The teacher should talk with the student about possible solutions, discussing the pros and cons of doing something. A student who self-advocates should feel supported and encouraged. Good self-advocates know how to ask questions and get help from other people. They do not let other people do everything for them.

Students need to practice newly acquired self-advocacy skills. Teachers should have student's role play various situations, such as setting up a class schedule, moving out of the home, and asking for accommodations needed for a course.

The impact of transition planning on a student with a disability is very great. The student should be an active member of the transition team, as well as the focus of all activities. Students often think that being passive and relying on others to take care of them is the way to get things done. Students should be encouraged to express their opinions throughout the transition process. They need to learn how to express themselves so that others listen and take them seriously. These skills should be practiced within a supportive and caring environment.

A major focus of special education is to prepare students to become working, independent members of society. IDEA 2004 (Individuals with Disabilities Education Act) also includes preparing students for *further education*. Certain skills beyond academics are needed to attain this level of functioning.

Affective and Social Skills-These skills transcend to all areas of life. When an individual is unable to acquire information on expectations and reactions of others or misinterprets those cues, he/she is missing an important element needed for success as an adult in the workplace and community in general.

Special education should incorporate a level of instruction in the affective/social area as many students will not develop these skills without instruction, modeling, practice, and feedback.

Affective social skills taught throughout the school setting might include: social greetings; eye contact with a speaker; interpretation of facial expression, body language, and personal space; ability to put feelings and questions into words; and use of words to acquire additional information as needed.

Career/Vocational Skills-Although counseling and, in some cases, medication can improve the difficulties (?) symptoms(?) of the emotionally disturbed adult in the workplace, there are many potential difficulties.

Initially, the individual may find it difficult to be hired for a job because of employer prejudice, difficulty with communication, behavioral issues, or environmental challenges.

Students with emotional disturbances should be taught responsibility for actions, a good work ethic, and independence in the academic setting. If students are able to regulate their overall work habits with school tasks, it is likely that the same skills will carry over into the work force.

The special education teacher may assess the student's level of career/vocational readiness by using the following list:

- Being prepared by showing responsibility for materials/school tools such as books, assignments, study packets, pencils, pens, assignment notebook.
- Knowing expectations by keeping an assignment notebook completed. Asking questions when unsure of the expectations.
- Use of additional checklists as needed.
- Use of needed assistive devices.
- Completing assignments on time to the best of his ability.

An additional responsibility of the special educator when teaching career/vocational skills is recognition that a variety of vocations and skills are present in the community.

If academics, per se, are not an area in which students excel, other exploratory or training opportunities should be provided. Such opportunities might include art, music, culinary arts, childcare, technical, or building instruction. These skills can often be included (although not to the exclusion of additional programs) within the academic setting.

For example, a student with strong vocation interest in art may be asked to create a poster to show learned information in a science or social studies unit. While addressing a career/vocational interest and skill this way, the teacher would also be establishing a program of differentiated instruction.

Cognitive Development-Children go through patterns of learning beginning with pre-operational thought processes and move to concrete operational thoughts. Eventually they begin to acquire the mental ability to think about and solve problems in their head because they can manipulate objects symbolically. Children of most ages can use symbols such as words and numbers to represent objects and relations, but they need concrete reference points.

It is essential children be encouraged to use and develop the thinking skills that they possess in solving problems that interest them. The content of the curriculum must be relevant, engaging, and meaningful to the students.

The teacher of special needs students must have a general knowledge of cognitive development. Although children with special needs cognitive development rate maybe different than other children, a teacher needs to be aware of some of the activities of each stage as part of the basis to determine what should be taught and when it should be taught.

The following information about cognitive development was taken from the Cincinatti Children's Hospital Medical Center at www.cincinattichildrens.org Some common features indicating a progression from more simple to more complex cognitive development include the following:

Children (ages 6-12)
- Begin to develop the ability to think in concrete ways.
- Concrete operations are operations performed in the presence of the object and events that are to be used.
- Examples: how to combine (addition), separate (subtract or divide), order (alphabetize and sort/categorize), and transform (change things such as 25 pennies=1 quarter) objects and actions.
-

Adolescence (ages 12-18)-Adolescence marks the beginning development of more complex thinking skills, including abstract thinking, the ability to reason from known principles (form own new ideas or questions), the ability to consider many points of view according to varying criteria (compare or debate ideas or opinions), and the ability to think about the process of thinking.

During adolescence (between 12 and 18 years of age), the developing teenager acquires the ability to think systematically about all logical relationships within a problem. The transition from concrete thinking to formal logical operations occurs over time. Every adolescent progresses at varying rates in developing his / her ability to think in more complex ways.

Each adolescent develops his/her own view of the world. Some adolescents may be able to apply logical operations to school work long before they are able to apply them to personal dilemmas. When emotional issues arise, they often interfere with an adolescent's ability to think in more complex ways. The ability to consider possibilities, as well as facts, may influence decision making, in either positive or negative ways.

Some common features indicating a progression from more simple to more complex cognitive development include the following:

Early adolescence-During early adolescence, the use of more complex thinking is focused on personal decision making in school and home environments, including the following:

a) Begins to demonstrate use of formal logical operations in schoolwork.
b) Begins to question authority and society standards.
c) Begins to form and verbalize his / her own thoughts and views on a variety of topics, usually more related to his / her own life, such as:

- Which sports are better to play.
- Which groups are better to be included in.
- What personal appearances are desirable or attractive.
- What parental rules should be changed.

Middle adolescence-With some experience in using more complex thinking processes, the focus of middle adolescence often expands to include more philosophical and futuristic concerns, including the following:

- Often questions more extensively.
- Often analyzes more extensively.
- Thinks about and begins to form his / her own code of ethics.
- Thinks about different possibilities and begins to develop own identity.
- Thinks about and begins to systematically consider possible future goals.
- Thinks about and begins to make his / her own plans.
- Begins to think long term.
- Use of systematic thinking begins to influence relationships with others.

Late adolescence-During late adolescence, complex thinking processes are used to focus on less self-centered concepts as well as personal decision making, including the following:

- Increased thoughts about more global concepts such as justice, history, politics, and patriotism.
- Develops idealistic views on specific topics or concerns.
- Debate and develop intolerance of opposing views.
- Begins to focus thinking on making career decisions.
- Begins to focus thinking on emerging role in adult society.

The following suggestions will help to encourage positive and healthy cognitive development in the adolescent:

- Include adolescents in discussions about a variety of topics, issues, and current events.
- Encourage adolescents to share ideas and thoughts with adults.
- Encourage adolescents to think independently and develop their own ideas.
- Assist adolescents in setting their own goals.
- Stimulate adolescents to think about possibilities of the future.
- Compliment and praise adolescents for well thought out decisions.
- Assist adolescents in re-evaluating poorly made decisions for themselves.

PHYSICAL DEVELOPMENT, INCLUDING MOTOR AND SENSORY

It is important for the teacher to be aware of the physical stage of development and how the child's physical growth and development affect the child's learning. Factors determined by the physical stage of development include: ability to sit and attend; the need for activity; the relationship between physical skills and self-esteem; and the degree to which physical involvement in an activity (as opposed to being able to understand an abstract concept) affects learning.

Children with physical impairments possess a variety of disabling conditions. Although there are significant differences among these conditions, similarities also exist. Each condition usually affects one particular system of the body: the cardiopulmonary system (i.e., blood vessels, heart, and lungs) and the musculoskeletal system (i.e., spinal cord, brain nerves). Some conditions develop during pregnancy, birth, or infancy because of the known or unknown factors, which may affect the fetus or newborn infant. Other conditions occur later due to injury (trauma), disease, or factors not fully understood.

In addition to motor disorders, individuals with physical disabilities may have multi-disabling conditions such as concomitant hearing impairments, visual impairments, perceptual disorders, speech defects, behavior disorders, or mental handicaps, performance, and emotional responsiveness.

Some characteristics in which may occur with individuals with physical disabilities and other health impairments are:

1. Lack of physical stamina; fatigue.
2. Chronic illness; poor endurance.
3. Deficient motor skills; normal movement may be prevented.
4. May cause physical limitations or impede motor development; a prosthesis or an orthosis may be required.
5. Mobility and exploration of one's environment may be limited.
6. Limited self-care abilities.
7. Progressive weakening and degeneration of muscles.
8. Frequent speech and language defects; communication may be prevented; echolatia orthosis may be present.
9. May experience pain and discomfort throughout the body.
10. May display emotional (psychological) problems, which require treatment.
11. Social adjustments may be needed; may display maladaptive social behavior.
12. May necessitate long-term medical treatment.
13. May have embarrassing side effects from certain diseases or treatment.
14. May exhibit erratic or poor attendance patterns.

Skill 1.6   Demonstrate knowledge of educator resources relevant to the education of students with emotional impairments.

Includes types and characteristics of unique services, networks, and consumer organizations for students with emotional impairments and their families; publications, journals, professional organizations, and activities relevant to the ongoing professional development of educators in the field; and types of information available from families, school officials, and legal, social, and health agencies.

Organization	Members	Mission
Alexander Graham Bell Association for the Deaf and Hard of Hearing 3417 Volta Place, N.W. Washington, D.C. 20007 http://www.agbell.org	Teachers of the deaf, speech-language pathologists, audiologists, physicians, hearing aid dealers	To promote the teaching of speech, lip reading, and use of residual hearing to persons who are deaf; encourage research; and work to further better education of persons who are deaf.
Alliance for Technology Access 1304 Southpoint Blvd., Suite 240, Petaluma, CA 94954 Phone (707) 778-3011 Fax (707) 765-2080 TTY (707) 778-3015 Email: ATAinfo@ATAccess.org http://ww.Ataccess.org	People with disabilities, family members, and professionals in related fields, and organizations with work in their own communities and ways to support our mission.	**To** increase the use of technology **by** children and adults with disabilities and functional limitations.
American Council of the Blind 1155 15th Street, NW, Suite 1004, Washington, DC 20005 Phone: (202) 467-5081 (800) 424-8666 FAX: (202) 467-5085 http://Acb.org		To improve the well-being of all blind and visually impaired people by: serving as a representative national organization of blind people and conducting a public education program to promote greater understanding of blindness and the capabilities of blind people.

Organization	Members	Mission
American Council on Rural Special Education (ACRES) Utah State University 2865 Old Main Hill Logan, Utah 84322 Phone: (435) 797 3728 E-mail: inquiries at acres-sped.org	Open to anyone interested in supporting their mission	To provide leadership and support that will enhance services for individuals with exceptional needs, their families, and the professionals who work with them, and for the rural communities in which they live
American Society for Deaf Children 3820 Hartzdale Drive, Camp Hill, PA 17011 Phone: (717) 703-0073 (866) 895-4206 FAX: (717) 909-5599 Email: asdc@deafchildren.org www.deafchildren.org	Open to all who support the mission of THE association	To provide support, encouragement and information to families raising children who are deaf or hard of hearing.
American Speech-Language-Hearing Association 10801 Rockville Pike Rockville, MD 20852	Specialists in speech-language pathology and audiology	To advocate for provision of speech-language and hearing services in school and clinic settings; advocate for legislation relative to the profession; and work to promote effective services and development of the profession.
Asperger Syndrome Education Network (ASPEN) 9 Aspen Circle Edison, NJ 08820 Phone: (732) 321-0880 Email: info@AspenNJ.org http://www.aspennj.org		Provides families and individuals whose lives are affected by Autism Spectrum Disorders and Nonverbal Learning Disabilities with education, support and advocacy.
Attention Deficit Disorder Association 15000 Commerce Pkwy, Suite C Mount Laurel, NJ 08054 Phone: (856) 439-9099 FAX: (856) 439-0525 http://www.add.org/	Open to all who support the mission of ADDA	Provides information, resources and networking to adults with AD/HD and to the professionals who work with them.

Organization	Members	Mission
Autism Society of America 7910 Woodmont Avenue, Suite 300 Bethesda, Maryland 20814 Phone: (800) 328-8476 http://www.autism-society.org	Open to all who support the mission of ASA	To increase public awareness about autism and the day-to-day issues faced by individuals with autism, their families and the professionals with whom they interact. The Society and its chapters share a common mission of providing information and education, and supporting research and advocating for programs and services for the autism community.
Brain Injury Association of America 8201 Greensboro Drive Suite 611 McLean, VA 22102 Phone: (703) 761-0750 http://www.biausa.org	Open to all	Provides information, education and support to assist the 5.3 million Americans currently living with traumatic brain injury and their families.
Child and Adolescent Bipolar Association (CABF) 1187 Wilmette Ave. P.M.B. #331 Wilmette, IL 60091 **http://www.bpkids.org**	Physicians, scientific researchers, and allied professionals (therapists, social workers, educators, attorneys, and others) who provide services to children and adolescents with bipolar disorder or do research on the topic	**educates** families, professionals, and the public about pediatric bipolar disorder; **connects** families with resources and support; **advocates** for and **empowers** affected families; and **supports research** on pediatric bipolar disorder and its cure.
Children and Adults with Attention Deficit/ Hyperactive Disorder (CHADD) 8181 Professional Place - Suite 150 Landover, MD 20785 Phone: (301) 306-7070 Fax: (301) 306-7090 Email: national@chadd.org http://www.chadd.org	Open to all	providing resources and encouragement to parents, educators and professionals on a grassroots level through CHADD chapters

Organization	Members	Mission
Council for Exceptional Children (CEC) 1110 N. Glebe Road Suite 300 Arlington, VA 22201 Phone: (888) 232-7733 TTY: (866) 915-5000 FAX: (703) 264-9494 http://www.cec.sped.org	Teachers, administrators, teacher educators, and related service personnel	Advocate for services for [disabled] and gifted individuals. A professional organization that addresses service, training, and research relative to exceptional persons.
Epilepsy Foundation of America (EFA) 8301 Professional Place Landover, MD 20785 Phone: (800) 332-1000 http://www.epilepsyfoundation.org	A non-membership organization	Works to ensure that people with seizures are able to participate in all life experiences; and to prevent, control and cure epilepsy through research, education, advocacy and services
Family Center on Technology and Disability (FCTD) 1825 Connecticut Avenue, NW 7th Floor Washington, DC 20009 Phone: (202) 884-8068 fax: (202) 884-8441 Email: fctd@aed.org http://www.fctd.info/	Non member association	A resource designed to support organizations and programs that work with families of children and youth with disabilities.
Hands and Voices P.O. Box 371926 Denver CO 80237 Phone: (866) 422-0422 Email: parentadvocate@handsandvoices.org http://www.handsandvoices.org	Families, professionals, other organizations, pre-service students, and deaf and hard of hearing adults who are all working towards ensuring successful outcomes for children who are deaf and hard of hearing.	To support families and their children who are deaf or hard of hearing, as well as the professionals who serve them.

Organization	Members	Mission
The International Dyslexia Association Chester Building, Suite 382 8600 LaSalle Road Baltimore, Maryland 21286 Phone: (410) 296-0232 Fax: (410) 321-5069 http://www.interdys.org	Anyone interested in IDA and its mission can become a member	Provides information and referral services, research, advocacy and direct services to professionals in the field of learning disabilities.
Learning Disabilities Association of America (LDA) 4156 Library Road Pittsburgh, PA 15234 Phone: (412) 341-1515 Fax: (412) 344-0224 http://www.ldanatl.org	Anyone interested in LDA and its mission can become a member	• Provides cutting edge information on learning disabilities, practical solutions, and a comprehensive network of resources. • Provides support to people with learning disabilities, their families, teachers and other professionals.
National Association of the Deaf (NAD) 8630 Fenton Street, Suite 820, Silver Spring, MD Phone: (209) 210-3819 TTY: (301) 587-1789, , FAX: (301) 587-1791 Email: NADinfo@nad.org http://nad.org	Anyone interested in NAD and its mission can become a member	To promote, protect, and preserve the rights and quality of life of deaf and hard of hearing individuals in the United States of America.
National Mental Health Information Center P.O. Box 42557 Washington, DC 20015 Phone: (800) 789-2647 http://www.mentalhealth.samhsa.gov	Government Agency	Developed for users of mental health services and their families, the general public, policy makers, providers, and the media.

Organization	Members	Mission
National Dissemination Center for Children with Disabilities (NIHCY) P.O. Box 1492 Washington, DC 20013 Phone: (800) 695-0285 · Fax: (202) 884-8441 Email: nichcy@aed.org http://www.mentalhealth.samhsa.gov	Non membership association	A central source of information on: • disabilities in infants, toddlers, children, and youth, • IDEA, which is the law authorizing special education, • No Child Left Behind (as it relates to children with disabilities), and • research-based information on effective educational practices.
US Department of Education Office of Special Education and Rehabilitative Services http://www.ed.gov/about/offices/list/osers/index.html	Government Resource	Committed to improving results and outcomes for people with disabilities of all ages.
Wrights Law Email: webmaster@wrightslaw.com http://wrightslaw.com	Non membership organization	Parents, educators, advocates, and attorneys come to Wrightslaw for accurate, reliable information about special education law, education law, and advocacy for children with disabilities. Provides parent Advocacy training and updates on the law through out the country.
TASH (Formerly The Association for Persons with Severe Handicaps) 29 W. Susquehanna Ave., Suite 210 Baltimore, MD 21204 Phone: (410) 828-8274 Fax: (410) 828-6706 http:// www.tash.org	Anyone interested in TASH and its mission can become a member	To create change and build capacity so that all people, no matter their perceived level of disability, are included in all aspects of society.

Organization	Members	Mission
American Psychological Association 750 First Street, NE, Washington, DC 20002-4242 Phone: (800) 374-2721; FAX: (202) 336-5500. TTY: (202) 336-6123 http://www.apa.org	Psychologists and professors of Psychology	Scientific and professional society working to improve mental health services and to advocate for legislation and programs that will promote mental health; facilitate research and professional development.
Association for Children and Adults with Learning Disabilities 4156 Library Road Pittsburgh, PA 15234 http://www.acldonline.org/	Parents of children with learning disabilities and interested professionals	Advanced the education and general well-being of children with adequate intelligence who have learning disabilities arising from perceptual, conceptual, or subtle coordinative problems, sometimes accompanied by behavior difficulties.
The Arc of the United States 1010 Wayne Avenue Suite 650 Silver Springs, MD 20910 Phone: (301) 565-3842 FAX: (301) 565-3843 http://www.the arc.org	Parents, professionals, and others interested in individuals with mental retardation	Work on local, state, and national levels to promote treatment, research, public understanding, and legislation for persons with mental retardation; provide counseling for parents of students with mental retardation.
National Association for Gifted Children 1707 L Street, NW Suite 550 Washington, DC 20036 Phone: (202) 785-4368 FAX: (202) 785-4248 Email: nagc@nagc.org http://nagc.org	Parents, educators, community leaders and, other professionals who work with Gifted children.	To address the unique needs of children and youth with demonstrated gifts and talents.

Organization	Members	Mission
Council for Children with Behavioral Disorders Two Ballston Plaza 1110 N. Glebe Road Arlington, VA 22201 Phone: (800) 224-6830 FAX: (703) 264-9494	Members of the Council for Exceptional Children who teach children with behavior disorders or who train teachers to work with those children	Promote education and general welfare of children and youth with behavior disorders or serious emotional disturbances. Promote professional growth and research on students with behavior disorders and severe emotional disturbances.
Council for Educational Diagnostic Services Two Ballston Plaza 1110 N. Glebe Road Arlington, VA 22201	Members of the Council for Exceptional Children who are school psychologists, educational diagnosticians, [and] social workers who are involved in diagnosing educational difficulties	Promote the most appropriate education of children and youth through appraisal, diagnosis, educational intervention, implementation, and evaluation of a prescribed educational program. Work to facilitate the professional development of those who assess students. Work to further development of better diagnostic techniques and procedures.
Council for Exceptional Children Two Ballston Plaza 1110 N. Glebe Road Arlington, VA 22201	Teachers, administrators, teacher educators, and related service personnel	Advocate for services for [disabled] and gifted individuals. A professional organization that addresses service, training, and research relative to exceptional persons.
Council of Administrators of Special Education Two Ballston Plaza 1110 N. Glebe Road Arlington, VA 22201	Members of the Council for Exceptional Children who are administrators, directors, coordinators, or supervisors of programs, schools, or classes for exceptional children; college faculty who train administrators	Promote professional leadership; provide opportunities for the study of problems common to its members; communicate through discussion and publications information that will facilitate improved services for children with exceptional needs.

Organization	Members	Mission
Division for Children with Communication Disorders Two Ballston Plaza 1110 N. Glebe Road Arlington, VA 22201	Members of the Council for Exceptional Children who are speech-language pathologists, audiologists, teachers of children with communication disorders, or educators of professionals who plan to work with children who have communication disorders	Promote the education of children with communication disorders. Promote professional growth and research.
Division for Early Childhood Two Ballston Plaza 1110 N. Glebe Road Arlington, VA 22201	Members of the Council for Exceptional Children who teach preschool children and infants or educate teachers to work with young children	Promote effective education for young children and infants. Promote professional development of those who work with young children and infants. Promote legislation and research.
Division for the Physically Handicapped Two Ballston Plaza 1110 N. Glebe Road Arlington, VA 22201	Members of the Council for Exceptional Children who work with individuals who have physical disabilities or educate professionals to work with those individuals	Promote closer relationships among educators of students who have physical impairments or are homebound. Facilitate research and encourage development of new ideas, practices, and techniques through professional meetings, workshops, and publications.
Division for the Visually Handicapped Two Ballston Plaza 1110 N. Glebe Road Arlington, VA 22201	Members of the Council for Exceptional Children who work with individuals who have visual disabilities or educate professionals to work with those individuals	Work to advance the education and training of individuals with visual impairments. Work to bring about better understanding of educational, emotional, or other problems associated with visual impairment. Facilitate research and development of new techniques or ideas in education and training of individuals with visual problems.

Organization	Members	Mission
Division on Career Development Two Ballston Plaza 1110 N. Glebe Road Arlington, VA 22201	Members of the Council for Exceptional Children who teach or in other ways work toward career development and vocational education of exceptional children	Promote and encourage professional growth of all those concerned with career development and vocational education. Promote research, legislation, information dissemination, and technical assistance relevant to career development and vocational education.
Division on Mental Retardation Two Ballston Plaza 1110 N. Glebe Road Arlington, VA 22201	Members of the Council for Exceptional Children who work with students with mental retardation or educate professionals to work with those students	Work to advance the education of individuals with mental retardation, research mental retardation, and the training o professionals to work with individuals with mental retardation. Promote public understanding of mental retardation and professional development of those who work with persons with mental retardation.
Gifted Child Society P.O. Box 120 Oakland, NJ 07436	Parents and educators of children who are gifted	Train educators to meet the needs of students with gifted abilities, offer assistance to parents facing special problems in raising children who are gifted, and seek public recognition of the needs of these children.
National Association for the Education of Young Children 1313 L St. N.W. Suite 500, Washington DC 20005 Phone: (800) 424-2460 Email: webmaster@naeyc.org http://www.naeyc.org		Promote service and action on behalf of the needs and rights of young children, with emphasis on provision of educational services and resources.
National Asociation for Retarded Citizens 5101 Washington Ave., N.W. Washington, D.C http://www.thearc.org .		Work to promote the general welfare of persons with mental retardation; facilitate research and information dissemination relative to causes, treatment, and prevention of mental retardation.

Organization	Members	Mission
National Easter Seal Society 230 West Monroe Street, Suite 1800 Chicago, IL 60606 Phone: (800) 221-6827 TTY: (312) 726-1494 http://www.easterseals.com	State units (49) and local societies (951); no individual members	Establish and run programs for individuals with physical impairments, usually including diagnostic services, speech therapy, preschool services, physical therapy, and occupational therapy.
The National Association of Special Education Teachers 1201 Pennsylvania Avenue, N.W., Suite 300Washington D.C. 20004 Phone: (800) 754-4421 **FAX:** 800-424-0371 Email: contactus@naset.org	Special Education Teachers	To render all possible support and assistance to professionals who teach children with special needs. to promote standards of excellence and innovation in special education research, practice, and policy in order to foster exceptional teaching for exceptional children.

COMPETENCY 2.0   EVALUATION, ASSESSMENT, AND INDIVIDUALIZED EDUCATION PROGRAMS (IEPS)

Skill 2.1   Demonstrate knowledge of types and characteristics of assessment instruments and methods.

The following terms are frequently used in behavioral as well as academic testing and assessment. They represent basic terminology and not more advanced statistical concepts.

Baseline—(Also known as establishing a baseline.) This procedure means collecting data about a target behavior or performance of a skill before certain interventions or teaching procedures are implemented. Establishing a baseline will enable a person to determine if the interventions are effective.

Criterion-Referenced Test – A test in which the individual's performance is measured against mastery of curriculum criteria rather than comparison to the performance of other students. Criterion-referenced tests may be commercially or teacher made. Since these tests measure what a student can or cannot do, results are especially useful for identifying goals and objectives for IEPs and lesson plans.

Curriculum-Based Assessment—Assessment of an individual's performance of objectives of a curriculum, such as a reading or math program. The individual's performance is measured in terms of what objectives were mastered.

Duration recording-- Measuring the length of time a behavior lasts i.e., tantrums, time out of class, or crying.

Error Analysis—The mistakes on an individual's test are noted and categorized by type. For example, an error analysis in a reading test could categorize mistakes by miscues, substituting words, omitted words or phrases, and miscues that are self corrected.

Event recording—The number of times a target behavior occurs during an observation period.

Formal Assessment—Standardized tests have specific procedures for administration, norming, scoring and interpretation. These include intelligence and achievement tests. (Is norming correct?)

Frequency—The number of times a behavior occurs in a time interval, such as out-of-seat behavior, hitting, and temper tantrums.

Frequency Distribution—Plotting the scores received on a test and tallying how many individuals received those scores. A frequency distribution is used to visually determine how the group of individuals performed on a test, illustrate extreme scores, and compare the distribution to the mean or other criterion.

Informal Assessment—Non-standardized tests such as criterion referenced tests and teacher-prepared tests. There are no rigid rules or procedures for administration or scoring.

Intensity—The degree of a behavior as measured by its frequency and duration.

Interval recording—This technique involves breaking the observation into an equal number of time intervals, such as 10-second intervals during a 5-minute period. At the end of each interval, the observer notes the presence or absence of the target behavior. The observer can then calculate a percentage by dividing the number of intervals in which the target behavior occurred by the total number of intervals in the observation period. This type of recording works well for behaviors which occur with high frequency or for long periods of time, such as on or off-task behavior, pencil tapping, or stereotyped behaviors. The observer does not have to constantly monitor the student, yet can gather enough data to get an accurate idea of the extent of the behavior.

Latency—The length of time that elapses between the presentation of a stimulus, e.g., a question and the response, e.g., the student's answer.

Mean—The arithmetic average of a set of scores, calculated by adding the set of scores and dividing the sum by the number of scores. For example, if the sum of a set of 35 scores is 2935, dividing that sum by 35 (the number of scores), yields a mean of 83.9.

Median—The middle score. 50% of the scores are above this number and 50% of the scores are below this number. In the example above, if the middle score were 72, 17 students would have scored less than 72, and 17 students would have scored more than 72.

Mode: The score most frequently tallied in a frequency distribution. In the example above, the most frequently tallied score might be 78. It is possible for a set of scores to have more than one mode.

Momentary time sampling-This is a technique used for measuring behaviors of a group of individuals or several behaviors from the same individual. Time samples are usually brief and may be conducted at fixed or variable intervals. The advantage of using variable intervals is increased reliability, as the students will not be able to predict when the time sample will be taken.

Norm-Referenced Test- An individual's performance is compared to the group that was used to calculate the performance standards in this standardized test. Some examples are the CTBS, WISC-R and Stanford-Binet.

Operational Definition-The description of a behavior and its measurable components. In behavioral observations the description must be specific and measurable so that the observer will know exactly what constitutes instances and non-instances of the target behavior. Otherwise, reliability may be inaccurate.

Pinpoint- Specifying and describing the target behavior for change in measurable and precise terms. "On time for class" may be interpreted as arriving physically in the classroom when the tardy bell has finished ringing, or it may mean being at the pencil sharpener, or it may mean being in one's in seat and ready to begin work when the bell has finished ringing. Pinpointing the behavior makes it possible to accurately measure the behavior.

Profile-Plotting an individual's behavioral data on a graph.

Rate-The frequency of a behavior over a specified time period, such as 5 talk-outs during a 30-minute period, or typing 85 words per minute. (is the typing relevant?)

Raw Score-The number of correct responses on a test before they have been converted to standard scores. Raw scores are not meaningful because they have no basis of comparison to the performance of other individuals.

Reliability—The consistency (stability) of a test over time to measure what it is supposed to measure. Reliability is commonly measured in four ways:

- Test-retest method-The test is administered to the same group or individual after a short period of time and the results are compared.

- Alternate form (equivalent form)-measures reliability by using alternative forms to measure the same skills. If both forms are administered to the same group within a relatively short period of time, there should be a high correlation between the two sets of scores if the test has a high degree of reliability.

- Interrater-This refers to the degree of agreement between two or more individuals observing the same behaviors or observing the same tests.

- Internal reliability—is determined by statistical procedures or by correlating one-half of the test with the other half of the test.

Standard Deviation—The standard deviation is a statistical measure of the variability of the scores. The more closely the scores are clustered around the mean, the smaller the Standard Deviation will be.

Standard Error of Measurement—This statistic measures the amount of possible error in a score. If the standard error of measurement for a test is + or - 3, and the individual's score is 35, then the actual score may be 32 to 35.

Standard Score—A derived score with a set mean (usually 100) and a standard deviation. Examples are T-scores (mean of 50 and a standard deviation of 10), Z-scores (mean of 0 and standard deviation of 1), and scaled scores. Scaled scores may be given for age groups or grade levels. IQ scores, for instance, use a mean of 100 and a standard deviation of 15.

Task Analysis-Breaking an academic or behavioral task down into its sequence of steps. Task analysis is necessary when preparing criterion-referenced tests and performing error analysis. A task analysis for a student learning to do laundry might include:

1. Sort the clothes by type (white, permanent press, delicate).
2. Choose a type and select the correct water temperature and setting.
3. If doing a partial load, adjust the water level.
4. Measure the detergent.
5. Turn on the machine.
6. Load the clothes.
7. Add bleach, fabric softener at the correct time.
8. Wait for the machine to stop spinning completely before opening it.
9. Remove the clothes from the machine and place in a dryer. (A task analysis could be done for drying and folding as well.)

Validity—The degree to which a test measures what it claims to measure, such as reading readiness, self-concept, or math achievement. A test may be highly reliable but it will be useless if it is not valid. There are several types of validity to examine when selecting or constructing an assessment instrument.

- Content –examines the question of whether the types of tasks in the test measure the skill or construct the test claims to measure. That is, a test, which claims to measure mastery in algebra, would probably not be valid if the majority of the items involved basic operations with fractions and decimals.

- Criterion – referenced validity involves comparing the test results with a valid criterion. For example, a doctoral student preparing a test to measure reading and spelling skills may check the test against an established test such as the WRAT-T or another valid criterion such as school grades.

- Predictive Validity - refers to how well a test will relate to a future criterion level, such as the ability of a reading test administered to a first-grader to predict that student's performance at third or fifth grade.

- <u>Concurrent validity</u> – refers to how well the test relates to a criterion measure given at the same time. The test results are compared using statistical measures. The recommended coefficient is .80 or better.

- <u>Construct validity</u> – refers to the ability of the test to measure a theoretical construct, such as intelligence, self-concept, and other non-observable behaviors. Factor analysis and correlation studies with other instruments that measure the same construct are ways to determine construct validity.

Having the knowledge of interpreting and applying formal and informal assessment data is very important to deciding placement. An educator must have knowledge of interpreting formal and informal assessment data to assist him/her in determining some of those strengths and weaknesses.

Results of formal assessments are given in derived scores, which compare the student's raw score to the performance of a specified group of subjects. Criteria for the selection of the group may be based on characteristics such as age, sex, or geographic area. The test results of formal assessments must always be interpreted in light of what type of tasks the individual was required to perform. The most commonly used derived scores follow.

A. Age and Grade Equivalents are considered developmental scores because they attempt to convert the student's raw score into an average performance of a particular age or grade group.

Age equivalents are expressed in years and months, eg, 7.3. In the standardization procedure, a mean is calculated for all individuals of the particular age who took the test. If the mean or median number of correct responses for children 7 years and 3 months was 80, then an individual whose raw score was 80 would be assigned an age-equivalent of 7 years and 3 months.

Grade Equivalents are written as years and tenths of years, e.g., 6.2 would read sixth grade, second month. Grade equivalents are calculated on the average performance of the group, and have been criticized for their use to measure gains in academic achievement and to identify exceptional students.

Quartiles, Deciles, and Percentiles indicate the percentage of scores that fall below the individual's raw score. Quartiles divide the score into four equal parts; the first quartile is the point at which 25% of the scores fall below, the full score. Deciles divide the distribution into ten equal parts where the seventh decile would mark the point below which 70% of the scores fall. Percentiles are the most frequently used, however, a percentile rank of 45 would indicate that the person's raw score was at the point below which 45% of the other scores fell.

B. Standard Scores are raw scores with the same mean (average) and standard deviation (variability of asset of scores). In the standardization of a test, about 68% of the scores will fall above or below 1 standard deviation of the mean of 100. About 96% of the scores will fall within the range of 2 standard deviations above or below the mean. A standard deviation of 20, for example, will mean that 68% of the scores will fall between 80 and 120, with 100 as the mean. The most common are T scores, z scores, stanines, and scaled scores. Standard scores are useful because they allow for direct comparison of raw scores from different individuals. In interpreting scores, it is important to note what type of standard score is being used.

C. Criterion Referenced Tests and Curriculum-based Assessments are interpreted on the basis of the individual's performance on the objectives being measured. Such assessments may be commercially prepared or teacher-made and can be designed for a particular curriculum or a scope and sequence. These assessments are made by selecting objectives, task analyzing those objectives, and selecting measures to test the skills necessary to meet those tasks. Results are calculated for each objective, such as Cindy was able to divide 2-digit numbers by 1-digit numbers 85% of the time and was able to divide 2-digit numbers by 2-digit numbers 45% of the time. These tests are useful for gaining insight into the types of error patterns the student makes. Because the student's performance is not compared to others in a group, results are useful for writing IEPs as well as for deciding what to teach.

INTERPRET THE RESULTS OF FORMAL/INFORMAL SOCIAL/EMOTIONAL ASSESSMENTS

Standardized measures of behavior involve direct observation with a behavior rating scale. Measurement of emotional state involves inference and subjectivity on the part of the examiner.

Behavior Rating Scales-Examples of these scales are the Revised Behavior Problem Checklist, Behavior Rating Profile, and Burks Behavior Rating Scales. Items may be grouped according to categorical characteristics.

For the Revised Behavior Problem Checklist, the four major scales are:
- Conduct Disorder.
- Socialized Aggression.
- Attention Problem-Immaturity.
- Anxiety-Withdrawn.

There are minor scales of:
- Psychotic Behavior.
- Motor Excess.

Behavior-rating scales involve the examiner using a Likert-type scale to rate student behaviors. Each scale has its own set of scoring procedures, therefore, the teacher must be sure to consult the test manual before attempting to interpret the results.

Other factors to consider in interpreting behavior-rating scales are:
- Reliability and validity information.
- Norming group information as well as relevant research on the test instrument.
- Sources of information. Some tests include parent and youth reports or measure behavior across a number of settings in and out of school.
- Suggested uses of the results. Some tests are intended for screening but not diagnostic purposes.
- Scoring and profile information. For example, the Child Behavior Checklist and Revised Behavior Profile lists three social competency scales and behavior problem scales identified by factor analysis for boys and girls in three separate age ranges.

Measures of Emotional State -These tests are designed to be administered by trained psychologists and psychiatrists. The child's emotional state is inferred by analyzing observable behavior. Types of tests include projective methods, measures of self-concept, and inventories and questionnaires.

Projective Methods -The theory of these methods is that a person will project his or her own meaning, patterns, feelings, and significance to ambiguous stimuli. Because these tests are subjective, it is difficult to establish reliability and validity. Therefore, their usefulness for educational purposes is limited. Some examples of these tests are:

- Rorschach Ink Blot Test. The individual states what he "sees" in each of the 10 inkblots. Diagnostic interpretation is based on clinical data.
- Thematic Apperception Test. The examiner uses a series of 31 pictures and asks the child to tell a story about them. The examiner looks for themes in the stories, especially those relating to the main character.

Interpretations of these tests should be read with the following advisories—the reliability and validity, the training of the examiner, and the subjective quality.

Self-concept Measures-Some familiar examples are the Tennessee Self-concept Scale and Piers-Harris Children's Self-Concept scale. Most instruments use a system of self-evaluation and self-report. Thus, there is the potential for the child to choose the answer that he or she believes the examiner wants to see. In addition, because self-concept is a difficult construct to define, there is the problem of adequate validity.

Inventories and Questionnaires-Many of these are designed for measuring emotional and personality characteristics of adolescents and adults. These tests are often self-reported, although some like the Personality Inventory for Children (PIC) include a parent report. Results are grouped into scales such as adjustment, achievement, depression, delinquency, and anxiety. These results are generally used with classification and placement decisions. Interpretation of these tests should be done with the issues of reliability and validity. A popular example of this type of test for use with children is the PIC.

Personality Inventory for Children (PIC) was designed specifically for evaluating children. The parent completes the true/false items, and three validity scales are included to determine the "truthfulness" of the responses. Thirteen of the thirty scales are considered the "profile scales" with the first three, adjustment, achievement, and intellectual screening, considered the "cognitive triad".

LIMITATIONS OF VARIOUS TYPES OF ASSESSMENT

Achievement tests are instruments that directly assess students' skill development in academic content areas. This type of test measures the extent to which a student has profited from educational and/or life experiences compared to others of like age or grade level. Emphasis needs to be placed upon the kinds of behaviors each tests samples, the adequacy of its norms, the test reliability, and its validity.

An achievement test may be classified as a diagnostic test if strengths and weaknesses in skill development can be delineated. Typically, when used as a diagnostic tool, an achievement test measures one basic skill and its related components. For example, a reading test may measure reading recognition, reading comprehension, reading fluency, decoding skills, and sound discrimination. Each skill measured is reported in sub-classifications.

In order to render pertinent information, achievement tests must reflect the content of the curriculum. Some achievement tests assess skill development in many subject areas, while others focus upon single content areas. Within similar content areas, the particular skills assessed and how they are measured differ from test to test. The more prominent areas assessed by achievement tests include math, reading and spelling.

Achievement test usages include screening, placement, progress evaluation, and curricula effectiveness. As screening tests, these instruments provide a wide index of academic skill development and may be used to pinpoint students for whom educational interventions may be necessary for purposes of remediation or enrichment. They offer a general idea of where to begin additional diagnostic assessment.

Placement decisions in special education include significant progress, or lack thereof, in academic achievement. It is essential that data from individually administered achievement tests allow the examiner to observe quantitative (i.e., scores) performance as well as to denote specific strengths and weaknesses inherent in qualitative (e.g., attitude, motivation, problem-solving) performance. Knowing how an individual reacts or produces answers during a testing situation is equally relevant to measured skill levels when making placement decisions.

Achievement tests are routinely given in school districts across the nation as a means of evaluating progress. Scores of students can be compared locally, statewide, and with national norms. Accountability and quality controls can be kept in check through the reporting of scores.

Achievement tests may be norm-referenced or criterion-referenced, and administered individually or with in groups. Results of norm-referenced achievements tests (e.g., Peabody Individualized Achievement Test [PIAT], Wide Range Achievement Test [WRAT]), thought important in making comparisons, may not provide information needed for individual program planning, types of behaviors testes, sub-skill data, or types of scores reported.

Criterion-referenced achievement tests (e.g., KeyMath Diagnostic Arithmetic Test, Brigance Diagnostic Inventories) contain items that correspond with stated objectives, thus enabling identification of cognitive deficiencies. Knowledge of specific skill deficits is needed for developing individualized education plans.

Lastly, teachers can be provided with measures showing the effectiveness of their instruction. Progress reflected by student scores should be used to review, and often revise, instructional techniques and content. Alternative methods of delivery (i.e., presentations, worksheets, tests) can be devised to enhance instruction provided students.

Skill 2.2   Demonstrate knowledge of procedures for evaluating and identifying students with emotional impairments.

Please refer to the state website at http://www.michigan.gov/mde/

Skill 2.3   Demonstrate knowledge of the development and implementation of Individualized Education Programs (IEPs) for students with emotional impairments.

Please refer to skill 2.4 for more information

The special educator is trained to work in a team approach. This occurs from the initial identification of students who appear to deviate from what is considered to be normal performance or behavior for particular age- and grade-level students.

The special education teacher serves as a consultant (or as a team member, depending on the school district) to the student support team. If the student is referred, the special education teacher may be asked to collect assessment data for the forthcoming comprehensive evaluation.

This professional generally serves on the multidisciplinary eligibility, individualized educational planning and placement committees. If the student is placed in a special education setting, the special educator continues to coordinate and collaborate with regular classroom teachers and support personnel at the school-based level.

Support professionals are available at both the district and school-based levels, and they contribute valuable services and expertise in their respective areas. A team approach between district ancillary services and local school-based staff is essential.

1. **School psychologist.** The school psychologist participates in the referral, identification, and program planning processes. She/he contributes to the multidisciplinary team by adding important observations, data and inferences about the student's performance. As she/he conducts an evaluation, she/he observes the student in the classroom environment, takes a case history, and administers a battery of formal and informal individual tests. The psychologist is involved as a member of a professional team throughout the stages of referral, assessment, placement and program planning.
2. **Physical therapist.** This person works with disorders of bones, joints, muscles and nerves following medical assessment. Under the prescription of a physician, the therapist applies treatment to the students in the form of heat, light, massage and exercise to prevent further disability or deformity. Physical therapy includes the use of adaptive equipment and prosthetic and orthotic devices to facilitate independent movement. This type of therapy helps individuals with disabilities to develop or recover their physical strength and endurance.

3. **Occupational therapist.** This specialist is trained in helping students develop self-help skills (e.g., self-care, motor, perceptual and vocational skills). The students are actively involved in the treatment process to quicken recovery and rehabilitation.

4. **Speech and language pathologist.** This specialist assists in the identification and diagnosis of children with speech or language disorders. In addition, she/he makes referrals for medical or habilitation needs, counsels family members and teachers, and works with the prevention of communicative disorders. The speech and language therapist concentrates on rehabilitative service delivery and continuing diagnosis.

5. **Administrators.** Building principals and special education directors (or coordinators) provide logistical as well as emotional support. Principals implement building policy procedures and control designation of facilities, equipment and materials. Their support is crucial to the success of the program within the parameters of the base school. Special education directors provide information about federal, state, and local policy which is vital to the operation of a special education unit. In some districts the special education director may actually control certain services and materials. Role clarification, preferably in writing, should be accomplished to ensure effectiveness of program services.

6. **Guidance counselors, psychometrists, and diagnosticians.** These persons often lead individual and group counseling sessions and are trained in assessment, diagnostic and observation skills as well as personality development and functioning abilities. They can apply knowledge and skills to multidisciplinary teams and assist in the assessment, diagnosis, placement and program planning process.

7. **Social worker.** The social worker is trained in interviewing and counseling skills. This person possesses knowledge of available community and school services, and makes these known to parents. She/he often visits homes of students, conducts intake and assessment interviews, counsels individuals and small groups, and assists in district enforcement policies.

8. **School nurse.** This person offers valuable information about diagnostic and treatment services. She/he is knowledgeable about diets, medications, therapeutic services, health-related services, and care needed for specific medical conditions. Reports of communicable diseases are filed with the health department to which a health professional has access. A medical professional can sometimes obtain cooperation with the families of children with disabilities in ways that are difficult for the special education teacher to achieve.

9. **Regular teachers and subject matter specialists.** These professionals are trained in general and specific instructional areas, teaching techniques, and overall child growth and development. They serve as a vital component to the referral process, as well as in the subsequent treatment program if the student is determined eligible. They work with the students with special needs for the majority of the school day and function as a link to the children's special education and medical programs.

10. **Paraprofessional.** This staff member assists the special educator and often works in the classroom with the special needs students. She/he helps prepare specialized materials, tutor individual students, lead small groups, and provide feedback to students about their work.

Skill 2.4 **Demonstrate knowledge of the development and implementation of goals and objectives on Individualized Education Programs (IEPs) for students with emotional impairments.**

STATE THE IMPORTANCE OF MULTIDISCIPLINARY TEAM DECISION

As the due process procedure is followed, a series of major decisions are made by multidisciplinary teams. A typical chain of events that occur as decisions are made is outlined in Figure 2.4-1. Multidisciplinary teams are composed of persons from various disciplines. Team members include teachers (regular and special education), building and district administrators, school psychologists, school social workers, parents, and medical experts.

Figure 2.4-1

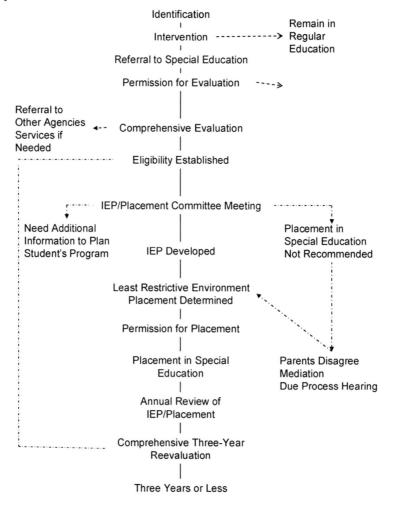

Identification-Identification of a student's learning problem occurs when comparisons are made within the general population about a student's academic or behavioral characteristics.

Teachers hold expectations for student behaviors, and those who exhibit actions that differ are singled out. The readers will want to review these behaviors as they have been specifically pinpointed as being necessary for success in the regular classroom by Salend and Lutz (1984).

All children and youth exhibit behaviors that deviate from normative expectations at times. But overall, it is the intensity of the behavior, the degree to which it is shown, and the length of time that it persists or has occurred that is significant. Behavior rating scales, checklists, inventories, and sociograms are used to determine whether a particular behavior is occurring and to what extent. Students with disabilities are identifiable by academic and social behaviors that deviate significantly from those of their classmates. The longer it takes to identify these students, the further they fall behind their age-mates in school.

Intervention-Once a student is identified as being at-risk academically or socially, remedial interventions are attempted within the regular classroom. Federal legislation requires sincere efforts be made to help the child learn in the regular classroom.

In some states, school-based teams of educators are formed to solve learning and behavior problems in the regular classroom. These informal problem-solving teams have a variety of names that include concepts of support (school support reams, student support teams), assistance (teacher assistant teams, school assistance teams, or building assistance teams), and appraisal (school appraisal teams - Pugach & Johnson 1989).

Regardless of what the teams are called, their purpose is similar. Chalfant, Pysh, and Moultrie (1979) state that teacher assistance teams are created to make professional suggestions about curricular alternatives and instructional modifications. These teams may be composed of a variety of participants including regular education teachers, building administrator, guidance counselor, special education teacher, and the student's parent(s). The team composition varies based on the type of referral, the needs of the student, and availability of educational personnel and state requirements. (Georgia department of Education 1986.)

Instructional modifications are tried in an attempt to accommodate the student in the regular classroom. Effective instruction is geared toward individual needs and recognizes differences in how students learn. Modifications are tailored to individual student needs. Some strategies for modifying regular classroom instruction shown on Table 2.4-2 are effective with at-risk students with disabilities, and students without learning or behavior problems.

Table 2.4-2 Strategies for Modifying Classroom Instruction

Strategy 1 Provide active learning experiences to teach concepts. Student motivation is increased when students can manipulate, weigh, measure, read or write using materials and skills that relate to their daily lives.

Strategy 2 Provide ample opportunities for guided practice of new skills. Frequent feedback on performance is essential to overcome student feelings of inadequacy. Peer tutoring and cooperative projects provide non-threatening practice opportunities. Individual student conferences, curriculum-based tests, and small group discussions are three useful methods for checking progress.

Strategy 3 Provide multi-sensory learning experiences. Students with learning problems sometimes have sensory processing difficulties. For instance, an auditory discrimination problem may cause misunderstanding about teacher expectations. Lessons and directions that include visual, auditory, tactile and kinesthetic modes are preferable to a single sensory approach.

Strategy 4 Present information in a manner that is relevant to the student. Particular attention to this strategy is needed when there is a cultural or economic gap between the lives of teachers and students. Relate instruction to a youngster's daily experience and interests.

Strategy 5 Provide students with concrete illustrations of their progress. Students with learning problems need frequent reinforcement for their efforts. Charts, graphs and check sheets provide tangible markers of student achievement.

Referral-Referral is the process through which a teacher, a parent, or some other person formally requests an evaluation of a student to determine eligibility for special education services.

The decision to refer a student may be influenced by: (1) student characteristics, such as the abilities, behaviors, or skills that students exhibit (or lack of them); (2) individual differences among teachers, in their beliefs, expectations, or skill in dealing with specific kinds of problems; (3) expectations for assistance with a student who is exhibiting academic or behavioral learning problems; (4) availability of specific kinds of strategies and materials; (5) parents' demand for referral or opposition to referral; and (6) institutional factors which may facilitate or constrain teachers in making referral decisions.

Fewer students are referred when school districts have complex procedures for referral, psychological assessments are backlogged for months, special education classes are filled to capacity, or principals and other administrators do not fully recognize the importance of special services. It is important that referral procedures be clearly understood and coordinated among all school personnel. All educators need to be able to identify characteristics typically exhibited by special needs students.

Also, the restrictiveness of special service settings must be known and the appropriateness of each clearly understood. The more restrictive special education programs tend to group students with similar disabilities for instruction. Last, the specialized services afforded through equipment, materials, teaching approaches, and specific teacher-student relations should be clearly understood.

Evaluation-If instructional modifications in the regular classroom have not proven successful, a student may be referred for multidisciplinary evaluation. The evaluation is comprehensive and includes norm and criterion-referenced tests (e.g., IQ and diagnostic tests), curriculum-based assessment, systematic teacher observation (e.g., behavior frequency checklist), samples of student work, and parent interviews.

The results of the evaluation are twofold: to determined eligibility for special education services; and to identify a student's strengths and weaknesses in order to plan an individual education program.

The wording in federal law is very explicit about the manner in which evaluations must be conducted, and about the existence of due process procedures that protect against bias and discrimination. Provisions in the law include the following as listed.

1.   The testing of children in their native or primary language unless it is clearly not feasible to do so.
2.   The use of evaluation procedures selected and administered to prevent cultural or ethnic discrimination.
3.   The use of assessment tools validated for the purpose for which they are being used (e.g., achievement levels, IQ scores, adaptive skills).
4.   Assessment by a multidisciplinary team utilizing several pieces of information to formulate a placement decision.

Furthermore, parental involvement must occur in the development of the child's educational program. According to the law, parents must:

1. Be notified before initial evaluation or any change in placement by a written notice in their primary language describing the proposed school action, the reasons for it, and the available educational opportunities.
2. Consent, in writing, before the child is initially evaluated.

Parents may:

1. Request an independent educational evaluation if they feel the school's evaluation is inappropriate.
2. Request an evaluation at public expense if a due process hearing decision is that the public agency's evaluation was inappropriate.
3. Participate on the committee that considers the evaluation, placement and programming of the student.

All students referred for evaluation for special education should have on file the results of a relatively current vision and hearing screening. This will determine the adequacy of sensory acuity and ensure that learning problems are not due to a vision and/or hearing problem.

Eligibility-Eligibility is based on criteria defined in federal law or state regulations, which vary from state to state. Evaluation methods correspond with eligibility criteria for the special education classifications.

For example, a multidisciplinary evaluation for a student being evaluated for intellectual disabilities would include the individual's intellectual functioning, adaptive behavior, and achievement levels.

Other tests are based on developmental characteristics exhibited (e.g., social, language and motor). A student evaluated for learning disabilities is given reading, math, and/or spelling achievement tests, an intelligence test to confirm average or above average cognitive capabilities, and tests of written and oral language ability.

Tests need to show a discrepancy between potential and performance. Classroom observations and samples of student work (such as impaired reading ability or impaired writing ability) also provide indicators of possible learning disabilities.

Eligibility for services in behavior disorders requires documented evidence of social deficiencies or learning deficits that are not due to intellectual, sensory, or physical conditions.

Therefore, any student undergoing multidisciplinary evaluation for this categorical service is usually given an intelligence test, diagnostic achievement tests, and social and/or adaptive inventories. Results of behavior frequency lists, direct observations, and anecdotal records collected over an extended period often accompany test results.

Additional information frequently used when making decisions about a child's eligibility for special education include:

- Developmental history
- Past academic performance
- Medical history or records
- Neurological reports
- Classroom observations
- Speech and language evaluations
- Personality assessment
- Discipline reports
- Home visits
- Parent interviews
- Samples of student work

If considered eligible for special education services, the child's disability should be documented in a written report stating specific reasons for the decision.

Three-year re-evaluations of a student's progress are required by law and serve the purpose of determining the growth and changing needs of the student. During the re-evaluation, continued eligibility for services in special education must be assessed using a range of evaluation tools similar to those used during the initial evaluation.

All relevant information about the student is considered when making a decision about continued eligibility or whether the student no longer needs the service and is ready to begin preparing to exit the program. If the latter transition is more appropriate, planning must occur.

Individual Education Plan - Before placement can occur, the multidisciplinary team must develop an Individualized Education Plan (IEP), a child-centered educational plan tailored to meet individual needs. IEPs acknowledge each student's requirement for a specially designed educational program.

Three purposes for IEPs are identified by Holloway, Patton, Payne, and Payne (1989):

1.   IEPs outline instructional programs. They provide specific instructional direction, which eliminates any pulling together of marginally related instructional exercises.
2.   IEPs function as the basis for evaluation.
3.   IEPs facilitate communication among staff members, teachers, and parents, and to some extent, teachers, and students.

Development of the IEP follows initial identification, evaluation and classification of students with disabilities. IEPs continue to be written annually as long as the student demonstrates an educational need for the services. These items should be included:

List format doesn't match list above.
1.   The student's present level of academic performance and functional performance.
2.   A statement of how the disability affects the student's involvement and progress in the general education curriculum. Preschool children must have a statement explaining how the disability effects the child's participation in appropriate activities.
3.   A statement of annual goals, or anticipated attainments.
4.   Short-term objectives are no longer required on every IEP. Students with severe disabilities or those taking an alternate assessment may need short term objectives, which lead to the obtainment of annual goals.
5.   A statement of when the parent will be notified of their child's progress which must be at least as often as the regular education student.
6.   Modifications or accommodations for participation in statewide or citywide assessments; stet f it is determined that the child cannot participate, why the assessment is inappropriate for the child and how the child will be assessed. Modifications and accommodations necessary for participation in the regular education curriculum are also included and are sometimes referred to as the specially designed instruction.
7.   Specific educational services, assistive technology, and related services, to be provided, and those who will provide them.
8.   Evaluate criteria and timeliness for determining whether instructional objectives have been achieved.
9.   Projected dates for initiating services with their anticipated frequency, location and, duration.
10.   The extent to which the child will not participate in the regular education program.

11. Transition:

- Beginning when a student is 14, and annually thereafter, the student's IEP must contain a statement of his or her transition service needs under the various components of the IEP that focus upon the student's courses of study (e.g., vocational education or advanced placement); and when appropriate include interagency responsibilities and links for possible future assistance

- Beginning at least one year before the student reaches the age of majority under State law, the IEP must contain a statement that the student has been informed of the rights under the law that will transfer to him or her upon reaching the age of majority.

Placement-The law defines special education and identifies related services that may be required if special education is to be effective. By law, placement in a special education delivery service must be the student's least restrictive environment.

Special education services occur at a variety of levels, some more restrictive than others. The largest number of students (i.e., mild disabilities) are served in settings closest to regular educational placements. Service delivery in more restrictive settings is limited to students with severe or profound disabilities who comprise a smaller population within special education. The exception is correctional facilities, which serve an even more limited and restricted populace.

Options for placement of special education students are given on what we call a "cascade of services," the term coined by Deno (1970). The multidisciplinary team must be able to match the needs of the student with an appropriate placement in the cascade system of services (see Figure 8-3). According to Polloway, et al. (1994), two assumptions are made when we place students using the cascade of services as a guide.

First, a child should be placed in an educational setting as close to the regular classroom as possible, and placed only as far away from this least restrictive environment as necessary to provide an appropriate education.

Second, program exit should be a goal. A student's placement may change when the team obtains data suggesting the advisability of an alternative educational setting. As adaptive, social, cognitive, motor and language skills are developed, the student may be placed in a lesser restrictive environment. The multidisciplinary team is responsible for monitoring and recommending placement changes when appropriate.

Figure 2.4-3 Cascade System of Special Education Services

Level 1   Regular classroom, including students with disabilities able to learn with regular class accommodations, with or without medical and counseling services.

Level 2   Regular classroom with supportive services (i.e., consultation, inclusion).

Level 3   Regular class with part-time special class (i.e., itinerant services, resource room).

Level 4   Full-time special class (i.e., self-contained).

Level 5   Special stations (i.e., special schools).

Level 6   Homebound

Level 7   Residential (i.e., hospital, institution)

Adapted from 1. Deno, "Special Education as Developmental Capital." Exceptional Children 1970, 37, 239, 237 Copyright 1970 by The Council for Exceptional Children Reprinted with permission from The Council for Exceptional Children.

Skill 2.5 Demonstrate knowledge of the uses of ongoing evaluation in the education of students with emotional impairments.

Special Education teachers must be associated with the various methods of alternative assessments in order to properly evaluate the goals and objectives of their students that are not able to be assessed by the use of standardized tests that utilize "paper and pencil methods."

Naturalistic Assessments (informal/authentic) address the functional skills that enhance a person's independence and social interactions in a variety of settings (i.e., school, home, community, etc.). Functional skills best addressed by this method are vocational skills such as following directions, socially acceptable behavior, and measurable work ethics. Naturalistic assessment requires planning for instruction to occur in various settings. The advantages of this method include a "real world setting" and allowing for the cultural appropriate materials. The disadvantages of this method are the requirements for long-range planning and reduced efficiency in both teaching and assessing the skill that is to be measured.

Performance-Based Assessments use a form of evaluation examining skills that are necessary to complete a project. An example of this method would be evaluating the math skill of "Order of Operations" by evaluating how an algebraic expression was solved. Another example would be observing how the skill of buttoning a shirt is progressing by having a student complete the task of putting a shirt on.

Portfolio Assessments are an evaluation tool which can be used to document the beginning, middle, and end of a student's yearly progress. This method utilizes compiling samples of work throughout a given period of time. Portfolio assessment is often used to track academic growth/progress in writing within regular education classrooms. The portfolio assessment also provides the teacher with a way to explain a student's present levels to parents.

Dynamic Assessment is a tailor made evaluation tool that looks at the manner in which a student learns and possible impediments to that learning process. Dynamic assessments look first at what must be taught and then how it will be taught to the student. Next, possible impediments to the student's success in this goal are examined to provide further insight.

When the impediments have been examined it is then possible to look at the goal and distinguish between performance and ability. For this reason it is an ideal method to use when evaluating student progress that may have been inhibited by a cultural norm. Identifying impediments allows for the evaluator to assess if a different teaching strategy may be more effective for students to attain objectives and goals on their IEPs.

Recommended Reading: Alternative Approaches to Assessing Young Children
By Angela Losardo, Ph.D., & Angela Notari-Syverson, Ph.D. © 2001 Paul H. Brookes Publishing Co.

Skill 2.6 **Demonstrate knowledge of a continuum of options for program and service delivery for students with emotional impairments.**

STATE CONDITIONS WHICH INDICATE THAT A CHILD SHOULD BE PLACED IN A REGULAR CLASSROOM

Most children whose learning and/or social-interpersonal problems tend to be of a mild and easily correctable nature can be successfully taught in the regular classroom by a general educator. These students are able to remain with age- and/or grade-level peers for the entire school day.

This least restrictive environment is especially suitable when certain indicators are present. These indicators will vary with individual children depending upon present disabilities. Indicators that tend to signify successful placement in regular classroom settings include ability to cope with disability, adjustment to the disability, adequate physical stamina, maturational level, motivation, cognitive development, interpersonal growth, and successful response to psychoactive drug intervention if needed.

Environmental modifications and special accommodations may need to be made for special education students in the regular classroom. Special needs students who receive special services through consultation or inclusion function for the entire day in the regular classroom.

Most students with mild disabilities remain in the regular classroom for the major portion of the school day. The special education teacher may deliver services to the youngster in his or her regular classroom, or he or she will receive pullout services through consultation through scheduled itinerant or resource room attendance.

An example of itinerant services is twenty minutes of speech correction from a speech/language teacher who goes to a particular school two or three times a week. Resource room services are generally delivered by a teacher certified in the exceptionality area in which the student in being served in special education. These services are given in a designated room at the school site. Students are scheduled to come to this delivery of service for one or several periods a day. Special modification and accommodations need to be made for these students in the regular classroom as well, since the majority of their school day is in this least restrictive environment.

Least restrictive Environment (LRE): There is no simple definition of LRE. LRE differs with the child's needs. LRE means that the student is placed in an environment which is not dangerous, overly controlling, or intrusive. The student should be given opportunities to experience what other peers of similar mental or chronological age are doing. Finally, LRE should be the environment that is the most integrated and normalized for the student's strengths and weaknesses. LRE for one child may be a regular classroom with support services, while LRE for another may be a self-contained classroom in a special school.

EXPLAIN SERVICE DELIVERY OPTIONS FOR PLACEMENT IN THE REGULAR CLASSROOM (CONSULTATION SERVICES AND INCLUSION)

Consultation Services-Two types of special education consultation models are presently being used in schools. The most traditional is the specially trained, special education teacher who provides consultation services to regular education teachers.

These consultants are available to regular teachers when they have questions about a child's academic or social-interpersonal needs, or when they require help with special materials, techniques, equipment, or instructional approaches. The assistance given is referred to as indirect services.

In contrast, the second type of consultant services provided by special education personnel are those in which special education personnel work directly with the student in the regular classroom in an effort to remediate difficulties, or to help the student make progress in the regular curriculum.

Preschool children who are placed in the regular classroom with a special education consultant are seen as having the potential to progress normally in a learning environment with sufficient maturation and development. These children who remain in the regular classroom with age-level peers are less likely to be labeled by others as special education students, and are given the opportunity to develop physically, intellectually, and socially before being placed in a special education setting.

School-age students who remain in the regular classroom with the assistance of a special education consultant receive the same benefits and considerations as the preschool children. They are typically characterized as having mild learning and/or social-interpersonal deficits. They are able to progress with their age-and grade-level peers in a regular classroom setting with specialized services and accommodations.

Inclusion-Inclusion is both a concept and a method of service delivery. It includes both indirect and direct services rendered by the special education teacher. With indirect services, the special education teacher consults with the regular classroom teacher about the type of instruction and instructional materials that would best meet the needs of a particular student.

Through direct services, the special education teacher comes into the regular classroom and team-teaches with the general education teacher. The special education teacher works with individuals, small groups, and large groups of students who are experiencing similar educational difficulties.

COMPOSITE SCENARIO OF AN INCLUSIVE EDUCATIONAL SETTING

The following composite scenario, published in the ERIC Clearinghouse Views (1993 pp. 66-67), provides a brief description of how regular and special teachers work together to address the individual needs of all of their students.

Jane Smith teaches 3rd grade at Lincoln Elementary School. Three days a week she co-teaches the class with Lynn Vogei, a special education teacher. Their 25 students include four who have special needs due to disabilities, and two others who currently need special help in specific curriculum areas. Each of the students with a disability has an IEP that was developed by a team that included both teachers. The teachers, paraprofessionals, and the school principal believe that these students have a great deal to contribute to the class and that they will achieve their best in the environment of a general education classroom.

All of the school personnel have attended in-service training designed to develop collaborative skills for teaming and problem solving. Mrs. Smith and the two professionals who work in the classroom also received special training on disabilities and how to create an inclusive classroom environment. The school's principal, Ben Parks, worked in special education many years ago and has received training on the impact of new special education developments and instructional arrangements on school administration. Each year, Mr. Parks works with the building staff to identify areas in which new training is needed. For specific questions that may arise technical assistance is available through a regional special education cooperative.

Mrs. Smith and Miss Vogel share responsibility for teaching and for supervising their paraprofessional. In addition to the time they spend together in the classroom, they spend two hours each week planning instruction, plus additional planning time with other teachers and support personnel who work with their students.

The teachers use their joint planning time to problem-solve and discuss the use of special instructional techniques for all students who need special assistance. Monitoring and adapting instruction for individual students is an ongoing activity. The teachers use curriculum-based measurement in systematically assessing their students' learning progress.

They adapt curricula so that lessons begin at the edge of the students' knowledge, adding new material at the students' pace and presenting it in a style consistent with the students' learning style. For some students, preorganizers or chapter previews are used to bring out the most important points of the material to be learned. For other students new vocabulary words may need to be highlighted or reduced reading levels may be required . Some students may use special activity worksheets, while others may learn best by using audiocassettes.

In the classroom the teachers group students differently for different activities. Sometimes the teachers and paraprofessionals divide the class, each teaching a small group or tutoring individuals. They use cooperative learning projects to help the students learn to work together and develop social relationships. Peer tutors provide extra help to students who need it. Students without disabilities are more than willing to help their friends who have disabilities, and vice versa.

While the regular classroom may not be the best learning environment for every child with a disability, it is highly desirable for all who can benefit. It provides contact with age-peers and prepares all students for the diversity of the world beyond the classroom.

SUCCESSFUL INCLUSION

Listed below are activities and support systems that are commonly found where successful inclusion has occurred.

Attitudes and Beliefs
- The regular teacher believes that the student can succeed.
- The school personnel are committed to accepting responsibility for the learning outcomes of students with disabilities.
- School personnel and the students in the class have been prepared to receive a student with disabilities.

Services and Physical Accommodation
- Services needed by the student are available (e.g., health, physical, occupational, or speech therapy).
- Adequate numbers of personnel, including aides and support personnel, are available.
- Adequate staff development and technical assistance, based on the needs of the school personnel, are being provided (e.g., information on disabilities, instructional methods, and awareness and acceptance activities for students, and team-building skills).
- Appropriate policies and procedures for monitoring individual students progress, including grading and testing, are in place.

Collaboration
- Special educators are part of the instructional or planning team.
- Teaming approaches are used for problem solving and program implementation.
- Regular teachers, special education teachers, and other specialists collaborate (e.g. co-teach, team teach, work together on teacher assistance teams).

Instructional Materials
- Teachers have the knowledge and skills needed to select and adapt curricula and instructional methods according to individual student needs.
- A variety of instructional arrangements is available (e.g., team teaching, cross-grade grouping, peer tutoring, and teacher assistance teams).
- Teachers foster a cooperative learning environment and promote socialization.

Source: ERJC Clearing House Views. Teaching Exceptional Children. Fall 1993 pp.66

DEMONSTRATE AN UNDERSTANDING OF THE CONCEPT OF THE RESOURCE ROOM

The resource room has been described as a regularly scheduled (specialized) instructional setting to which students go during the day for brief periods of special work. The emphasis is on teaching specific skills the student may be lacking. For the remainder of the school day the student is in his regular classroom. It is important the resource room teacher consult with the regular teacher and cooperatively develop a program that is intended eventually to eliminate the need for resource room assistance.

Students with mild disabilities comprise approximately 75 to 87 percent of all school-age students with disabilities. The majority of these students are enrolled in the regular classroom with resource room services. Causes of mild intellectual, learning, and behavioral disabilities are virtually unknown, and physical appearance is like that of the normal population.

Students with mild learning and behavior disorders are characterized as unable to meet the academic or behavioral standards of the regular education program. Therefore, the resource room provides a means of instructional programming to meet unique needs even though these students remain in the regular classroom during the greater portion of the day. They may be seen as discipline problems, slow learners, or poorly motivated. After exiting formal schooling, these students appear to assume a better adaptive fit into society. Most are not perceivably different when they enter the world of work.

PLACEMENT OF PRESCHOOL OR SCHOOL-AGE CHILDREN IN A FULL-TIME INSTRUCTIONAL SETTING

When students with disabilities are assigned to one classroom and one teacher for the entire day, the class is called a self-contained special education class, and the teacher is often referred to as a self-contained special class teacher.

This type of special education teacher assumes the major responsibility for educating the students assigned to her full-time placement. The students are generally assigned by exceptionality category (e.g., physically disabled, emotionally/behaviorally disordered, learning disabled). Exceptions to this practice occur in preschool sites where labeling rarely occurs.

Students enrolled in self-contained special education classrooms usually have moderate impairments. Often these students are among the most impaired in the regular school setting. Intensively administered and specially designed instruction is generally required in order for these students to gain academic or social-adaptive proficiency.

Preschool youngsters with moderate disabilities generally demonstrate difficulties in the areas of developing language and gross motor abilities, relating to peers and family, and are recognized during their early years.

In the preschool environment, these disabling conditions are more apt to be manifested in an inability to learn adequate readiness skills or to demonstrate successful self-help, adaptive, social-interpersonal, communication, or gross motor skills.

For school age students, the most typical symptoms exhibited by this population of special education students are inattention, disruptiveness, inability to learn to read, write, spell, or perform mathematical calculations, unintelligible speech, an appearance of not being able to see or hear adequately, frequent daydreaming, excessive movement, and in general, clumsiness and ineptitude in most school-related activities.

Regardless of the specified manifestations or symptoms reported, behaviors at the moderate level of severity are characterized by several factors. In general, the behaviors are significantly excessive, disruptive, and inappropriate. The number, as well as the degree and intensity of the behavior, is comparatively high. Moreover, the problem behaviors interfere with the student's expected performance (e.g., intellectual, social-interpersonal, and adaptive) relative to chronological age.

PLACEMENT AT A SPECIAL SCHOOL

Some self-contained special class settings are housed in separate schools, which primarily serve students with disabilities. These schools are referred to as special day schools or residential centers. This type of setting serves special needs students in specific categories, such as emotionally/behaviorally disordered, severely or profoundly intellectually disabled, physically disabled, deaf, blind, and multiple disabled. The student may attend the special school and return home after classes each day, or may be in residence at the school.

The advantage of this type of placement is the focused depth of the remedial services, including specialized instruction, techniques, and equipment. Due to the restrictive environment of the placement there is currently a trend toward reducing the number of special schools, particularly for exceptionality areas such as physical disabilities who typically can make progress when placed with regular students. This placement should be viewed as an alternative for students who cannot be accommodated in a less restrictive setting.

Students enrolled in special schools are usually among the most disabled in the public school setting. Identification of the severity levels, when applied across disabling conditions, more accurately corresponds with low moderate to severe disabilities. The individuals within this range of functioning are capable of developing skills that will allow some independence within their physical environment. These self-help skills include the ability to dress and feed themselves, to care for their personal health and grooming needs (e.g., toileting, bathing) and to develop adequate personal safety habits.

Some means of communication can generally be established by children functioning at this level. Most can develop verbal language skills however, some may use manual communication solely. Social-interpersonal skills are limited. The more severe the disability, the more completely the etiology of the condition is known. Furthermore, as the level of severity progresses the number of individuals in this population decreases proportionately.

PLACEMENT OF STUDENTS IN TRANSITIONAL PROGRAMS OF VOCATIONAL TRAINING

Vocational Training-Vocational education programs prepare students for entry into occupations in the labor force. Through these programs, it is intended that students become self-sufficient, self-supporting citizens.

This training has typically incorporated work-study programs at the high school and post-secondary levels. These programs include training while students are in school and on-the-job training after leaving school. Instruction focuses on particular job skills and on integral activities such as job opportunities, skill requirements, personal qualifications in relation to job requirements, work habits, money management, and academic skills needed for particular jobs.

Such vocational training programs are based on three main ideas (Blake, 1976):

1.   Students need specific training in job skills. They must acquire them prior to exiting school.
2.   Students need specific training and supervision in applying skills learned in school to requirements in job situations.
3.   Vocational training can provide instruction and field-based experience, which will meet these needs and help the student become able to work in specific occupations.

Career Education -Curricular aspects of career education include the phases of (1) career awareness (diversity of available jobs); (2) career exploration (skills needed for occupational groups); and (3) career preparation (specific training and preparation required for the world of work).

The concept of career education (1) extended this training into all levels of public school education (i.e., elementary through high school); (2) emphasized the importance of acquiring skills in the areas of daily living and personal-social interaction, as well as occupational training and preparation; and (3) focused upon integrating these skills into numerous areas of academic and vocational curricula. In general, career education attempts to prepare the individual for all facets of life.

Vocational Training in Special Education-Vocational training in special education has typically focused upon the exceptionality area of intellectual disabilities. Special guidance and training services have more recently been directed toward students with learning disabilities, emotional behavior disorders, physically disabled, visually impaired, and hearing impaired.

Individuals with disabilities are mainstreamed with non-disabled students in vocational training programs when possible. Special sites provide training for those persons with more severe disabilities who are unable to be successfully taught in an integrated setting. Specially trained vocational counselors monitor and supervise student work sites.

Regardless of the disabling condition, aptitude testing is considered an important component in vocational training for the students in a mild or moderate setting. This assessment is necessary in order to identify areas of interest and capability. Attitudes and work habits are deemed important by many prospective employers, and so these competencies are included in the training.

Training provisions for individuals with severe intellectual disabilities have expanded. They include special programs for school-aged children and secondary-level adolescents, and sheltered workshop programs for adults.

Instruction focuses upon self-help skills, social-interpersonal skills, motor skills, rudimentary academic skills, simple occupational skills, and lifetime leisure and recreational skills. In addition, secondary-level programs offer on-the-job supervision and sheltered workshop programs provide work supervision and pay a small wage for contract labor. Some persons with moderate to severe intellectual disabilities can be trained for employment in supervised unskilled occupations, while others are only able to perform chores and other simple tasks in sheltered workshops.

COMPETENCY 3.0   BEHAVIOR MANAGEMENT

Skill 3.1   Demonstrate knowledge of strategies and techniques used to improve students' social skills.

One of the components of Bower's definition of emotional handicaps is an inability to form satisfactory interpersonal relationships with others. Social skill deficits may compound academic problems because time spent engaged in negative encounters with others, or maladaptive behavior, takes valuable time away from learning.

Many children with behavior disorders display deficits in such areas as popularity with others, ability to adapt to changes and demands of different situations. Social skills instruction also included "survival skills" such as asking for assistance, communication skills, and problem solving.

Possible reasons for social skills deficits may be:

- Lack of suitable role models (e.g., family members who are constantly aggression in resolving conflicts).
- Lack of opportunity to observe and practice certain social skills (e.g., a young child who has not had much interaction with children may find it difficult to allow his peers to take turns in games).
- Lack of previous instruction in certain skills (e.g., a child who has never had to travel on public transportation will probably not know how to read schedules and ask for help in using public transportation).
- Cultural differences which may create conflicts but may not in themselves be maladaptive (i.e., differences in "personal space" boundaries between persons having a conversation)

Methods of identifying and assessing social skills deficits include:

1. Social Skills Checklists: Examples of commercial checklists include the Walker Problem Behavior Identification Checklist, Revised Behavior Problem Checklist, and the Deveraux Scales for Elementary and Adolescent Children. Checklists are used to report the presence or absence of a behavior, while rating scales indicate the frequency of a particular behavior and often include teacher as well as parent report forms.

2. Direct Observation: These observations of the child in various settings help to identify problem behaviors across settings. The child's behavior can also be compared to that of his or her peers in similar settings. Observations should include the components of the child's environment as well as how others interact with the child. It is possible that adjustments in the environment can decrease or eliminate the undesirable behavior.

3. Role Playing: In this type of observation, a social situation is staged, and the teacher observes the student's behavior. The teacher can determine if the student does not know the skill, or knows the skill but does not practice it. These activities may be part of commercially prepared training activities or designed by the teacher.

4. Self-Reports: The student may complete a checklist, a questionnaire, (questions with open-ended statements), or a direct interview with the teacher.

5. Sociometric Measures: Three basic formats are (a) peer nominations (based on nonbehavioral criteria such as preferred playmates), (b) peer ratings (where students rate all of their peers on nonbehavioral criteria such as work preferences) and (c) peer assessments (where peers are rated with respect to specific behaviors).

Mercer and Mercer (1993) recommend five general teaching techniques to build positive self-concepts in students and can do much to eliminate the frustration, anxiety and resulting acting-out behaviors in children. These suggestions are:
- Incorporate learning activities that provide opportunities for success
- Establish goals and expectations
- Monitor progress and provide regular feedback
- Provide a positive and supportive learning environment
- Teach students to be independent learners

There are commercial programs to teach specific social skills, but the teacher can take advantage of opportunities throughout the day to teach social skills. Examples of such opportunities include:

- Teacher modeling of positive social behaviors throughout the day
- Reinforcing instances when students display positive behaviors
- Planning instances for students to practice social behaviors
- Assigning responsibilities to students
- Assisting students in identification of their strengths and in finding behaviors to be targeted for change
- Assist students in setting goals and in making plans to achieve those goals

Teaching techniques that have been used to teach social skills include:

1. **Bibliotherapy:** Selected children's books are used to help the child identify with the problems faced with the main character, release emotions regarding the problems, and develop insight into his own behavior. Through reading about others with similar problems, the child can discuss the situation in the book, relate them to his own situation and analyze the problem-solving methods used in the story.

2. **Attribution Retraining:** Often, students with learning and behavior problems attribute their success or failure to outside causes rather than their own ability or lack of effort. Through attribution retraining, students are taught to attribute success to their own efforts (i.e., studying rather than the test being "too easy") and failure to ineffective strategies, rather than being "dumb". Students are taught study skills and other learning strategies to help them become better learners.

3. **Modeling:** The teacher gives positive reinforcement to students who exhibit desirable behaviors as well as model positive social skills in his daily interactions. For example, if the teacher wants students to learn how to initiate a conversation, he can select the student models, set up a demonstration of appropriate ways to initiate a conversation, and have the other students observe the model. The teacher should provide opportunities for the students to practice, and consistently reinforce students who perform the behavior.

4. **Behavior Modification**: This topic is discussed in Competency 14.

5. **Cognitive Behavior Modification**: Meichenbaum's research in this technique is well known in the field of learning disabilities. CBM involves a three-step process to teach academic as well as social skills. The goal of CBM is to encourage the student to think through his or her actions before acting. As part of this process, the teacher should build in errors or obstacles in order to teach students how to deal with mistakes and set-backs. In the CBM process,

   a. The teacher or another adult performs the task or social skill while verbalizing the thinking process aloud
   b. The student performs the task or social skill while verbalizing the process aloud, while the teacher reinforces and provides feedback,
   c. The student performs the task while thinking to himself, and the teacher provides reinforcement and feedback.

6. **Self-management:** Self-management is an important part of social skills training, especially for older students preparing for employment. Components of self-management include:
   a. Self-monitoring: choosing behaviors and alternatives and monitoring those actions.
   b. Self-evaluation: deciding the effectiveness of the behavior in solving the problem.
   c. Self-reinforcement: telling oneself that one is capable of achieving success.

7. **Interview techniques**: There are many different interview techniques such as Life-space Interviewing and Reality Therapy. These techniques assist the student in solving interpersonal problems and managing crisis situations through discussing the problem and the maladaptive behaviors, generating alternatives, and assuming responsibility for one's actions.

8. **Commercial Programs:** These programs teach skills such as friendship skills (i.e., giving compliments) problem-solving (asking for help), successful classroom behaviors (complying with rules), conversation skills (asking skills), and skills for difficult situations (rejection by peers, criticism from an employer). Examples of these programs include:
   - ASSET: A Social Skills Program for Adolescents.
   - CLASS: Contingencies for Learning Academic and Social Skills.
   - Getting Along with Others.
   - Skill Streaming the Elementary School Child and Skill Streaming the Adolescent.
   - Social Skills for Daily Living.
   - Coping With Series.
   - Walker Social Skills Curriculum, which includes ACCEPTS and ACCESS.

Teaching is usually done through a process of:

- Providing a description of the behavior and rationale for learning the appropriate behavior.
- Modeling of the behavior.
- Rehearsal and practice.
- Feedback.
- Generalization.

For many students, generalizing skills learned in class to other situations (on campus, on the job, or in the home and community) is the most difficult part of social skills training. Thus, the teacher should periodically review the skills with the students and encourage them to learn the skills outside class. By recruiting others on campus to help with reinforcement (such as setting up situations where students must ask the media teacher for assistance in finding a reference, or asking the administrators to reinforce and reward them when they observe students exhibiting social skills), students can have additional instances to use and experience the value of using the skill(s) they learned in class.

Skill 3.2 Demonstrate knowledge of strategies and techniques used to improve students' independent learning skills.

Many students with learning and behavior problems are characterized as poor independent workers. Too frequently these students do not know how to study or work without adult supervision, nor do they view themselves as responsible for their own learning or behavior.

Several concerns must be addressed prior to expecting independent functioning. First, the child must understand the nature of the assignment and the content on which they are based. Next, it must be determined whether the child cannot, rather than will not, do the work. Then it needs to be determined whether the child is able to ask for help in a positive, appropriate manner. Finally, the task expectations held by the teacher need to be accurately conveyed to the student (i.e., how they should be done and criteria for successful completion).

Modeling: Modeling is often used as a mechanism for moving the learner from dependence to independence. Modeling refers to the use of significant adults or peers to demonstrate to the learner appropriate performance behaviors. Initially, the teacher models the appropriate performance, which is a form of demonstration. She/he may then encourage the student to copy her; thus imitation occurs. Next, she/he might encourage the learner to undertake the task himself, but with her/his guidance, assistance, and prompting if necessary. Finally, she/he would provide verbal instruction without prompting, hopefully leading the learner to the point at which he/she can perform the task him/herself upon request.

Training in self-instruction can be combined with modeling. The underlying purpose for this approach is to encourage the learner to develop verbal control of behavior. Meichenbaum (1975) advocates the use of the following components:

1. Cognitive Modeling. The adult model performs a task while verbally instructing himself.
2. Overt, Self-Guidance. The child performs the same task, imitating instructions spoken by the model.
3. Faded, Overt, Self-Guidance. The child softly repeats the instructions while repeating the task.
4. Covert Self-Instruction. The child performs the task while silently instructing himself.

Self-monitoring refers to procedures by which the learner records whether he is engaging in certain behaviors, particularly those that would lead to increased academic achievement and/or social behavior. Self-reinforcement is important to the success of self-monitoring and may be administered as verbal self-acknowledgment or as tangible rewards. Checklists, or other means of keeping track, may be faded upon evidence of progress. This system encourages self-responsibility and independence.

See skill 1.5 for information on self-advocacy

Self Concept-Self-concept may be defined as the collective attitudes or feelings that one holds about oneself. Children with disabilities perceive early in life that they are deficient in skills that seem easier for their peers without disabilities.

They also receive expressions of surprise or even disgust from both adults and children in response to their differing appearance and actions, again resulting in damage to the self-concept. The special education teacher, for these reasons, will want to direct special and continuing effort to bettering each child's own perception of him/herself.

1. The poor self-concept of a child with disabilities causes that student at times to exhibit aggression or rage over inappropriate things. The teacher can ignore this behavior unless it is dangerous to others or too distracting to the total group, thereby reducing the amount of negative conditioning in the child's life. Further, the teacher can praise this child quickly and frequently for the correct responses he/she makes, remembering that these responses may require special effort on the student's part to produce. Further, correction, when needed, can be done tactfully and in private.

2. The child whose poor self-concept manifests itself in withdrawn behavior should be pulled gently into as many social situations as possible by the teacher. This child must be encouraged to share experiences with the class, to serve as teacher helper for projects, and to be part of small groups for tasks. Again, praise for performing these group and public acts is most effective if done immediately.

3. The teacher can plan, in advance, to structure the classroom experiences so that aversive situations will be avoided. Thus, settings that stimulate the aggressive child to act out can be redesigned and situations that stimulate group participation can be set up in advance for the child who acts in a withdrawn manner. Frequent, positive, and immediate are the best terms to describe the teacher feedback required by children with disabilities. Praise for very small correct acts should be given immediately, and repeated when each correct act is repeated. Criticism or outright scolding should be done, whenever needed and possible, in private. The teacher should first check the total day's interactions with students to ensure that the number and qualitative content of verbal stimuli is heavily on the positive side. While this trait is desirable in all good teaching, it is fundamental and utterly necessary to build the fragile self-concept of youngsters with disabilities.

4. The teacher must have a strategy for use with the child who persists in negative behavior outbursts. One system is to intervene immediately and break the situation down in to three components. First, the teacher requires the child to identify the worst possible outcome from the situation, the thing that he/she fears. To do this task, the child must be required to state the situation in the most factual way he/she can. Second, the child is required to state what would really happen if this worst possible outcome happened, and to evaluate the likelihood of it happening. Third, the child is asked to state an action or attitude that he/she can take after examining the consequences in a new light. This process has been termed <u>rational emotive therapy.</u>

Skill 3.3 **Demonstrate knowledge of strategies and techniques used to improve students' individual and group problem-solving and decision-making skills.**

Teachers should have a toolkit of instructional strategies, materials and technologies to encourage and teach students how to problem solve and think critically about subject content.

With each curriculum chosen by a district for school implementation comes an expectation that students must master benchmarks and standards of learning skills. There is an established level of academic performance and proficiency in public schools that students are required to master in today's classrooms. Research of national and state standards indicate that there additional benchmarks and learning objectives in the subject areas of science, foreign language, English language arts, history, art, health, civics, economics, geography, physical education, mathematics and social studies that students are required to master in state assessments (Marzano & Kendall, 1996).

Students use basic skills to understand things that are read such as a reading passage, a math word problem, or directions for a project. However, students apply additional thinking skills to fully comprehend how what was read could be applied to their own life and how to make comparatives or choices based on the factual information given.

These higher-order thinking skills are called critical thinking skills as students think about thinking. Teachers are instrumental in helping students use these skills in everyday activities such as:
- Analyzing bills for overcharges.
- Comparing shopping ads or catalogue deals.
- Finding the main idea from readings.
- Applying what's been learned to new situations.
- Gathering information/data from a diversity of sources to plan a project.
- Following a sequence of directions.
- Looking for cause and effect relationships.
- Comparing and contrasting information in synthesizing information.

Attention to learner needs during planning is foremost and includes identification of that which the students already know and still need to know. The matching of learner needs with instructional elements such as content, materials, activities and goals is an important part of the instructional design process..

Since most teachers want their educational objectives to use higher level thinking skills, teachers need to direct students to these higher levels on the taxonomy. Questioning is an effective tool to increase students' higher order thinking skills.

Low order questions are useful to begin the process. They insure the student is focused on the required information and understands what needs to be included in the thinking process. For example, if the objective is for students to be able to read and understand the story "Goldilocks and the Three Bears," the teacher may wish to start with low order questions (i.e., "What are some things Goldilocks did while in the bears home?" [Knowledge] or "Why didn't Goldilocks like the Papa Bear's chair?" [Analysis]).

Through a series of questions, the teacher can move the students up the taxonomy. (For example, "If Goldilocks had come to your house, what are some things she may have used?" [Application], "How might the story differ if Goldilocks had visited the three fishes?" [Synthesis], or "Do you think Goldilocks was good or bad? Why?" [Evaluation]). The teacher, through questioning, can control the thinking process of the class. As students become more involved in the discussion they are systematically being lead toward higher level thinking.

Teachers can use semester portfolios to gauge student academic progress and personal growth of students. Using graphic organizers and concept web guides is an instructional strategy teachers can use to guide students into further inquiry of the subject matter.

Imagine the research of the German chemist Fredrich August Kekule when he looked into a fire one night and solved the molecular structure of benzene and you can imagine fostering that same creativity in students. Helping students understand the art of "visualization" and the creativity of discovery may impart a student visualizing the cure for AIDS or Cancer, or how to create reading programs for the next generation of readers.

Helping students become effective note-takers and stimulating a diversity of perspectives for spatial techniques that can be applied to learning is a proactive teacher strategy. Teachers create a visual learning environment where art and visualization become natural art forms for learning. In today's computer environment, students must understand that computers cannot replace the creative thinking and skill application that comes from the greatest computer on record, the human mind.

Motivation-Before the teacher begins instruction, he or she should choose activities that are at the appropriate level of student difficulty, are meaningful, and relevant. Teacher behaviors that motivate students include:

- Maintain Success Expectations through teaching, goal setting, establishing connections between effort and outcome, and self-appraisal and reinforcement.
- Have a supply of intrinsic incentives such as rewards, appropriate competition between students, and the value of the academic activities.
- Focus on students' intrinsic motivation through adapting the tasks to students' interests, providing opportunities for active response, including a variety of tasks, providing rapid feedback, incorporating games into the lesson, allowing students the opportunity to make choices, create, and interact with peers.
- Stimulate students' learning by modeling positive expectations and attributions. Project enthusiasm and personalize abstract concepts. Students will be better motivated if they know what they will be learning about. The teacher should also model problem-solving and task-related thinking so students can see how the process is done.

For adolescents, motivation strategies are usually aimed at getting the student actively involved in the learning process. Since the adolescent has the opportunity to get involved in a wider range of activities outside the classroom (job, car, being with friends), stimulating motivation may be the focus even more than academics.

Motivation may be achieved through extrinsic reinforcers or intrinsic reinforcers. This is accomplished by allowing the student a degree of choice in what is being taught or how it will be taught. The teacher will, if possible, obtain a commitment either through a verbal or written contract between the student and the teacher. Adolescents also respond to regular feedback, especially when that feedback shows that they are making progress.

Rewards for adolescents often include free time for listening to music, recreation or games. They may like extra time for a break or exemption from a homework assignment. They may receive rewards at home for satisfactory performance at school. Other rewards include self-charting progress, and tangible reinforcers. In summary, motivational activities may be used for goal setting, self-recording of academic progress, self-evaluation, and self-reinforcement.

Problem Solving-The skills of analysis and interpretation are necessary for problem solving. Students with learning disabilities find problem solving difficult, and therefore sometimes attempt to avoid them.

Skills necessary for problem solving include:

1) Identification of the main idea- what is the problem about?
2) *Main question of the problem- what is the problem asking for?*
3) *Identifying important facts- what information is necessary to solve the problem?*
4) *Choose a strategy and an operation* –how will the student solve the problem and with what operation?
5) *Solve the problem* – perform the computation.
6) *Check accuracy of computation and compare the answer to the main question* –Does it sound reasonable?
7) *If solution is correct* –*Repeat the steps.*

IDENTIFY EFFECTIVE TEACHING METHODS FOR DEVELOPING THE USE OF MATH SKILLS IN PROBLEM-SOLVING

One of the main reasons for studying mathematics is to acquire the ability to perform problem-solving skills. Problem solving is the process of applying previously acquired knowledge to new and novel situations.

Mathematical problem solving is generally thought of as solving word problems. However, there are more skills involved in problem solving than merely reading word problems, deciding on correct conceptual procedures, and performing the computations.

Problem solving has proven to be the primary area of mathematical difficulty for many students. The following methods for developing problem solving skills have been recommended.

1. Allot time for the development of successful problem solving skills. It is complex process and needs to be taught in a systematic way.
2. Be sure prerequisite skills have been adequately developed. The ability to perform the operations of addition, subtraction, multiplication, and division are necessary sub-skills.
3. Use error analysis to diagnose areas of difficulty. One error in procedure or choice of mathematical operation, once corrected, will eliminate subsequent mistakes following the initial error like the domino effect. Look for patterns of similar mistakes to prevent a series of identical errors. Instruct children on the usage of error analysis to perform self-appraisal of their own work.
4. Teach students appropriate terminology. Many words have a different meaning when used in a mathematical context than in every day life. For example "set" in mathematics refers to a grouping of objects, but it may be used as a very, such as in "set the table. Other words that should be defined include "order," "base," "power," and "root."
5. Have students estimate answers. Teach them how to check their computed answer, to determine how reasonable it is. For example, Teddy is asked how many hours he spent doing his homework. If he worked on it two hours before dinner and one hour after dinner, and his answer came out to be 21, Teddy should be able to conclude that 21 hours is the greater part of a day, and is far too large to be reasonable.
6. Remember that development of math readiness skills enables students to acquire prerequisite concepts and to build cognitive structures. These prerequisite skills appear to be related to problem solving performance.

Skill 3.4   Demonstrate knowledge of various strategies used to manage the behavior of individual students with emotional impairments.

APPROPRIATE USES OF IMMEDIATE AND DELAYED FEEDBACK

Feedback is essential in behavioral situations if a student is to examine his behavior and make appropriate choices concerning behavior. Timing of feedback is very important. Reactions to a particular situation should be given as soon as possible so that the student will know exactly which behavior is being discussed. The teacher should, when feasible, give a student feedback about a particular behavior during the encounter itself. For example, if a student says, "I don't want your help!" I don't like you," a teacher's immediate feedback might be a statement such as, "What you just said is the kind of remark that makes me feel pushed away."

In situations involving behavior and feelings, the more immediate the feedback, the more helpful it is. Disturbing situations should be discussed as they occur. Collective hurt feelings and annoyances that are dropped on a person at one time lead to more hurt feelings and frustrations.

Similarly, inappropriate behaviors that are not dealt with immediately are more likely to re-occur, as the student might not understand which behavior was inappropriate or why it was so if it is discussed later and in another context or unrelated situations.

Only those situations in which the student is out of control or temporarily "loses his cool" might call for delayed feedback from the teacher. In these instances, feedback is delayed until the student regains control of himself and is able to be receptive to the teacher's attempt to provide feedback.

In learning situations there are appropriate uses for both immediate and delayed feedback. In general, student learning is enhanced when students are provided with immediate and specific feedback about their performance.

When learning new skills or practicing tasks still to be mastered, students should be provided with prompt information about the correctness of their responses. Affirmative feedback that uses words such as "good" and "fine," other expressions or praise, or the delivery of tokens, are ways of confirming correctness of responses through the use of appropriate feedback.

If the responses are incorrect, there are techniques a teacher can use in guiding a student to analyze and discover his/her own errors, thus turning a failure situation into a successful venture. A teacher reinforces attempts or efforts by stating an affirmation and then follows it be a suggested modification. "Good job! You got two correct. Now just do this one the same way."

When students are asked to complete assignments in a self-directed manner without assistance from the teacher, it is especially important that materials contain clear instructions and provide immediate, self-corrective feedback that prevents the students from practicing their mistakes.

Immediate feedback increases motivation and reinforces correct learning. Delayed feedback can lead to frustration and can cause an easily frustrated or poorly motivated student to stop performing. However, for students who are self-motivated, delayed feedback can actually encourage learning by giving them an opportunity to correct their own mistakes and discover their own answers. Delayed feedback also serves as a good review of previously learned skills.

WAYS OF FACILITATING POSITIVE STUDENT BEHAVIOR IN AN ACADEMIC SETTING

Social skills training are an essential part of working with students who exhibit academic and social problems. Often these two problem areas, academic and social deficits, appear together. This issue presents a "chicken-and-egg" situation. Does the learning problem cause the behavior problem, or does the behavior problem cause the learning problem?

Typically, social skills are taught within the academic setting in special education. This is accomplished through classroom rules and contingency point systems that focus upon both areas at the same time. Rules, few in number, written in a positive direction, and designed jointly with students, help to set standards for acceptable behavior within the classroom.

Contingency point systems are established to reinforce the occurrence of these behaviors, as well as other academic and social behaviors that are considered appropriate. Reinforcement contingencies are an important means of encouraging their use.

It is important that the physical environment be arranged so that preventive discipline can occur. By this means, the teacher assumes responsibility for creating and maintaining an environment in which the needs of his/her charges are met. She/he may modify the physical aspects of the room, create a warm, motivating atmosphere, adapt instructional materials to the respective functioning levels of the students, and deliver specialized services through the use of systematic, reinforcing methods and techniques.

According to Henley, Ramsey, and Algozzine (1993, 1995), positive student behavior is facilitated by the teacher through techniques such as the following:

1. Provide students with cues about expected behavior. Both verbal and non-verbal signals may become a part of the general classroom routine. The teacher provides cues about acceptable and un-acceptable behavior in a consistent manner.

2. Provide appropriate and necessary structure. Based upon individual differences and needs, structure should be built into the environment. Children with aggressive and anxious traits may need a high degree of structure, while others with less significant conditions will require lesser, but varied, amounts of structure. Structure related to teacher direction, physical arrangement of environment, routine and scheduling, and classroom rules.

3. Involve each student in the learning process. Allow them to manipulate things, to explore surroundings, to experiment with alternative solutions, to compare findings with those of classmates, and to pose questions and seek answers. This helps to instill an internal focus of control while meaningful involving the child in the learning process.

4. Enable the student to experience success. If the student is not provided tasks or activities in which success can be experienced, the teacher can expect misbehavior or withdrawal.

5. Having successful experiences are vital in developing feelings of self-worth and confidence in attempting new activities. (Jones & Jones, 1986).

6. Use interest boosting. If signs of disinterest or restlessness occur, the teacher quickly shows interest in the student. Conversing with the student may stimulate renewed interest or enthusiasm.

7. Diffuse tension through humor. A humorous comment may bring forth laughter that lessens the tension in a stressful situation.

8. Help the student hurdle lessons that produce difficulty. The teacher can get a student back on track by assisting in the answering of difficult problems. Thus, the hurdle is removed and the student is back on task.

9. Use signal interference. Cue the student with signals so that a potential problem can be extinguished. Individualized signals may be designed and directed toward specific students.

10. Incorporate antiseptic bouncing when it is obvious that a student needs to be temporarily removed from the classroom situation. This technique is useful in dispelling uncontrollable laughter or hiccups and in helping the student get over feelings of anger, or disappointment. This approach involves no punishment, and removal may be in the form of delivering a message, getting a drink of water, or other chores that appear routine.

11. Use teacher reinforcing. The teacher "catches the child engaged in appropriate behavior" and reinforces him at that time. For example, the teacher praises the student's task-oriented behavior in an effort to keep him from getting off task.

12. Employ planned ignoring. Unless the behavior is of a severe, harmful, or self-injurious nature, the teacher purposefully ignores the child. This strategy helps to extinguish inappropriate behavior by removing a viable reinforcer, that of teacher attention. The key is to deliver substantial reinforcement for appropriate behavior.

13. Use teacher commanding. The teacher uses direct verbal commands in an effort to stop the misbehavior. This technique should not be continued, however, if the student does not stop the inappropriate behavior upon the first instance he/she is told to do so. Inappropriate behavior will probably worsen upon repeated verbal commands.

14. Try teacher focusing. The teacher expresses empathy or understanding about the student's feelings, situation or plight. The teacher uses inquiry to obtain information from the student, and then offers reasons or possible solutions to the problem.

15. Utilize teacher redirecting. The student exhibiting an inappropriate behavior is brought back on-task by having him performing an action that is compatible to the previous appropriate behavior. For example, the child who stops singing and starts poking a peer might be asked to play a musical instrument.

See also skill 3.5

Skill 3.5   Demonstrate knowledge of various strategies to manage the classroom behavior of students with emotional impairments.

CLASSROOM MANAGEMENT TECHNIQUES

Classroom management plans should be in place when the school year begins. Developing a management plan takes a proactive approach. That is, decide what behaviors will be expected of the class as a whole, anticipate possible problems, and teach the behaviors early in the school year.

Behavior management techniques should focus on positive procedures that can be used at home as well as at school. Involving the students in the development of the classroom rules lets the students know the rationale for the rules, and allows them to assume responsibility in the rules because they had a part in developing them. When students get involved in helping establish the rules, they will be more likely to assume responsibility for following them. Once the rules are established, enforcement and reinforcement for following the rules should begin right away.

Consequences should be introduced when the rules are introduced, clearly stated, and understood by all of the students. The severity of the consequence should match the severity of the offense and must be enforceable. The teacher must apply the consequence consistently and fairly so the students will know what to expect when they choose to break a rule.

Like consequences, students should understand what rewards to expect for following the rules. The teacher should never promise a reward that cannot be delivered, and follow through with the reward as soon as possible. Consistency and fairness is also necessary for rewards to be effective. Students will become frustrated and give up if they see that rewards and consequences are not delivered timely and fairly.

About four to six classroom rules should be posted where students can easily see and read them. These rules should be stated positively, and describe specific behaviors so they are easy to understand. Certain rules may also be tailored to meet target goals and IEP requirements of individual students. (For example, a new student who has had problems with leaving the classroom may need an individual behavior contract to assist him or her with adjusting to the class rule about remaining in the assigned area.) As the students demonstrate the behaviors, the teacher should provide reinforcement and corrective feedback. Periodic "refresher" practice can be done as needed, for example, after a long holiday or if students begin to "slack off." A copy of the classroom plan should be readily available for substitute use, and the classroom aide should also be familiar with the plan and procedures.

The teacher should clarify and model the expected behavior for the students. In addition to the classroom management plan, a management plan should be developed for special situations, (i.e., fire drills) and transitions (i.e., going to and from the cafeteria). Periodic review of the rules, as well as modeling and practice, may be conducted as needed, such as after an extended school holiday.

Procedures that use social humiliation, withholding of basic needs, pain, or extreme discomfort should never be used in a behavior management plan. Emergency intervention procedures used when the student is a danger to himself or others are not considered behavior management procedures. Throughout the year the teacher should periodically review the types of interventions being used, assess the effectiveness of the interventions used in the management plan, and make revisions as needed for the best interests of the child.

Motivation-Before the teacher begins instruction, he or she should choose activities that are at the appropriate level of student difficulty, are meaningful, and relevant. Teacher behaviors that motivate students include:

- Maintain Success Expectations through teaching, goal setting, establishing connections between effort and outcome, and self-appraisal and reinforcement.
- Have a supply of intrinsic incentives such as rewards, appropriate competition between students, and the value of the academic activities.
- Focus on students' intrinsic motivation through adapting the tasks to students' interests, providing opportunities for active response, including a variety of tasks, providing rapid feedback, incorporating games into the lesson, allowing students the opportunity to make choices, create, and interact with peers.
- Stimulate students' learning by modeling positive expectations and attributions. Project enthusiasm and personalize abstract concepts. Students will be better motivated if they know what they will be learning about. The teacher should also model problem-solving and task-related thinking so students can see how the process is done.

For adolescents, motivation strategies are usually aimed at getting the student actively involved in the learning process. Since the adolescent has the opportunity to get involved in a wider range of activities outside the classroom (job, car, being with friends), stimulating motivation may be the focus even more than academics.

Motivation may be achieved through extrinsic reinforcers or intrinsic reinforcers. This is accomplished by allowing the student a degree of choice in what is being taught or how it will be taught. The teacher will, if possible, obtain a commitment either through a verbal or written contract between the student and the teacher. Adolescents also respond to regular feedback, especially when that feedback shows that they are making progress.

Rewards for adolescents often include free time for listening to music, recreation or games. They may like extra time for a break or exemption from a homework assignment. They may receive rewards at home for satisfactory performance at school. Other rewards include self-charting progress, and tangible reinforcers. In summary, motivational activities may be used for goal setting, self-recording of academic progress, self-evaluation, and self-reinforcement.

Classroom interventions-Classroom interventions anticipate student disruptions and nullify potential discipline problems. Every student is different and each situation is unique. Therefore, student behavior cannot be matched to specific interventions. Good classroom management requires the ability to select appropriate interventions strategies from an array of alternatives. The following non-verbal and verbal interventions were explained in Henley, Ramsey, and Algonzzine (1993).

- **Nonverbal Intervention** - The use of nonverbal interventions allows classroom activities to proceed without interruption. These interventions also enable students to avoid "power struggles" with students.
- **Body Language** - Teachers can convey authority and command respect through body language. Posture, eye contact, facial expressions, and gestures are examples of body components that signal leadership to students.
- **Planned Ignoring** - Many minor classroom disturbances are best handled through planned ignoring. When teachers ignore attention-seeking behaviors, often students do likewise.
- **Signal Interference** - There are numerous non-verbal signals that teachers can use to quiet a class. Some of these are eye contact, snapping fingers, a frown, shaking the head, or making a quieting gesture with the hand. A few teachers present signs like flicking the lights, putting her finger over her lips, or wink at a selective student.
- **Proximity Control** - Teachers who move around the room merely need to stand near a student or small group of students, or gently place a hand on a student's shoulder to stop a disturbing behavior. Teachers who stand or sit as if rooted are compelled to issue verbal directions in order to deal with student disruptions.
- **Removal of Seductive Objects** - Some students become distracted by objects. Removing seductive objects eliminates the need some students have to handle, grab, or touch objects that distract their attention.
- **Verbal Interventions**-Because non-verbal interventions are the least intrusive, they are generally preferred to the use of verbal interventions. Verbal interventions are useful after it is clear that non-verbal interventions have been unsuccessful in preventing or stopping disruptive behavior.
- **Humor** - Some teachers have been successful in dispelling discipline problems with a quip or an easy comment that produces smiles or gentle laughter from students. This does not include sarcasm, cynicism, or teasing, which increase tension and often creates resentment.
- **Sane Messages**. Sane messages are descriptive and model appropriate behavior. They help students understand how their behavior affects others. "Karol, when you talk during silent reading, you disturb everyone in your group," is an example of a sane message.

- **Restructuring.** When confronted with student disinterest, the teacher makes the decision to change activities. This is an example of an occasion when restructuring could be used by the teacher to regenerate student interest.
- **Hypodermic Affection.** Sometimes students get frustrated, discouraged, and anxious in school. Hypodermic affection lets students know they are valued. Saying a kind word, giving a smile, or just showing interest in a child give the encouragement that is needed.
- **Praise and Encouragement.** Effective praise is directed at student behavior rather than at the student personally. Catching a child being good is an example of an effective use of praise that reinforces positive classroom behavior. Comments like, "you are really trying hard," encourages student effort.
- **Alerting.** Making abrupt changes from one activity to another can bring on behavior problems. Alerting helps students to make smooth transitioning by giving them time to make emotional adjustments to change.
- **Accepting Student Feelings.** Providing opportunities for students to express their feelings, even those that are distressful, helps them to learn to do so in appropriate ways. Role playing, class meetings or discussions, life space interviews, journal writings, and other creative modes help students to channel difficult feelings into constructive outlets.

Transfer between classes and subjects-Effective teachers use class time efficiently. This results in higher student subject engagement and will likely result in more subject matter retention. One way teachers use class time efficiently is through a smooth transition from one activity to another; this activity is also known as "management transition." Management transition is defined as "teacher shifts from one activity to another in a systemic, academically oriented way." One factor that contributes to efficient management transition is the teacher's management of instructional material.

Effective teachers gather their materials during the planning stage of instruction. Doing this, a teacher avoids flipping through things looking for the items necessary for the current lesson. Momentum is lost and student concentration is broken when this occurs.

Additionally, teachers who keep students informed of the sequencing of instructional activities maintain systematic transitions because the students are prepared to move on to the next activity. For example, the teacher says, "When we finish with this guided practice together, we will turn to page twenty-three and each student will do the exercises. I will then circulate throughout the classroom helping on an individual basis. Okay, let's begin." Following an example such as this will lead to systematic smooth transitions between activities because the students will be turning to page twenty-three when the class finishes the practice without a break in concentration.

Another method that leads to smooth transitions is to move students in groups and clusters rather than one by one. This is called "group fragmentation." For example, if some students do seat work while other students gather for a reading group, the teacher moves the students in pre-determined groups. Instead of calling the individual names of the reading group, which would be time consuming and laborious, the teacher simply says, "Will the blue reading group please assemble at the reading station. The red and yellow groups will quietly do the vocabulary assignment I am now passing out." As a result of this activity, the classroom is ready to move on in a matter of seconds rather than minutes.

Additionally, the teacher may employ academic transition signals, defined as academic transition signals— "teacher utterance that indicate[s] movement of the lesson from one topic or activity to another by indicating where the lesson is and where it is going." For example, the teacher may say, "That completes our description of clouds, now we will examine weather fronts." Like the sequencing of instructional materials, this keeps the student informed on what is coming next so they will move to the next activity with little or no break in concentration.

Therefore, effective teachers manage transitions from one activity to another in a systematically oriented way through efficient management of instructional matter, sequencing of instructional activities, moving students in groups, and by employing academic transition signals. Through an efficient use of class time, achievement is increased because students spend more class time engaged in on-task behavior.

Transition refers to changes in class activities that involve movement. Examples are:
  (a) Breaking up from large group instruction into small groups for learning centers and small-group instructions.
  (b) Classroom to lunch, to the playground, or to elective classes.
  (c) Finishing reading at the end of one period and getting ready for math the next period.
  (d) Emergency situations such as fire drills.

Successful transitions are achieved by using proactive strategies. Early in the year the teacher pinpoints the transition periods in the day and anticipates possible behavior problems, such as students habitually returning late from lunch. After identifying possible problems with the environment or the schedule, the teacher plans proactive strategies to minimize or eliminate those problems.

Proactive planning also gives the teacher the advantage of being prepared, addressing behaviors before they become problems, and incorporating strategies into the classroom management plan right away. Transition plans can be developed for each type of transition and the expected behaviors for each situation taught directly to the students.

Assertive discipline-Assertive discipline, developed by Canter and Canter, is an approach to classroom control that allows the teacher to constructively deal with misbehavior and maintain a supportive environment for the students. The assumptions behind assertive discipline are:

- Behavior is a choice.
- Consequences for not following rules are natural and logical, not a series of threats or punishments.
- Positive reinforcement occurs for desired behavior.
- The focus is on the behavior and the situation, not the student's character.

The assertive discipline plan should be developed as soon as the teacher meets the students. The students can become involved in developing and discussing the needs for the rules. Rules should be limited to 4 to 6 basic classroom rules that are simple to remember and positively stated (e.g. "Raise hand to speak" instead of "Don't talk without permission").

1. *Recognize and remove roadblocks to assertive discipline.* Replace negative expectations with positives, and set reasonable limits for students.
2. *Practice an assertive response style.* That is, clearly state teacher expectations and expect the students to comply with them.
3. *Set limits.* Take into consideration the students' behavioral needs, the teacher's expectations, and set limits for behavior. Decide what you will do when the rules are broken or complied with.
4. *Follow through promptly with consequences when students break the rules.* However, the students should clearly know in advance what to expect when a rule is broken. Conversely, follow through with the promised rewards for compliance and good behavior. This reinforces the concept that individuals choose their behavior and that there are consequences for their behavior.
5. *Devise a System of Positive Consequences.* Positive consequences do not always have to be food or treats. However, rewards should not be promised if it is not possible to deliver them. The result is a more positive classroom.

All teachers who work with special education have a need for knowledge that includes skills required for classroom management. It is the teacher's responsibility to use whatever techniques and strategies he or she can to develop each child's learning potential to the fullest. In order to accomplish this goal, a teacher must know how to make a learning environment attractive, comfortable, safe, and motivating.

Careful structuring of the classroom environment and attention to variables such as student scheduling, time of day allotments, and use of equipment and materials are essential to effective management of the classroom. The teacher must know which factors promote selective attention and facility in learning. Above all, she/he must remain an effective facilitator for children who may otherwise become discouraged in the school environment.

Competencies in this section emphasize preventive discipline, behavior modification, social skills instruction, and techniques for enhancing the self-concept of students. Identification of inappropriate behaviors, along with knowledge of procedures for the modification of behavior, must be known and used consistently in order to obtain results.

The conditions under which antecedent and consequent stimuli influence behaviors in the educational setting must be thoroughly understood. Therefore, the teacher must be able to apply behavior analysis in a scientific manner with a view toward understanding behavior and its functional relationship to environmental events.

Students must be able to practice newly learned social skills in a learning environment that support and accept student attempts to acquire them and try them out with others. The teacher will sometimes use other counseling and discipline approaches that are effective generally if applied in a systematic manner. And, self-concept training is generally needed for students who have experienced frustration and failure.

The effective teacher will acquire conceptual understanding of these principles, model them, and utilize them in a wide range of teaching situations. Students will be assisted toward generalizing behaviors across settings.

See also skill 3.4

COMPETENCY 4.0   METHODOLOGY AND INSTRUCTION

Skill 4.1   Apply principles and methods involved in individualizing instruction for students with emotional impairments.

Teachers are generally trained to teach the masses of students who progress through our American education system. Today, with emphasis upon inclusion and mainstreaming to the fullest extent possible, educators must not only be taught the fundamental processes and procedures used in general education, but they must be able to apply specialized methodology that is needed by special needs students.

Their specialized approaches must be tailored to meet individual needs. After all, these students are receiving delivery of services through a special education teacher in a general or special education setting because they were unable to make sufficient progress in a regular classroom without supportive services.

Teachers must be able to diagnose individual learning styles because the way in which students learn differs just as abilities vary. Learning can be affected by environmental elements like sound, room arrangement, and physical elements such as time of day or mobility. Coupled with the concern for learning styles is the use of sensory channels such as visual, auditory and haptic. The special needs teacher must identify modality channels through which students process information most proficiently.

Special techniques are needed in order to teach basic skills due to the fact that students vary in their rate of learning, need for routine, and ability to memorize or retain what they learn, reasoning skills, and ability to generalize newly acquired concepts. Students must be able to learn from simple to more complex levels within a task hierarchy in order to experience success, and become independent learners to the greatest extent possible.

Effective communication must occur between teacher and students, as well as among students. Clarity of expression as well as appropriate feedback is essential to successful teaching.

Thus, the special educator needs to be able to teach students who require varying techniques and approaches. She or he must be able to recognize specific needs, must possess diagnostic capabilities, and must make the necessary environment and instruction adaptations, all on an individual basis.

IDENTIFY VARIABLES WHICH INFLUENCE INDIVIDUAL LEARNING STYLES

According to Dunn and Dunn (1994), studies have shown students can identify their own learning styles; that students score higher on tests, factual knowledge, attitude, and efficiency when exposed to a teaching style consistent with the ways they believe they learn; and that it is advantageous to teach and test students in their preferred modality. Individual learning styles are influenced by environmental, emotional, sociological and physical elements.

Environment elements that affect learning include sound, light, temperature and design. Knowing some students can block out sound and some students require complete silence before they can concentrate, the teacher can design an instructional environment that includes areas and sections where talking, interacting, and sharing are permitted, and areas where students may work to meet these individual needs.

Temperature is an environmental element that is difficult to control to suit every student's preference, since individualized reactions to temperature are unique. The teacher can be aware of which sections of each room provide the most and least warmth at various times of the years, and then permit students to choose the section that best meets their needs in which to work and learn.

Finally, the teacher can accommodate individual differences by including sections where students can work at tables or in lounge chairs during learning tasks, and other areas that provide desks and chairs for students who learn better in a more formal design.

Emotional elements such as motivation, persistence, responsibility, and structure also influence learning styles. Motivated students present few problems for the teacher, whereas unmotivated students may need an individualized program to become more interested in achieving.

Similarly, some students need to complete assignments in their own way, in a flexible period, and in accordance with their total learning style. Responsible students usually follow through with a given task, complete it to the best of their ability, and do so without direct or frequent direction.

However, many less responsible students need encouragement, frequent supervision, and praise for task completions. Structure should vary in the amount and kind that is provided for each student. Some learners are creative and thrive when offered opportunities to organize their own learning situations, while other students are unable to function effectively unless they receive well-defined directions and procedures. Some students are able to self-pace, whereas others do better with incremental programmed materials.

Students learn in a variety of social groupings that include working alone, working with one or two peers, working in a small group, and working with adults. Recognizing the social setting in which each student learns best is easy when the students themselves are permitted to select the ways they will complete their assignments. Once preferences are recognized, the teacher can assign individuals to the correct groupings, methods, and resources.

Physical elements greatly influence learning styles. Some students perform well at one time of the day, and others perform better at another time. Some students require extensive mobility, and others are able to complete a task while in one physical position for a long period. Some students even seem to learn better when they are permitted to eat or drink while learning.

Perhaps the most influential of all physical elements are sensory modalities. Learning style is greatly affected by information processing capabilities. It is commonly accepted that students learn through different senses. Some students learn best through their visual sense, others through their auditory sense, and still others by doing, touching and moving.

Visual learners acquire information most proficiently by seeing and watching demonstrations. This type of student typically enjoys reading books, viewing filmstrips and videotapes, looking at pictures, or playing a game of concentration. Students who are looked upon as auditory learners learn best by hearing. This kind of learner generally listens to people, follows verbal directions, and enjoys heaving records, cassette tapes, and stories.

There are students who best learn by touching and those who require experiential or whole body experiences in order to learn. These persons learn by doing or touching. This type of student is able to draw, manipulate objects, work with clay or paints, play action games, perform experiments, and operate a cassette recorder, calculator, and operate a computer. By identifying the preferred preferences, it shows assessment techniques and educational implications for differing students who are predominately auditory, visual, or tactile-kinesthetic.

DEMONSTRATE AN UNDERSTANDING OF THE PRINCIPLES OF TASK ANALYSIS AND CRITERION MEASUREMENT OF TASK PERFORMANCE

After completing an adaptive behavior scale, it is important to look specifically at the skills which are shown as at a deficit level for the student and complete a task analysis. This task analysis can then be used to provide IEP goals and objectives in order to have the deficit areas become part of the student's instructional content.

A teacher can use the set of behavioral specifications that are the result of the task an analysis to prepare tests that will measure the student's ability to meet those specifications. These tests are referred to as criterion measurements. If task analysis identifies which skills will be needed to perform a task successfully, then the criterion measurements will further identify whether the student possesses the necessary skills or knowledge for that task. The level of performance that is acceptable is the "criterion level."

Criterion measurements must be developed along certain guidelines if they are to accurately measure a task and its sub-areas. Johnson and Morasky (1977) give the following guidelines for establishing criterion measurement:

1. Criterion measurement must directly evaluate a student's ability to perform a task.
2. Criterion measurements should cover the range of possible situations in order to be considered an adequate measure.
3. Criterion measurements should measure whether or not a student can perform the task without additional or outside assistance. They should not give any information that the student is expected to possess.
4. All responses in the criterion measurement should be relevant to the task being measured.

Behavioral objectives offer descriptive statements defining the task that the student will perform, state the conditions under which the task will occur, and show the criterion measurement required for mastery. The criterion measurement is the process for evaluating what the student can do. For the instruction to be meaningful there must be a precise correspondence between the capabilities determined in a criterion measurement and the behavioral demands of the objective.

Learning should be logically sequenced, presenting lower order skills and concepts before moving on to higher order or more complex ones. By considering the structure of the task to be learned and using task analysis to specify the sub-skills and concepts necessary for reaching the goal, or target behavior, a learning hierarchy can be developed. Successful learning depends on presentation in a logically sequenced curriculum.

Task sequences may be forward chained or backward chained. Backward chaining is called descending task analysis, because it begins with a target task, the terminal behavior, and works backwards to prerequisite sub-skills. Descending task analysis works backward to subsidiary tasks on the theory that the successful mastery of those easier skills that precede them in the learning hierarchy.

In forward chaining or ascending task analysis, the teacher initiates instruction on the first sub-skill of a task sequence. Once the designated criterion mastery is reached, instruction continues on the next sub-skill, linking it to the previously mastered response that now serves as a prerequisite. More complex ones in the learning hierarchy are introduced, as preceding ones are mastered.

Effectiveness of instruction is keyed to the teacher's ability to know when mastery criterion has been reached on each one in ascending order. If instruction begins before mastery of a lower level skill is achieved, performance gaps will weaken the chances of that student reaching the target task, or terminal behavior. Too slow a pace creates boredom and may lessen the student's enthusiasm for progressing through subsequent steps. Therefore, successful learning depends not only on presentation of skills in a logically sequenced learning hierarchy, but also upon the responsiveness to criteria mastery and appropriate movement through levels of difficulty.

Figure 4.1-1 Descending Task Analysis

TEACHER DOES	TEACHER ASKS
Step 1 Statement of Target Task	Is it significant? Is it relevant?
Step II Statement of Sub-skills 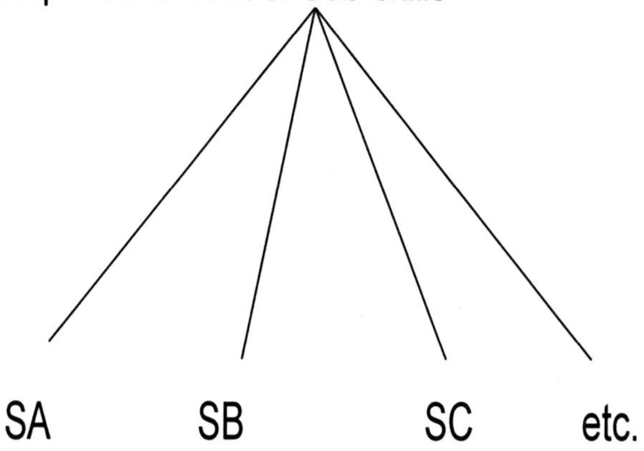 SA SB SC etc.	Are these sub-skills necessary for performing target tasks? Are these sub-skills sufficient for performing target tasks? Are these sub-skills relevant for performing target tasks? Are there any missing or redundant sub-skills? Can the child perform any of these tasks?
Step III Statement of Sub-skills 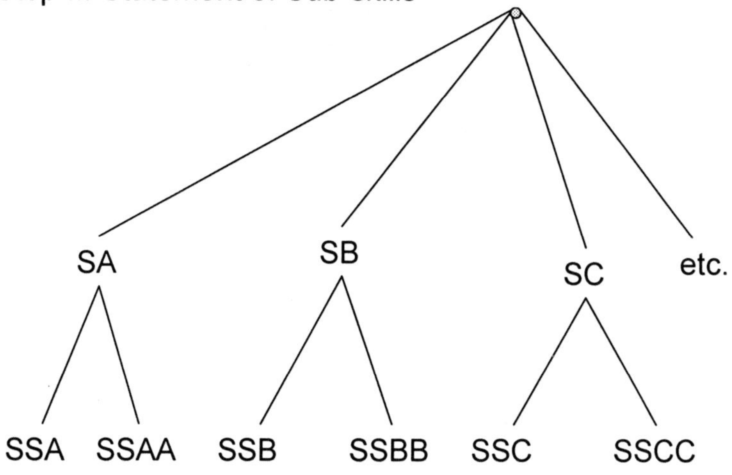 SA SB SC etc. SSA SSAA SSB SSBB SSC SSCC	Are these sub-skills necessary for performing target tasks? Are these sub-skills sufficient for performing target tasks? Are these sub-skills relevant for performing target tasks? Are there any missing or redundant sub-skills? Can the child perform any of these tasks?

DESCRIBE METHODS FOR ALTERING THE PRESENTATION OF TASKS TO MATCH THE STUDENT'S RATE OF LEARNING

The pacing of selected subject content and the pace at which tasks are presented are two ways in which a teacher can use pacing to complement an individual student's rate of learning.

Deciding when a special needs student should be introduced to new concepts or materials is largely based upon whether the student has mastered skills prerequisite to the new topic. New tasks are introduced when the student demonstrates mastery of the previous task in the learning hierarchy.

Content pacing is another way of altering the presentation of tasks. Deciding how much of a topic to present during a learning session, and during each consecutive session, is based on a student's individual rate of learning. For many, smaller steps must be planned when building concepts and assignments may have to be shortened to achieve success. Generally, the more severe the disability, the more adjustments need to be made.

The following suggestions by Jones and Jones (1981) serve as guidelines and specialized needs.

1. Develop an awareness of one's own teaching tempo. Self-evaluation such as videotaping during group instruction can assist a teacher in determining if she is effectively generating interest and enthusiasm. She may find it necessary to adjust her instructional pace.
2. Observe non-verbal cues given by students that signal confusion, boredom, or general restlessness. The teacher might decide, based on student reaction or body language, that too much material is being covered. She/he may need to shorten the lesson and incorporate several personalized questions or examples to increase student involvement and attention.
3. Teach several short sessions rather than infrequent long sessions. Studies have reported findings of positive correlation between learning and time on task; however, optimum time segments need to be determined (e.g. 15, 20, 30 minutes) based on learner characteristics, subject comment, and type of learning activity.
4. Vary the style as well as the content of instructional lessons. The teacher must learn to apply a variety of approaches in teaching content, just as she/he varies content material to maintain student interest.

5.   Avoid burying students in an avalanche of worksheets. Just as the style and content of instructional lessons are varied, so, too, should written activities presented as learning tasks differ. Mastery of a new skill can often be demonstrated with a few problems rather than a larger number, and with one or a few written activities instead of a continuous procession of worksheets. Written work is used to practice or review a learned skill and to indicate mastery of a new one.

There are two reasons a teacher would measure a student's rate of learning on a specific task: (1) to evaluate the instructional program of which the task was a part, and (2) to measure the student's individual progress. In order to measure rate of learning, the teacher should administer an appropriate commercial or teacher-made criterion-referenced test specific to the task being taught.

This is done before, after, and sometimes during the learning of the task. By comparing the student's test scores, rate of learning may be determined. If time is an important factor, a record might be kept of the dates the tests were administered, and the increase in learning that occurred during time intervals between the tests.

UNDERSTAND INTENTIONAL LEARNING AND MEMORY CATEGORIES AND IDENTIFY EDUCATIONAL SITUATIONS IN WHICH THEY ARE NECESSARY TO ASSURE EFECTIVE LEARNING

Two realms of learning are intentional learning versus incidental learning and memory. There are several relationships between these two realms that are not totally unique to special education, but awareness of both concepts is required to teach special needs students.

Intentional Learning-With intentional learning, a student consciously works toward learning something, and afterwards he is aware he knows it. Conversely, with incidental learning, the student does not consciously undertake learning something specifically, and he may be unaware he knows it.

Purposeful instruction and practice are usually necessary components of intentional learning, and more learning occurs through application of effort. Intentional learning has the effect of increasing attention and persistence while undertaking a task. It requires that learners organize information or ideas, use self-questioning strategies, and compare new information to what they already know.

Incidental learning occurs more frequently with regular students than with those identified as having learning and/or behavioral problems. Incidental learning happens without direct instruction or practice. Students are often amazed when they discover the acquisition of information, or trivia, through this means.

Memory-Memory can be visualized as a series of cognitive process. Retention problems are related to specific perceptual processes such as visual or auditory learning.

Moreover, memory refers to the recall of non-verbal as well as verbal experiences (e.g., the ability to remember meaning conveyed by body language, sounds made by familiar objects, or certain voice qualities). Until information is remembered, it cannot be retrieved, verbalized, or generalized for later purposes. Differentiation can be made for other categories of memory, to include rote memory, short-term memory, sequential memory, and long-term memory.

Rote Memory refers to mechanical repetitions with lack of understanding.

Short-Term Memory is required in tasks whenever information is retained for immediate recall.

Both rote and short-term memory learning can be effectively utilized in educational situations in which it may be needless or impractical for the student to undertake study in more depth.

For example, irregular, non-phonetic, spelling words are memorized for short-term weekly tests. A series of digits is remembered just long enough to repeat them to a test administrator. And instructions are retained through performance, with no need for further retention. Math facts are memorized for the sake of speed and accuracy and no further application is made except mere recognition.

Short-term memory can be measured by methods as simple as questioning the student about the content he/she has learned immediately or shortly after being taught. Queries include both recognition such as locating the answer to a factual question in the text, and recall like remembering the answer to a factual question. These vary in difficulty, with recognition considered to be the easiest and recall the most difficult.

Sequential memory is another type of automatic response. It requires serialization or a specified order to items being recalled. Sentence formation entails sequential memory as does recall of events and happenings. Remembering the days of the week or months in a year necessitates serial memory.

Long-term memory requires the storage of information for an extended period prior to retrieval efforts. The ability to assimilate, store and retrieve needed information is largely dependent on the student's ability to perceive the relevancy of the material and relate it to past knowledge. Trivial Pursuit games are based on players' skills in remembering informational details learned long ago through intentional and incidental learning efforts. Furthermore, long-term memory tracers are sometimes triggered by unusual associations or occurrences.

Situational variables, cognitive abilities, and the learning of effective memory strategies affect the quality of long-term memory. Specific situational factors include intensity of attention, meaningfulness of the content, interests in the topic, and the amount of drill/over-learning provided.

Multiple cognitive functions are involved, such as perception, selective attention, language, thought, and memory. Effective teaching can assist student in developing strategies that enhance the ability to retain knowledge.

Long-term memory or learning can be measured by an educational testing instrument, formal or informal, comprised of items covering a specified amount of subject matter that has been taught previously, and administered after allowing a substantial amount of time to pass between teaching and assessment. This type of long-term memory assessment would lose its validity if the student were allowed to review the previously learned material just prior to being teased.

EXHIBIT KNOWLEDGE OF HOW TO SELECT AND ADAPT INSTRUCTIONAL STRATEGIES AS APPROPRIATE

The choice of instructional strategy depends primarily on the needs of the students. Information from the IEP and assessment reports can give the teacher guidelines on what type of instructional modifications are recommended for a particular child.

Interviews with the student as well as interest inventories can also help the teacher select instructional strategies that students identify as helping them learn best. Interest inventories can be teacher-made, commercially prepared, or from computer programs. The teacher can construct a class profile from these inventories.

From the profiles, the teacher should be able to determine learning styles; whether the student is a visual, auditory, or kinesthetic learner. With a group of primarily visual learners, for example, a lecture would probably not be very effective unless it were accompanied by visual aids.

Students also have preferences for certain types of materials over others, such as manipulative materials over worksheets. The cognitive level of the students will also affect the type of strategy employed. Students who have difficulty with abstract concepts will need hands-on, concrete instructional strategies to help them make the transition from concrete to semi-concrete and finally to the more abstract concepts.

The type of task also influences choice of instructional strategy. Teaching a mnemonic device is effective in helping students remember the names of the planets in order, whereas an outline is more useful for reviewing a history chapter. Other factors influencing choice of strategy involves the frustration level, motivation, and attitude towards the task. The need for supervision, and assistance, the ability to work independently, or in groups, and variations in time needed to complete the task also affect choice of strategy.

EXPLAIN HOW TO UTILIZE ACTIVITIES DESIGNED FOR LARGE GROUP/SMALL GROUP/INDIVIDUAL WORK

Small group instruction is excellent for teaching basic skills such as math, reading, and writing and is often used in the elementary grades. The groups should be as homogenous as possible, and flexible to allow students to move from group to group as the need arises. Motivation activities that are especially suited to small group work include positive praise, descriptive praise, group praise, a fast pace, and enthusiasm from the teacher.

Content area subjects such as science and social studies are usually taught in large groups. The variety of individuals in a large group is ideal for class discussions, cooperative learning, playing games, and brainstorming. However, the pace and scope of large group instruction can become too slow or too fast for higher achievers and lower achievers.

Instruction should, therefore, include a balance of higher-level and lower-level questions that involves all students in the lesson. Large group instruction should be lively paced and have plenty of visual aids such as diagrams, concept maps, and story maps to help students understand the relationships between concepts.

Individual tutoring and seatwork can be done for short periods of time daily to help students learn or consolidate a new concept. These tutoring sessions can be scheduled or may be spontaneous as the teacher observes students with difficulties.

Peer tutoring is effective with materials that the teacher has already given to the students, as long as the teacher has established the goals of the tutoring session, planned specific materials and academic skills to focus on, trained the students who will act as tutors, and matched the student pairs appropriately.

Skill 4.2   Demonstrate knowledge of strategies and techniques used to improve the communication skills of students with emotional impairments.

UNDERSTAND WHAT CONSTITUTES EFFECTIVE COMMUNICATION SKILLS BETWEEN THE SENDER AND THE RECEIVER

Communication occurs when one person sends a message and gets a response from another person. In fact, whenever two people can see or hear each other they are communicating. The receiver changes roles and becomes the sender once the response is given. The communication process may break down if the receiver's interpretation differs from that of the sender.

Effective teaching depends on communication. By using good sending skills, the teacher has more assurance that he/she is getting his/her message across to the members of the education team, the students, and their families.

Effective communication skills include attending skills, clarity of expression, paraphrasing, and evaluative feedback.

Special education teachers of students with mild to moderate disabilities are moving toward consultative/collaborative models of service delivery. This movement has resulted in more team teaching in the regular classroom, and a higher degree of mainstreaming of students.

Education of students with more severe disabilities has moved closer in proximity to non-disabled peers. Technology enables a wide range of learners to participate meaningfully in learning and social interaction. Thus, the special education teacher must be able to identify student access needs, and match technology resources with appropriate learning activities and curricula.

While the regular classroom may not be the best learning environment for every child with a disability, it is highly desirable for all who can benefit. It provides contact with age-peers and prepares all students for the diversity of the world beyond the classroom.

Close contact and communication must be established and maintained between the school district staff, each base school, and the various specialists (or consultants) providing ancillary services. These persons often serve special needs students in auxiliary (i.e., providing help) and supplementary (i.e., in addition to) ways. Thus, the principles and methods of special education must be shared with regular educators, and tenets and practices of regular education must be conveyed to special educators. Job roles and unique responsibilities and duties of support specialists like speech/language therapists, physical and occupational therapists, social workers, school psychologists and nurses, and others need to be known by all teachers.

Attending Skills- Attending skills are used to receive a message. Some task-related attending skills that have been identified include: (1) looking at the teacher when information or instructions are being presented, (2) listening to assignment directions, (3) listening for answers to questions, (4) looking at the chalkboard, (5) listening to others speak when appropriate.

For some students, special techniques must be employed to gain and hold attention. For example, the teacher might first call the student by name when asking a question to assure attending by that individual, or she/he may ask the question before calling the name of a student to create greater interest. Selecting students at random to answer questions helps to keep them alert and listening. Being enthusiastic and keeping lessons short and interactive assists in maintaining the attention of those students who have shorter attention spans. Some students may be better able to focus their attention when environmental distraction are eliminated or at least reduced, and non-verbal signals can be used to draw students' attention to the task. Finally, arranging the classroom so that all students can see the teacher helps direct attention to the appropriate location.

Clarity of Expression- Unclear communication between the teacher and special needs students sometimes contributes to problems in academic and behavioral situations. In the learning environment, unclear communication can add to the student's confusion about certain processes or skills he is attempting to master.

There are many ways in which the teacher can improve the clarity of her communication. Giving clear, precise directions is one. Verbal directions can be simplified by using shorter sentences, familiar words, and relevant explanations. Asking a student to repeat directions or to demonstrate understanding of them by carrying out the instructions is an effective way of monitoring the clarity of expression. In addition, clarification can be achieved by the use of concrete objects, multidimensional teaching aids, and by modeling or demonstrating what should be done in a practice situation.

Finally, a teacher can clarify his/her communication by using a variety of vocal inflections. The use of intonation juncture can help make the message clearer, as can pauses at significant points in the communication. For example, verbal praise should be spoken with inflection that communicates sincerity. Pausing before starting key words, or stressing those that convey meanings, helps students learn concepts being taught.

Paraphrasing- Paraphrasing, that is, restating what the student says using one's own words, can improve communication between the teacher and that student. First, in restating what the students has communicated, the teacher is not judging the content but is simply relating what he/she understands the message to be. If the message has been interpreted differently from the way intended, the student is asked to clarify. Clarification should continue until both parties are satisfied that the message has been understood.

The act of paraphrasing sends the message that the teacher is trying to better understand the student. Restating the student's message as fairly and accurately as possible assists the teacher in seeing things from the student's perspective.

Paraphrasing if often a simple restatement of what has been said. Lead-ins such as "Your position is..." or "it seems to you that..." are helpful in paraphrasing a student's messages. A student's statement, "I am not going to do my math today" might be paraphrased by the teacher as, "Did I understand you to say that you are not going to do your math today?" By mirroring what the student has just said, the teacher has telegraphed a caring attitude for that student and a desire to respond accurately to his message.

To paraphrase effectively a student's message, the teacher should: (1) restate the student's message in his/her own words; (2) preface the paraphrasing with such remarks as, "You feel..." or "I hear you say that..." (3) avoid indicating any approval or disapproval of the student's statements. Johnson (1978) states the following as a rule to remember when paraphrasing: "Before you can reply to a statement, restate what the sender says, feels, and means correctly and to the sender's satisfaction." (p.139)

Descriptive feedback is a factual, objective (i.e., unemotional) recounting of a behavioral situation or message sent by a student. Descriptive feedback has the same effect as paraphrasing, in that: (1) when responding to a student's statement, the teacher restates (i.e., paraphrases) what the student has said, or factually describes what she/he has seen, and (2) it allows the teacher to check her/his perceptions of the student and the message. A student may do or say something but because of the teacher's feelings or state of mind, the student's message or behavior might be totally misunderstood. The teacher's descriptive feedback, which Johnson (1972) refers to as "understanding," indicates that the teacher's intent is to respond only to ask the student whether his/her statement has been understood, how he/she feels about the problem, and how he/she perceives the problem. The intent of the teacher is to more clearly "understand" what the student is saying, feeling, or perceiving, in relation to a stated message or a behavioral event.

Evaluative feedback is verbalized perception by the teacher that judges, evaluates, approves, or disapproves of the statements made by the student. Evaluative feedback occurs when the student makes a statement and the teacher responds openly with "I think you're wrong," "That was a dumb thing to do," or "I agree with you entirely." The tendency to give evaluative responses is heightened in situations where feelings and emotions are deeply involved. The stronger the feelings, the more likely it is that two persons will each evaluate the other's statements solely from their own point of view.

Since evaluative feedback intones a judgmental approval or disapproval of the student's remark or behavior in most instances, it can be a major barrier to mutual understanding and effective communication. It is a necessary mechanism for providing feedback of a quantitative (and sometimes qualitative) instructional nature (e.g. test scores, homework results, classroom performance). In order to be effective, evaluative feedback must be offered in a factual, constructive manner. Descriptive feedback tends to reduce defensiveness and feelings of being threatened because it will most likely communicate that the teacher is interested in the student as a person, has an accurate understanding of the student and what he/she is saying, and encourages the students to elaborate and further discuss his problems.

To summarize, in the learning environment, as in all situations, effective communication depends upon good sending and receiving skills. Teaching and managing students involves good communication. By using clear, non-threatening feedback, the teacher can provide students with information that helps them to understand themselves better, at the same time providing a clearer understanding of each student on the teacher's part.

UNDERSTAND THT THE TEACHER MAY NEED TO RESPOND TO FEELINGS AS WELL AS WORDS

Not all communication is delivered in a verbal manner. Indeed, words spoken are not always true indicators of what a person means and feels. Non-verbal communication, such as body language, facial expression, tone of voice, and speaking patterns, are all clues to the underlying message the student is attempting to deliver. The teacher demonstrates her/his willingness to listen by sitting close, leaning forward, making eye-to-eye contact, and showing understanding by nodding or smiling. By so doing, she/he is sending the message that she/he cares, is concerned about the student's feelings, and will take the time necessary to understand what is really being communicated.

To facilitate further communication, the teacher must become an active listener. This involves much more than just restating what the person has said. Her Responses must reflect feelings rather than the spoken language. It is essential that the teacher says back what she/he understands the student's message to mean, as well as the feelings she/he perceives, and ask for correctness of interpretation.

Often, teachers enter into active listening with body language conveying a willingness to listen, but respond in such a way that judgment or disapproval of the underlying message is conveyed. Evaluative responses from the listener will decrease attempts to communicate. Encouragement toward communicative efforts is enhanced by use of statements rather than questions, spoken in the present tense and with use of personal pronouns, reflective of current feelings about the situation, and offering self-disclosure of similar experiences or feelings if the teacher feels inclined to do so.

Response to the child's feelings is particularly important since his/her message may not convey what he/she really feels. For example, a student who has failed a test may feel inadequate and have the need to blame someone else, such as the teacher, for this failure. The might say to, "You didn't tell me that you were including all the words from the last six weeks on the spelling test." The teacher, if she/he were to respond solely to the spoken message might say, "I know I told you that you would be tested over the entire unit. You just weren't listening!" The intuitive, sensitive teacher would look beyond the spoken words by saying, "You're telling me that it feels bad to fail a test." By responding to the child's feelings, the teacher lets him/her know the teacher understands the feeling of personal crisis, and the student is encouraged to communicate further.

Skill 4.3   Demonstrate knowledge of strategies and techniques used to promote students' acquisition of learning strategies and study skills.

Transfer of Learning- Transfer of Learning-Transfer of learning occurs when experience with one task influences performance on another task. Positive transfer occurs when the required responses are about the same and the stimuli are similar, such as moving from handball to racquetball, or field hockey to soccer. Negative transfer occurs when the stimuli remain similar, but the required responses change, such as shifting from soccer to football, tennis to racquetball, and boxing to sports karate. Instructional procedures should stress the similar features between the activities and the dimensions that are transferable. Specific information should emphasize when stimuli in the old and new situations are the same as or similar, and when responses used in the old situation apply to the new.

To facilitate learning, instructional objectives should be arranged in order according to their patterns of similarity. Objectives involving similar responses should be closely sequenced; thus, the possibility for positive transfer is stressed. Likewise, learning objectives that involve different responses should be programmed within instructional procedures in the most appropriate way possible. For example, students should have little difficulty transferring handwriting instruction to writing in other areas. However, there might be some negative transfer when moving from manuscript to cursive writing. By using transitional methods and focusing upon the similarities between manuscript and cursive writing, negative transfer can be reduced.

Generalization- Generalization is the occurrence of a learned behavior in the presence of a stimulus other than the one that produced the initial response (e.g., novel stimulus). It is the expansion of a student's performance beyond conditions initially anticipated. Students must be able to generalize what is learned to other settings (e.g., reading to math, word problems; resource room to regular classroom).

Generalization training is a procedure in which a behavior is reinforced in each of all series of situations until it generalizes to other members of the same stimulus class. Stimulus generalization occurs when responses, which have been reinforced in the presence of a specific stimulus, the <u>discriminative stimulus</u> (SD), occur in the presence of related stimuli (e.g. bathrooms labeled women, ladies, dames). In fact, the more similar the stimuli, the more likely it is that stimulus generalization will occur. This concept applies to inter-task similarity, in that the more one task resembles another, the greater the probability the student will be able to master it. For example, if Johnny has learned the initial consonant sounds of "b" and "d," and he has been taught to read the word "dad," it is likely that when he is shown the word "bad," he will be able to pronounce this formerly unknown word upon presentation.

Generalization may be enhanced by the following:

1. Use many examples in teaching to deepen application of learned skills.
2. Use consistency in initial teaching situations, and later introduce variety in format, procedure, and use of examples.
3. Have the same information presented by different teachers, in different settings, and under varying conditions.
4. Include a continuous reinforcement schedule at first, later changing to delayed, and intermittent schedules as instruction progresses.
5. Teach students to record instances of generalization and to reward themselves at that time.
6. Associate naturally occurring stimuli when possible.

STRATEGIES AND TECHNIQUES FOR ENSURING THE EFFICIENT AND EFFECTIVE USE OF INSTRUCTIONAL TIME

Schedule development depends upon the type of class (elementary or secondary) and the setting (regular classroom or resource room). There are, however, general rules of thumb that apply to both types and settings:

1. Allow time for transitions, planning, and setups.
2. Aim for maximum instructional time by pacing the instruction quickly and allotting time for practice of the new skills.
3. Proceed from short assignments to long ones, breaking up long lessons or complex tasks into short sessions or step-by-step instruction.
4. Follow a less preferred academic or activity with a highly preferred academic or activity.

5. In settings where students are working on individualized plans, do not schedule all the students at once in activities that require a great deal of teacher assistance. For example, have some students work on math or spelling while the teacher works with the students in reading, which usually requires more teacher involvement.
6. Break up a longer segment into several smaller segments with a variety of activities.

SPECIAL CONSIDERATIONS FOR ELEMENTARY CLASSROOMS

1. Determine the amount of time that is needed for activities such as P.E., lunch, or recess.
2. Allow about 15 to 20 minutes each for opening and closing exercises. Spend this time for "housekeeping" activities such as collecting lunch money, going over the schedule, cleaning up, reviewing the day's activities, getting ready to go home.
3. Schedule academics for periods when the students are more alert and motivated, usually in the afternoon.
4. Build in time for slower students to finish their work; others may work at learning centers or other activities of interest. Allowing extra time gives the teacher time to give more attention where it is needed, conduct assessments, or for students to complete or correct work.

SPECIAL CONSIDERATIONS FOR SECONDARY CLASSES

Secondary school days are usually divided into five, six, or seven periods of about 50 (or 90 if using a 4 class block scheduling system) minutes, with time for homeroom and lunch. Students cannot stay behind and finish their work, since they have to leave for a different room. Resource room time should be scheduled so that the student does not miss academic instruction in his classroom or miss desirable nonacademic activities. In schools where special education teachers also co-teach or work with students in the regular classroom, coordination and consultation time will also have to be budgeted into the schedule.

Skill 4.4   Demonstrate knowledge of strategies and techniques used to improve students' transition to adult life roles.

TRANSITION PLANNING

Transition planning is mandated in the Individuals with Disabilities Education Act (IDEA). The transition planning requirements ensure planning is begun at age 14 and continued through high school. Transition planning and services focus on a coordinated set of student-centered activities designed to facilitate the student's progression from school to post-school activities. Transition planning should be flexible and focus on the developmental and educational requirements of the student at different grades and times.

Transition planning is a student-centered event that necessitates a collaborative endeavor. In reference to secondary students, the responsibilities are shared by the student, parents, secondary personnel, and postsecondary personnel, who are all members of the transition team.

In most cases when transition is mentioned, it is referring to a child 14 or over, but in some cases children younger than 14 may need transition planning and assistance. Depending on the child's disability and its severity, a child may need assistance with transitioning to school from home, or to school from a hospital or institution, or any other setting. In those cases the members of the transition team may also include doctors or nurses, social workers, speech therapist, and physical therapists.

It is important that the student play a key role in transition planning. This will entail asking the student to identify preferences and interests and to attend meetings on transition planning. The degree of success experienced by the student in postsecondary educational settings depends on the student's degree of motivation, independence, self-direction, self-advocacy, and academic abilities developed in high school. Student participation in transition activities should be implemented as early as possible, and no later than age 16.

In order to contribute to the transition planning process, the student should: understand his learning disability and the impact it has on learning and work; implement achievable goals; present a positive self-image by emphasizing strengths, while understanding the impact of the learning disability; know how and when to discuss and ask for needed accommodations; be able to seek instructors and learning environments that are supportive and establish an ongoing personal file that consists of school and medical records, individualized education program (IEP), resume, and samples of academic work.

The primary function of parents during transition planning is to encourage and assist students in planning and achieving their educational goals. Parents also should encourage students to cultivate independent decision-making and self-advocacy skills.

Transition planning involves input from four groups: the student, parents, secondary education professionals, and postsecondary education professionals. The result of effective transition from a secondary to a postsecondary education program is a student with a learning disability who is confident, independent, self motivated, and striving to achieve career goals. This effective transition can be achieved if the team consisting of the student, parents, and professional personnel work as a group to create and implement effective transition plans. The transition team of a student entering the workforce may also include community members, organizations, company representatives, vocational education instructor, and job coaches.

Transition services will be different for each student. They must take into account the student's interests and preferences, evaluation of career interests, aptitudes, necessary and obtained skills and training may be considered.

The transition activities that have to be addressed, unless the IEP team finds it uncalled for, are:

1. Instruction – The instruction part of the transition plan deals with school instruction. The student should have a portfolio completed upon graduation. They should research and plan for further education and/or training after high school. Education can be in a college setting, technical school, or vocational center. Goals and objectives created for this transition domain depend upon the nature and severity of the student's disability, the students interests in further education, plans made for accommodations needed in future education and training, identification of post-secondary institutions that offer the requested training or education.

2. Community experiences – this part of the transition plan investigates how the student utilizes community resources. Resources entail places for recreation, transportation services, agencies, and advocacy services. It is essential for students to deal with the following areas:
   - Recreation and leisure - examples: movies, YMCA, religious activities.
   - Personal and social skills - examples: calling friends, religious groups, going out to eat.
   - Mobility and transportation - examples: passing a driver's license test or utilizing Dial-A-Ride.
   - Agency access - examples: utilizing a phone book and making calls.
   - System advocacy- example: have a list of advocacy groups to contact.
   - Citizenship and legal issues - example: registering to vote.

3. Development of employment -This segment of the transition plan investigates becoming employed. Students should complete a career interest inventory. They should have chances to investigate different careers. Many work skill activities can take place within the classroom, home, and community. Classroom activities may concentrate on employability, community skills, mobility, and vocational training. Home and neighborhood activities may concentrate on personal responsibility and daily chores. Community based activities may focus on part-time work after school and in the summer, cooperative education or work-study, individualized vocational training, and volunteer work.

4. Daily Living Skills – This segment of the transition plan is also important although not essential to the IEP. Living away from home can be an enormous undertaking for people with disabilities. Numerous skills are needed to live and function as an adult. In order to live as independently as possible, a person should have an income, know how to cook, clean, shop, pay bills, get to a job, and have a social life. Some living situations may entail independent living, shared living with a roommate, supported living, or group homes. Areas that may need to be looked into include personal and social skills, living options, income and finances, medical needs, community resources, and transportation.

Skill 4.5 **Apply principles of and procedures for supporting students' transition from school to employment and/or post-secondary education and training.**

Career development is the complex process of acquiring the knowledge, skill, and attitudes necessary to create a plan of choosing and being successful in a particular career field. Career development typically has four different stages. The stages of career development are awareness, exploration, preparation, and placement.

1. **Career Awareness** -Career Awareness activities focus on introducing students to the broad range of career options. First, students must be provided with current, in-depth information about careers, which includes job-related skills, necessary education and training, and a description of typical duties, responsibilities, and tasks. Students must be instructed on how to access the variety of available resources, such as Internet, professional magazines, newspapers and periodicals. Guest speakers and career fairs are provided for students to speak with and interview workers with first hand experiences.

2. **Career Exploration** -Career exploration focuses on learning about careers through direct, hands on activities. This stage is also important to gain insight into the characteristics of these occupations as well as personal interests and strengths. These activities can be provided through in-school and work-based experiences. In-school activities include contextual learning activities, simulated work experiences, and career fairs. Work-based experiences range from non-paid to paid activities. These activities include job shadowing, mentors, company tours, internship, service learning, cooperative education, and independent study.

3. **Career Preparation**-Career preparation provides students with the specific academic and technical knowledge and skills needed in order to be successful at a particular occupation. This may include Career and Technical Education programs or postsecondary education. They include the core activities of career assessments (formal and informal) and work-readiness (soft-skills development, computer competency and job search Skills). Community organizations, employers, and professional organizations are also available to provide training and insight on accommodations that may be provided for students with special needs.

4. **Career Placement**-Students transitioning from high school need to work collaboratively with involved parents, teachers, and guidance counselors to successfully enter either the workplace or post-secondary education. Placement should depend on the student's aptitude, skills, experiences, and interest.

Skill 4.6   Identify non-school resources that provide educational and transitional services for students with emotional impairments.

See skill 2.3

PARENT AND PROFESSIONAL ADVOCACY ACTIVITY AND PARENT ORGANIZATION

There have always been, and will always be, exceptional children with special needs, but special education services have not always been in existence to provide for these needs.

Private school and state institutions were primary sources of education for individuals with retardation in earlier years. The 9th and 10th amendments to the U.S. Constitution leave education as an unstated power, and therefore vested in the states. As was the practice in Europe, government funds in America were first appropriated to experimental schools to determine whether students with disabilities actually could be educated.

During the mid-twentieth century, legislators and governors in control of funds, faced with evidence of need and the efficacy of special education programs, refused to expend funds adequately, thus creating the ultimate need for federal guidelines in PL 94-142 to mandate flow-through money.

Concurrently, due process rights and procedures were outlined, based on litigation and legislation enacted by parents of children with disabilities, parent organizations, and professional advocacy groups. "Public support in the form of legislation and appropriation of funds has been achieved and sustained only by the most arduous and persevering efforts of individuals who advocate for exceptional children." (Hallahan & Kauffman, 1986 p. 26).

Parents, professionals, and other members of advocacy groups and organizations finally succeeded in bringing to the attention of legislators astounding data about the population of youth with disabilities in our country.

Among the findings revealed, Congress noted that: (1) there were more than eight million children with disabilities in the United States, and more than half were not receiving an appropriate education; (2) more than one million children with disabilities were excluded from the educational system, and many other children with disabilities were enrolled in regular education classes where they were not benefiting from the educational services provided because of their undetected conditions; and (3) due to inadequate educational services within the public school systems, families were forced to seek services outside the public realm. Years of advocacy effort resulted in the current laws and court decisions mandating special education at a federal level.

COMPETENCY 5.0 PROGRAM AND SERVICE DELIVERY

Skill 5.1   Understand the major concepts, current and historical trends, and legal foundations of special education.

LEGAL MANDATES AND HISTORICAL ASPECTS

Special education is precisely what the term denotes: education of a special nature for students who have special needs. The academic and behavioral techniques that are used today in special education are a culmination of "best practices" and evolved from a number of disciplines (e.g., medicine, psychology, sociology, language, ophthalmology, otology) to include education. Each of these disciplines contributed uniquely to their field so that the needs of special students might be better met in the educational arena.

Unfortunately, during the earlier part of the 1900s and mid-1950s, too many educators placed in positions of responsibility refused to recognize their professional obligation for assuring all children a free, appropriate, public education. Today, this door can no longer be shut, eyes cannot be closed, and heads cannot be turned since due process rights have been established for special needs students and their caregivers. Specific mandates are now stated in national laws, state regulations, and local policies. These mandates are the result of many years of successful litigation and politically advocacy, and they govern the delivery of special education.

What special educators do is one thing; how services are delivered is yet another. The concept of **inclusion** stresses the need for educators to rethink the continuum of services, which was designed by Evelyn Deno and has been in existence since the early 1970s. Many school districts developed educational placement sites, which contain options listed on this continuum. These traditional options extend from the least restrictive to the most restrictive special education settings. The least restrictive environment is the regular education classroom. The present trend is to team special education and regular classroom teachers in regular classrooms. This avoids pulling out students for resource room services, and provides services by specialists for students who may be showing difficulties similar to those of special education students.

The competencies in this section include the mandates (i.e., laws, regulations, policies) that apply to or have a bearing upon the respective states and local districts, as well as the major provisions of federal laws implemented twenty or more years ago, such as Public Laws 94-142 (1975), 93-112 (1973) and 101-476 (1990). These laws culminated into the comprehensive statute, IDEA (Individuals with Disabilities Education Act), which requires the states to offer comprehensive special education service programs to students with disabilities, and to plan for their transition into the work world. Most local districts have elaborately articulated delivery systems, which are an extension of national or state

KNOW THE MAJOR DEVELOPMENTS IN THE HISTORY OF SPECIAL EDUCATION

The Early Years: The Beginning

Although the origin of special education services for youngsters with disabilities is relatively recent, the history of public attitude toward people with disabling conditions was recorded as early as 1552. The Spartans practiced infanticide and the killing or abandonment of malformed or sickly babies. The ancient Greeks and Romans thought people with disabilities were cursed and forced them to beg for food and shelter. Those who could or could not fend for themselves were allowed to perish. Some with mental disabilities were employed as fools for the entertainment of the Greco-Roman royalty.

In the first century current era, people with disabilities were thought to be suffering the punishment of God. Those with emotional disturbances were considered to be possessed by the devil, and although early Christianity advocated humane treatment of those who were not normal physically or mentally, many remained outcasts of society, sometimes pitied and sometimes scorned.

During the Middle Ages, persons with disabilities were viewed within the aura of the unknown, and were treated with a mixture of fear and reverence. Some were wandering beggars, while others were used as jesters in the courts. The Reformation brought about a change of attitude, however. Individuals with disabilities were accused of being possessed by the devil and exorcism flourished. Many innocent people were put in chains and cast into dungeons.

The early seventeenth century was marked by a softening of public attitude toward persons with disabilities. Hospitals began to provide treatment for those with emotional disturbances and mental retardation. A manual alphabet for those with deafness was developed, and John Locke became the first person to differentiate between persons who were mentally retarded and those who were emotionally disturbed.

In America, however, the colonists treated people with severe mental disorders as criminals, while those who were harmless were left to beg or were treated as paupers. At one time, it was common practice to sell them to the person who would provide for them at the least cost to the public. When this practice was stopped, persons with mental retardation were put into poorhouses, where conditions were often extremely squalid.

The Nineteenth Century: The Beginning of Training

In 1799, Jean Marc Itard, a French physician, found a 12-year old boy who had been abandoned in the woods of Averyron, France. His attempts to civilize and educate the boy, Victor, established many of the educational principles presently in use in the field of special education, including developmental and multi-sensory approaches, sequencing of tasks, individualized instruction, and a curriculum geared toward functional life skills.

Itard's work had an enormous impact upon public attitude toward individuals with disabilities. They began to be seen as educable. During the late 1700s, rudimentary procedures were devised by which those with sensory impairments (i.e., deaf, blind) could be taught, closely followed in the early 1800s by attempts to teach students with mild intellectual disabilities and emotional disorders (i.e., at that time referred to as the "idiotic" and "insane"). Throughout Europe, schools for students with visual and hearing impairments were erected, paralleled by the founding of similar institutions in the United States. In 1817, Thomas Hopkins Gallaudet founded the first American school for students who were deaf, known today as Gallaudet University in Washington, D.C., one of the world's best institutions of higher learning for those with deafness. Gallaudet's work was followed closely by that of Samuel Gridley who was instrumental in the founding of the Perkins Institute for students who were blind in 1829.

The mid-1800s saw the further development of Itard's philosophy of education of students with mental disabilities. Around that time, his student, Edward Seguin, immigrated to the United States, where he established this philosophy of education for persons with mental retardation in a publication entitles Idiocy and Its Treatment by the Physiological Method in 1866. Seguin was instrumental in the establishment of the first residential school for individuals with retardation in the United States.

State legislatures began to assume the responsibility for housing people with physical and mental disabilities - the institutional care was largely custodial. Institutions were often referred to as warehouses due to the deplorable conditions of many. Humanitarians like Dorothea Dix helped to relieve anguish and suffering in institutions for persons with mental illnesses.

1900 - 1919: Specific Programs

The early twentieth century saw the publication of the first standardized test of intelligence by Alfred Binet of France. The test was designed to identify educationally substandard children, but by 1916, the test was revised by an American Louis Terman, and the concept of the intelligence quotient (IQ) was introduced. Since then the IQ test has come to be used as a predictor of both retarded (delayed) and advanced intellectual development.

At approximately the same time, Italian physician Maria Montessori was concerned with the development of effective techniques for early childhood education. Although she is known primarily for her contributions to this field, her work included methods of education for children with mental retardation as well, and the approach she developed is used in preschool programs today.

Ironically, it was the advancement of science and the scientific method that led special education to its worst setback in modern times. In 1912, psychologist Henry Goddard published a study based on the Killikak family, in which he traced five generations of the descendants of a man who had one legitimate child and one illegitimate child. Among the descendants of the legitimate child were numerous mental defectives and social deviates. This led Goddard to conclude that mental retardation and social deviation were inherited traits, and therefore that mental and social deviates were a threat to society, an observation that he called the Eugenics Theory.

Reinforcing the concept of retardation as hereditary deviance was a popular philosophy called positivism, under which these unscientific conclusions were believed to be fixed, mechanical laws that were carrying mankind to inevitable improvement. Falling by the wayside was seen as the natural, scientific outcome for the defective person in society. Consequently, during this time mass institutionalization and sterilization of persons with mental retardation and criminals were practiced.

Nevertheless, public school programs for persons with retardation gradually increased during this same period. Furthermore, the first college programs for the preparation of special education teachers were established between 1900 and 1920.

1919 - 1949: Professional and Expansion of Services

An awareness of the need for medical and mental health treatment in the community was evidenced during the 1920s. Halfway houses became a means for monitoring the transition from institution to community living and outpatient clinics were established to provide increased medical care. Social workers and other support personnel were dispensed into the community to coordinate services for the needy. The thrust toward humane treatment within the community came to an abrupt halt during the 1930s and 1940s, primarily due to economic depression and widespread dissatisfaction toward the recently enacted social programs.

Two factors related to the Word Wars I and II helped to improve public opinion toward persons with disabilities. First, there was the intensive screening of the population of young men with physical and mental disabilities in the United States. Second, patriotism caused people to regard the enormous number of young men who returned from the wars with physical and emotional disabilities in a different light than they would have been regarded before that time. People became more sensitive to the problems of the veterans with disabilities, and this acceptance generalized to other groups in the special needs population.

With increased public concern for people with disabilities came new research. John B. Watson introduced behaviorism, which shifted the treatment emphasis from psychoanalysis to learned behavior. He demonstrated in 1920 that maladaptive (or abnormal) behavior was learned by Albert, an 11-month old boy, through conditioning. B.F. Skinner followed with a book entitled the <u>Behavior of Organisms,</u> which outlined principles of operant behavior (i.e., voluntary) behavior.

In 1922, the Council for Exceptional Children (first called the International Council for Exceptional Children) was founded. During the 1920s, many comprehensive statewide programs were initiated. The number of special education programs in public schools increased at a rapid rate until the 1930s, when the push for humane and effective treatment of people with disabilities began to diminish once again.

The period of the Depression was marked by large-scale institutionalization and lack of treatment. Part of the cause was inadequately planned programs and poorly trained teachers. WW II did much to swing the pendulum back in the other direction, however, and inaugurated the most active period in the history of the development of special education.

1950 - 1969: The Parents, the Legislators, and the Courts Become Involved

The first two decades of the second half of the 20th century were characterized by increased federal involvement in general education, gradually extending to special education.

In 1950 came the establishment of the National Association of Retarded Children, later renamed the National Association of Retarded Citizens (NARC). It was the result of the efforts among concerned parents who felt the need of an appropriate public education. Increased media coverage exposed the miserable conditions in some of the institutions devoted to caring for people with disabilities, especially those with intellectual and emotional disabilities, and treatment consequently became more humane.

It was at about this time that parents of children with disabilities discovered the federal courts as a powerful agent on behalf of their children. The 1954 decision in the Brown v. the Topeka Board of Education case guaranteed equal opportunity rights to a free public education for all citizens, and the parents of children and youth with disabilities insisted that their children be included in that decision. From this point on, the court cases and public laws enacted[1] as a result of court decisions are too numerous to include in their entirety.

Only those few which had the greatest impact on the development of special education, as we know it today, are listed. Collectively, they are part of a movement in U.S. Supreme Court history known as the Doctrine of Selective Incorporation, under which the states are compelled to honor various substantive rights under procedural authority of the 14th Amendment.

1954: The Cooperative Research Act was passed, the first designation of general funds for the use of students with disabilities.

1958: Public Law 85-926 provided grants to intuitions of higher learning and to state education agencies for training professional personnel who would, in turn, train teachers of students with mental retardation.

1963: Public Law 88-164 (Amendment to Public Law 85-926) extended support to the training of personnel for teaching those with other disabling conditions (i.e., hard of hearing, speech impaired, visually impaired, seriously emotionally disturbed, crippled and other health impaired).

1965: Elementary and Secondary Education Act provided funds for the education of children who were disadvantaged and disabled (Public Law 89-10).

Public Law 89-313 (Educational Consolidation and Improvement Act -State Operated Programs) provided funds for children with disabilities who are or have been in state-operated or state-supported schools.

1966: Public Law 89-750 authorized the establishment of the Bureau Education for the Handicapped (BEH) and a National Advisory Committee on the Handicapped.

1967: Hanson v. Hobson ruled that ability grouping (tracking) based on student performance on standardized tests is unconstitutional.

1968: Public Law 80-538 (Handicapped Children's Early Education Assistance Act) funded model demonstration programs for preschool students with disabilities

1968: Public law 90-247 included provisions for dear-blind centers, resource centers and expansion of media services for students with disabilities.

Public Law 90-576 specified that 10 percent of vocational education funds be earmarked for youth with disabilities.

1969: Public Law 91-230 (Amendments to Public Law 89-10). Previous enactment relating to children with disabilities was consolidated into one act: Education of the Handicapped.

1970-Present: Federal Involvement in the Education of Children and Youth with Disabilities

During early involvement of the government in the education of individuals with disabilities, states were encouraged to establish programs, and they were rewarded with monetary assistance for compliance. Unfortunately, this assistance is often abused by those in control of services and funds.

Therefore, a more dogmatic attitude arose and the states were mandated to provide education for those with disabilities or else experience the cutoff of education funds from the federal government. Federal legal authority for this action was the 14th Amendment due process denial, paralleling enforcement of the 1954 Brown v. Topeka desegregation decision.

High proportions of minority students in programs for mental retardation resulted in a mandatory reexamination of placement procedures, which in turn brought about a rigid legal framework for the provision of educational services for students with disabilities.

1970: Diana v. the State Board of Education resulted in the decision that all children must be tested in their native language.

1971: Wyatt v. Stickney established the right to adequate treatment (education) for institutionalized persons with mental retardation.

The decision in Pennsylvania Association for Retarded Children (PARC) v. the Commonwealth of Pennsylvania prohibited the exclusion of students with mental retardation from educational treatment at state schools.

1972: Mills v. the Board of Education of the District of Columbia asserted the right of children and youth with disabilities to a constructive education, which includes appropriate specialized instruction.

1973: Public Law 93-112 (Rehabilitation Amendments of 1973) was the first comprehensive federal statute to address specifically the rights of disabled youth. It prohibited illegal discrimination in education, employment, or housing on the basis of a disability.

1974: Public Law 93-380 (Education Amendments of 1974. Public Law 94-142 is the funding portion of this act). It requires the states to provide full educational opportunities for children with disabilities. It addressed identification, fair evaluation, alternative placements, due process procedures, and free, appropriate public education.

1975: Public Law 94-142 (Education for all Handicapped Children Act) provided for a free, appropriate public education for all children with disabilities, defined special education and related services, and imposed rigid guidelines on the provisions of those services. (Refer to Objectives 2 and 3 in this section.) It paralleled the provision for a free and appropriate public education in Section in 504 of Public Law 94-142, and extended these services to preschool children with disabilities (ages 3-5) through provisions to preschool incentive grants.

1975: Goss v. Lopez ruled that the state could not deny a student education without following due process. While this decision is not based on a special education issue, the process of school suspension and expulsion is obviously critical in assuring an appropriate public education to children with disabilities.

1978: Public Law 95-56 (Gifted and Talented Children's Act) defined the gifted and talented population, and focused upon this exceptionally category, which was not included in Public Law 94-142.

1979: Larry P. v. Riles ordered the reevaluation of black students enrolled in classes for educable mental retardation (EMR) and enjoined the California State department of Education from the use of intelligence tests in subsequent EMR placement decisions.

1980: Parents in Action on Special Education (PASE) v. Hannon ruled that IQ tests are necessarily biased against ethnic and racial subcultures.

1982: The appeal for services of an interpreter during the school day for a deaf girl was denied by the Supreme Court in Hendrick Hudson Board of Education v. Rowley. This ruling established that an "appropriate" education does not mean the "best" education has to be provided. What is required is that individuals benefit and those due process procedures are followed in developing the educational program.

1983: Public Law 98-199 (Education of the Handicapped Act [EHA] Amendments). Public Law 94-142 was amended to provide added emphasis on parental education and preschool, secondary, and post-secondary programs for children and youth with disabilities.

1984: Irving Independent School District v. Tarro (468 U.S. 883) established that catheterization and similar health-type services are "related services" when they are relatively simple to provide and medical assistance is not needed in providing them.

1985: Public Law 99-457 mandated service systems for infants and young children.

1986: Public Law 99-372 (Handicapped Children's Protection Act of 1985). This law allowed parents who are unsuccessful in due process hearings or reviews to seek recovery of attorney's fees.

Public Law 99-457 (Education of the Handicapped Act Amendments of 1986). This re-authorized existing EHA, amended Public Law 94-142 to include financial incentives for states to educate children 3 to 5 years old by the 1990-1991 school years, and established incentive grants to promote programs serving infants with disabilities (birth to 2 years of age).

Public Law 99-506 (Rehabilitation Act Amendments of 1986). This authorized formula grant funds for the development of supported employment demonstration projects.

1987: School Board of Nassau County v. Arline Established that contagious diseases are a disability under Section 504 of the Rehabilitation Act and that people with them are protected from discrimination, if otherwise qualified (actual risk to health and safety to others may cause persons to be regarded as unqualified).

1988: Honig v. Doe established that expulsion from school programs for more than ten days constitutes a change in placement for which all due process provisions must be met. Temporary removals are permitted in emergencies.

1990: Public Law 101-336 (American with Disabilities Act ADA) gives civil rights protection to individuals with disabilities in private sector employment, all public services, public accommodations, transportation, and telecommunications. (Patterned after Section 504 of the Rehabilitation Act of 1973.)

The U.S. House of Representatives opened for citizen comment the issue of a separate exceptionality category for students with attention deficit disorders. The issue was tabled without legislative action.

Public Law 101-476 (Individuals with Disabilities Education Act IDEA) reauthorized and renamed existing EHA. This amendment to EHA changed the term "handicapped" to "disability," expanded related services, and required individual education programs (IEPs) to contain transitional goals and objectives for adolescents (ages 16 and above, special situations).

1993: Florence County School Dist Four v. Shannon Carter established that when a school district does not provide FAPE for a student with disability, the parents may seek reimbursement for private schooling. This decision has encouraged districts to be more inclusive of students with Autism who receive ABA/Lovaas therapy.

1994: Goals 2000: Educate America Act, Pub. L. 103-227, established national education goals to help guide state and local education systems.
1997: Reauthorization of IDEA—required involvement of a regular education teacher as part of the IEP team. Provided additional strength to school administrators for the discipline of students with special needs.

2002: No Child Left Behind Act (NCLB). (Read the NCLB section time line below.)

2004: M.L. v. Federal Way School District (WA) in the Ninth Circuit Court of Appeals ruled that absence of a regular education teacher on an IEP team was a serious procedural error.

Reauthorization of IDEA—Required all Special Education Teachers on a Secondary Level to be no less qualified than other teachers of the subject areas.

DEMONSTRATE AN UNDERSTANDING OF THE PHILOSOPHY OF SPECIAL EDUCATION THAT LED TO THE PASSAGE OF PUBLIC LAW 94-142

The passage of Public Law (PL) 94-142 , signed in 1975 and renamed Individuals with Disabilities Education Act (IDEA) in 1990, was a culmination of many years' struggle to achieve equal educational opportunity for children and youth with disabilities.

The 1960s was an era when much national emphasis was placed upon civil rights of the U.S. citizenry. Special education was supported by such leaders President John F. Kennedy, Vice-President Hubert Humphrey, President Lyndon B. Johnson, and many more in Congress.

Unlike rights legislation of a racial or ethnic nature, the reform laws for persons with disabilities mostly enjoyed bipartisan support. From the late 1960s to the mid-1970s, much legislation and litigation from the courts included decisions supporting the need to assure an appropriate education to all persons, regardless of race, creed, or disabling conditions. Much of what was stated in separate court rulings and mandated legislation was brought together into what is now considered to be the "backbone" of special education. PL 94-142, which was formally signed into law by President Gerald R. Ford in 1975.

Three important political forces were instrumental in obtaining the forerunner legislation and litigation, which is now within PL 94-142. These important forces included: (1) parent and professional support groups, (2) reform legislation, and (3) adversary litigation. These three were compacted to provide public education programs, which by law, are required to meet each child's unique educational needs.

NO CHILD LEFT BEHIND - No Child Left Behind, Public Law 107-110, was signed on January 8, 2002. It addresses accountability of school personnel for student achievement with the expectation that every child will demonstrate proficiency in reading, math, and science.

The first full wave of accountability will be in 12 years when children who attended school under NCLB graduate, but the process to meet that accountability begins now. In fact, as students progress through the school system, testing will show if an individual teacher has effectively met the needs of the students. Through testing, each student's adequate yearly progress or lack thereof will be tracked.

NCLB affects regular and special education students, gifted students and slow learners, and children of every ethnicity, culture and environment. NCLB is a document that encompasses every American educator and student.

Educators are affected as follows:
- Elementary teachers (K-3) are responsible for teaching reading and using different, scientific-based approaches as needed.
- Elementary teachers of upper grades will teach reading, math and science.
- Middle and high school teacher will teach to new, higher standards. Sometimes, they will have the task of playing catch up with students who did not have adequate education in earlier grades.
- Special educators are responsible for teaching students to a level of comparable proficiency as their non-disabled peers. This will raise the bar of academic expectations throughout the grades. For some students with disabilities, the criteria for getting a diploma will be more difficult. Although a small percentage of students with disabilities will need alternate assessment, they will still need to meet grade appropriate goals.

In order for special education teachers to meet the professional criteria of this act, they must be *highly qualified*, that is certified or licensed in their area of special education and show proof of a specific level of professional development in the core subjects that they teach.

Litigation-Over the years, court decisions have reflected different opinions about whether public school attendance should be: "(1) a privilege that may be awarded or withheld from an individual child at the discretion of local school officials; (2) the right of every child, regardless of his or her handicap; or (3) a means of assuring that every child receives an education appropriated for his or her individual needs." (Hallahan & Kauffman, 1986, p.27).

Around the turn of the twentieth century, courts aided in the protection of the school-aged majority from the minority who were disabled. Other children were spared the pain of seeing those with disabilities and teachers were protected from being overburdened by them. The 1950s and 1960s brought about equal protection rights in the field of education, and in 1975 Congress passed the most comprehensive legislation in history to assure appropriate education and treatment of students with disabilities.

A series of landmark legal decisions laid the foundation for the passage of Public Law 94-142. The Brown v. Topeka (1954) case guaranteed equal resources through equal ethnic and racially non-segregated educational environments. This case, based upon ethnic and racial issues with socioeconomic outcomes, set the precedent for civil rights in the area of special education.

Pennsylvania (1971) resulted in a consent agreement that ensured (1) a free and appropriate public education for all mentally retarded children, (2) education in the least restrictive educational environment appropriate to the learner, (3) periodic review and evaluation of the educational program, and (4) procedural due process.

Mills v. Board of Education of the District of Columbia extended this mandate to include not only those with mental retardation, but also all children and youth with disabilities. Institutionalized persons with disabilities were secured the right to education through the ruling, which occurred in Wyatt v. Stickney (1972), Diana v. State Board of Education (1970), and later Larry P. v. Riles (1979), guaranteed the use of proper evaluation procedures that led to appropriate placement of learners with disabilities.

Along with equalization suits, litigation has more recently included legal suits filed for inclusionary and exclusionary reasons, the former by parents who contended their children were not being provided with appropriate special education services, and the latter by parent whose children were considered by the schools in need of special education services but the parents believed their children not to be in need of them. Courts have been asked to make decisions based on children's physical, intellectual, and emotional characteristics. Schools and teachers are increasingly being held accountable for providing every child with an appropriate education.

Legislation-The court rulings have comprised the framework for the comprehensive legislation passed on behalf of students with disabilities. Collectively, these landmark rulings paved the way to significant legislation assuring education for those with disabilities, and ultimately to the Education of all Handicapped Children Act of 1975.

Other significant legislation acted as a forerunner to PL 94-142. Congress passed the Elementary and Secondary Education Act (ESEA) in 1965. Shortly thereafter, Title I of ESEA was amended to establish grants to state agencies, enabling them to provide a free, appropriate public education for students with disabilities. Funds were authorized to facilitate recruitment of personnel, as well as to disseminate information about special education services.

Funding for model demonstration programs for preschool students with disabilities was obtained through the Handicapped Children's Early Education Act of 1968. Provisions for students determined gifted and talented were made as amendments to ESEA in 1970.

The vocational Rehabilitation Act of 1973 extended funds which had been granted ten years before. Section 503 of this act mandated affirmative action in personnel practices (e.g., interviewing, hiring, promoting, and retention) for those with disabilities, while Section 504 authorized the inclusion of persons with severe disabilities in federally supported programs and facilities through non-barrier, as well as schedule accessibility.

All these driving forces culminated in the formation of a major comprehensive act, considered by many to be the "backbone" of special education. The results of litigation, legislative authorization, and principles advocated by parent groups resulted in the provisions of Public Law 94-142.

Present and Future Perspectives-What is the state of special education today? What can we anticipate as far as changes that might occur in the near future? It has been two decades since the passage of the initial Individuals with Disabilities Education Act as Public Law 93-142 in 1975.

So far, mandates stand with funding intact. The clients are still here, and in greater numbers due to improved identification procedures and to medical advances that have left many, who might had died in the past, with conditions considered disabling. Among the disabling conditions afflicting the population with recently discovered lifesaving techniques are blindness, deafness, amputation, central nervous system or neurological impairments, brain dysfunction, and mental retardation from environmental, genetic, traumatic, infectious, and unknown etiologies.

Despite challenges to the principles underlying PL 94-142 in the early 1980s, total federal funding for the concept increased as new amendments were passed throughout the decade. These amendments expanded services to infants, preschoolers, and secondary students. (Rothstein, 1995).

Following public hearings, Congress voted in 1990 not to include Attention Deficit Disorders (ADD) as a new exceptionality area. Determining factors included the alleged ambiguity of the definition and eligibility criteria for students with ADD, the large number of students who might be identified it is became a service delivery area, the subsequent cost of serving such a large population, and the fact that many of these students are already served in the exceptionality areas of learning disabilities and behavior disorders.

The revision of the original law that we now call IDEA included some other changes. These changes were primarily in language (terminology), procedures (especially transition), and addition of new categories (autism and traumatic brain injury).

Thus, we can see that despite challenges to federal services and mandates in special education as an extension of the Fourteenth Amendment since 1980, there has actually been growth in mandated categories and net funding.

The Doctrine of Selective Incorporation is the name for one major set of challenges to this process. Lobbyists and activists representing coalition and advocacy groups for those with disabilities have combined with bi-partisan congressional support to avert the proposed changes, which would have meant drastic setbacks in services for persons with disabilities.

Nevertheless, there remain several philosophical controversies in special education for the late 1990s. The need for labels for categories continues to be questioned. Many states are serving special needs students by severity level rather than by the exceptionality category.

Presently, special educators are faced with possible changes in what is considered to be the least restrictive environment for educating students with special needs. Following upon the heels of the Regular Education Initiative, the concept of **inclusion** has come to the forefront.

Both of these movements were, and are, an attempt to educate special needs students in the mainstream of the regular classroom. Both would eliminate pulling out students from regular classroom instructional activities, and both would incorporate the services of special education teachers in the regular classroom in collaboration with general classroom teachers.

IDENTIFY THE MAJOR PRINCIPLES OF PUBLIC LAW 101-476 AND EXPLAIN THE SPECIFIC REGULATIONS PERTAINING TO EACH PRINCIPLE

Public Law 94-142 was enacted by Congress in 1975. This law was reauthorized as Public Law 101-476 in 1990, and at that time was renamed Individuals with Disabilities Education Act (IDEA). Six basic principles are specified in the regulations. These principles are zero reject, nondiscriminatory testing, individualized education programs, least restrictive environment, due process, and parent participation. Knowledge of these interrelated principles enables educators to understand better the cornerstone of the Act, which is the provision of a free, appropriate public education for student with disabilities.

Zero Reject-The principle of zero reject requires that all children with disabilities be provided with a free, appropriate public education. This legal requirement was made for all school-age children, as for those in the 3 to 5 and 18 to 21 age groups, unless a state law or a court order makes an exception to the extended age ranges.

A documented report is filed annually by each local education agency (LEA) reporting all attempts to locate, identify, and evaluate children with disabilities residing within jurisdiction. Priorities identified in the legislation for the delivery of services and appropriation of federal funds is: (1) children with disabilities not receiving any education, and (2) children with the most severe disabilities receiving an inappropriate education.

Ethically, zero reject exists to guard against both total and functional exclusion. "Total exclusion refers to past situations in which children with disabilities have been denied access to any educational services at all. Functional exclusion occurs in cases in which educational services have been provided, but they have been inappropriate to the needs of the student with a disability." (Turnbull, Strickland, & Brantley, 1978, p. 4).

IDENTIFY THE MAJOR PRINCIPLES OF PUBLIC LAW 101-476 AND EXPLAIN THE SPECIFIC REGULATIONS PERTAINING TO EACH PRINCIPLE

Public Law 94-142 was enacted by Congress in 1975. This law was reauthorized as Public Law 101-476 in 1990, and at that time was renamed Individuals with Disabilities Education Act (IDEA). Six basic principles are specified in the regulations. These principles are: zero reject, nondiscriminatory testing, individualized education programs, least restrictive environment, due process, and parent participation. Knowledge of these interrelated principles enables educators to understand better the cornerstone of the Act, which is the provision of a free, appropriate public education for student with disabilities.

DUE PROCESS

"Due process is a set of procedures designed to ensure the fairness of educational decisions and the accountability of both professionals and parents in making these decisions" (Kirk and Gallagher, 1986, p. 24). These procedures serve as a mechanism by which the child and his family can voice their opinions or concerns, and sometimes dissents. Due process safeguards exist in all matters pertaining to identification, evaluation, and educational placement.

Due process occurs in two realms, substantive and procedural. Substantive due process is the content of the law (e.g. appropriate placement for special education students). Procedural due process is the form through which substantive due process is carried out (.e. parental permission for testing). The federal law provides many specific aspects of due process with which to be aware including:

1. A due process hearing may be initiated by parents of the LEA as an impartial forum for challenging decisions about identification, evaluation, or placement. Either party may present evidence, cross-examine witnesses, obtain a record of the hearing, and be advised by counsel or by individuals having expertise in the education of individuals with disabilities. Findings may be appealed to the State Education Agency (SEA) and if still dissatisfied, either party may bring civil action in Federal District Court. Hearing timelines are set by legislation.

2. Parents may obtain an independent evaluation if there is disagreement about the education evaluation performed by the LEA. The results of such an evaluation:
    a. Must be considered in any decision made with respect to the provision of a free, appropriate public education for the child.
    b. May be presented as evidence at a hearing.
    c. Further, the parents may request this evaluation at public expense:
        i. If a hearing officer requests an independent educational evaluation.
        ii. If the decision from a due process hearing is that the LEA's evaluation was inappropriate. If the final decision holds, the evaluation performed is appropriate, the parent still has the right to an independent educational evaluation, but not at public expense.
3. Written notice must be provided to parents prior to a proposal or refusal to initiate or make a change in the child's identification, evaluation, or educational placement.
    d. A listing of parental due process safeguards.
    e. A description and a rationale for the chosen action.
    f. A detailed listing of components (e.g. tests, records, reports) which was the basis for the decision.
    g. Assurance that the language and content of notices were understood by the parents.
4. Parental consent must be obtained before evaluation procedures can occur, unless there is a state law specifying otherwise.
5. Sometimes parents or guardians cannot be identified to function in the due process role. When this occurs, a suitable person must be assigned to act as a surrogate. This is done by the LEA in full accordance with legislation.

PARENTAL PARTICIPATION

The involvement of parents, though included directly or indirectly in other major provisions (i.e., principles) under Public Law 94-142 (and subsequent reauthorizations of said special education law), is presented as a separate category. Parental participation specific to this section assures access to educational records and participation in developing educational policy.

The Family Educational Rights and Privacy Act (1974), also known as the Buckley Amendment, assures confidentiality of student records. Parents are afforded the right to examine, review, request changes in information deemed inaccurate, and stipulate persons who might access their child's records.

The development and approval of educational policy is another means for involving parents. Membership on advisory boards, participation at public hearings, and review of local and state special education plans are examples of ways in which parents might participate in the formulation of policy and later monitoring of these guidelines.

MAJOR COMPONENTS RETAINED AND CHANGES MADE IN THE 1990 AMENDMENTS TO PUBLIC LAW 94-142

The Education for All Handicapped Children Act of 1975, (EHA Public Law 94-142) established principles requiring a free appropriate education for all students with disabling conditions between the ages of three and twenty-one by September, 1980 (Review Objective 3, this section).

It prohibited exclusion of these students from public education and mandated that federal funds be made available to school districts that compiled these provisions. This law provided assurances protecting students with disabilities and their parents or guardians through due process, protection in evaluation procedures, least restrictive environment, and individualized education programs.

The components due process and non-discriminatory evaluation practices were formulated to alleviate problems in determining eligibility for and classification in special education. The least restrictive environment and individualized education program provisions focused on decisions about placement of students in educational settings and how learning would differ from that of the general school curriculum.

The EHA Amendments of 1990 (Public Law 101-476), were signed into law by President Bush on October 30, 1990. This action renamed the EHA as the Individuals with Disabilities Education Act (IDEA), reauthorized the discretionary programs under Parts C through G, and made certain of changes in Parts A, B, and H of the act. Contemporary thinking was reflected in replacing all references to "handicapped children" with "children with disabilities."

Changes in Public Law 101-476, which are of most interest to teachers were primarily in terminology (language), procedural planning, and formation of new categories. "Children" became "Individuals," meaning that some of the students with special needs are adolescents and young adults - not just children. "handicapped" was changed to "with disabilities," signifying the difference between limitations imposed by society (handicap) and an inability to do certain things (disability).

The phrase "with disabilities" demonstrates that the person is thought of first, and the disabling condition in only one characteristic of the individual, who has other characteristics as well. Procedurally, special education was required to expand the IEP to include transition plans for every older student with a disability (usually beginning at age 14 or 16).

Specific goals and objectives would help make the transition work or further education following high school. The law recognizes two new categories (autism and traumatic brain injury) as separate entities, since they had both been preciously subsumed under other categorical services (Hallahan & Kauffman, 1994: Ysseldyke, Algozzine, & Thurlow, 1992).

GOALS 2000: EDUCATE AMERICA ACT (P.L. 103-227)

Goals 2000 established national education goals to help guide state and local education systems, by making the following goals for the year 2000. This was the first law in America that was modeled after the United Nations.

1. All children in America will start school ready to learn.
2. The high school graduation rate will increase to at least 90 percent.
3. All students will leave grades 4, 8, and 12 having demonstrated competency over challenging subject matter including English, mathematics, science, foreign languages, civics and government, economics, the arts, history, and geography, and every school in America will ensure that all students learn to use their minds well, so they may be prepared for responsible citizenship, further learning, and productive employment in our nation's modern economy.
4. United States students will be first in the world in mathematics and science achievement.
5. Every adult American will be literate and will possess the knowledge and skills necessary to compete in a global economy and exercise the rights and responsibilities of citizenship.
6. Every school in the United States will be free of drugs, violence, and the unauthorized presence of firearms and alcohol, and will offer a disciplined environment conducive to learning.
7. The nation's teaching force will have access to programs for the continued improvement of their professional skills and the opportunity to acquire the knowledge and skills needed to instruct and prepare all American students for the next century.
8. Every school will promote partnerships that will increase parental involvement and participation in promoting "the social, emotional, and academic growth of children."

STATE MAJOR COMPONENTS RETAINED AND CHANGES OF IDEA 97

In 1997, IDEA was revised and reauthorized as Public Law 105-17 as progressive legislation for the benefit of school age children with special needs, their parents and those who work with these children. The 1997 reauthorization of IDEA made major changes in the areas of the evaluation procedures, parent rights, transition and, discipline.

The evaluation process was amended to require members of the evaluation team to look at previously collected data, tests and information and to use it when it is deemed appropriate. Previous to IDEA 97 an entire re-evaluation had to be conducted every three years in relation to determine if the child continued to be a "child with a disability." This was changed to allow existing information/evaluations to be considered which would prevent unnecessary assessment of students and reduce the cost of evaluations.

Parent participation was not a requirement under the previous IDEA for an evaluation team to make decisions regarding a student's eligibility for special education and related services. Under IDEA 97, parents were specifically included as members of the group making the eligibility decision.

IEP Amendments-The IEP was modified under IDEA 97 to emphasize the involvement of students with special needs in a general education classroom setting, with the services and modifications deemed necessary by the evaluation team.

The "Present Levels of Educational Performance"(PLEP) was changed to require a statement of how the child's disability affects his or her involvement and progress in the general curriculum.

IDEA 97 established that there must be a connection between the special education and general education curriculum. For this reason the PLEP was required to include an explanation of the extent to which the student will *not* be participating with non-disabled children in the general education class and in extracurricular and non-academic activities.

The IEP now had an established connection to the general education setting and had to provide the needed test accommodations that would be provided on all state and district wide assessments of the student with special needs. IDEA 97's emphasis on raising the standards of those in special education placed an additional requirement of a definitive reason why a standard general education assessment would not be deemed appropriate for a child, and how the child should then be assessed.

IDEA 97 looked at how parents were receiving annual evaluations on their child's IEP goals and determined that this was not sufficient feedback for parents and required Schools to make reports to parents on the progress of their child at least as frequently as progress of their non-disabled peers.

The IEP was also modified to include a review of the student's transitional needs and services specifically:

- Beginning when a student is 14, and annually thereafter, the student's IEP must contain a statement of his or her transition service needs under the various components of that IEP that focus upon the student's courses of study (e.g., vocational education or advanced placement); and

- Beginning at least one year before the student reaches the age of majority under State law, the IEP must contain a statement that the student has been informed of the rights under the law that will transfer to him or her upon reaching the age of majority.

Discipline-IDEA 97 broadened the schools' right to take a disciplinary action with children who have been classified as needing special education services with those students that knowingly possess or use illegal drugs or sell or solicit the sale of a controlled substance while at school or school functions.

Manifest Determination Review-Under IDEA 97, suspensions/disciplinary consequences could result in an alternative educational placement. This possibility was to be weighed by a Manifest Determination Review, which is held by an IEP Team. Manifest Determination Reviews must occur no more than 10 days after the disciplinary action. This review team has the sole responsibility of determining:
1) Does the child's disability impaired his/her understand the impact and consequences of the behavior under disciplinary action?
2) Did the child's disability impair the ability of the child to control the behavior subject to discipline?

Determination of a relationship of the student's disability and an inappropriate behavior could allow current placement to occur.

When no relationship between the "inappropriate" behavior is established, IDEA 97 utilized FAPE to allow the relevant disciplinary procedures applicable to children without disabilities may be applied to the child in the same manner in which they would be applied to children without disabilities,

Functional Behavioral Assessments (FBAs) and Behavior Intervention Plans (BIPs) now became a requirement in many situations for schools to both modify and provide disciplinary consequences.

MAJOR COMPONENTS RETAINED AND CHANGES OF IDEA 2004

The second revision of IDEA occurred in 2004, IDEA was re-authorized as the Individuals with Disabilities Education Improvement Act of 2004 (IDEIA 2004) is commonly referred to as IDEA 2004. IDEA 2004 (effective July 1, 2005).

It was the intention to improve IDEA by adding the philosophy/understanding that special education students need preparation for further study beyond the high school setting by teaching compensatory methods. Accordingly, IDEA 2004 provided a close tie to PL 89-10, the Elementary and Special Education Act of 1965, and stated that students with special needs should have maximum access to the general curriculum.

This was defined as the amount for an individual student to reach his fullest potential. Full inclusion was stated not to be the only option by which to achieve this, and specified that skills should be taught to compensate students later in life in cases where inclusion was not the best setting.

IDEA 2004 added a new requirement for special education teachers on the secondary level enforcing NCLBs "Highly Qualified" requirements in the subject area of their curriculum. The rewording in this part of IDEA states that they shall be "no less qualified" than teachers in the core areas.

Free and Appropriate Public Education (FAPE), was revised by mandating that students have maximum access to appropriate general education. Additionally, LRE placement for those students with disabilities must have the same school placement rights as those students who are not disabled.

IDEA 2004 recognizes that due to the nature of some disabilities, appropriate education may vary in the amount of participation/placement in the general education setting. For some students, FAPE will mean a choice as to the type of educational institution they attend (private school for example), any of which must provide the special education services deemed necessary for the student through the IEP.

The definition of *assistive technology devices* was amended to exclude devices that are surgically implanted (i.e., cochlear implants), and clarified that students with assistive technology devices shall not be prevented from having special education services. Assistive technology devices may need to monitored by school personnel, but schools are not responsible for the implantation or replacement of such devices surgically. An example of this would be a cochlear implant.

The definition of *Child with a disability* is the term used for children ages 3-9 with a developmental delay now has been was changed to allow for the inclusion of Tourettes Syndrome.

IDEA 2004 recognized that all states must follow the National Instructional Materials Accessibility Standards which states that students who need materials in a certain form will get those at the same time their non-disabled peers receive their materials. Teacher recognition of this standard is important.

Changes in Requirements for Evaluations-The clock/time allowance between the request for an initial evaluation and the determination if a disability is present may be requested has been changed to state the finding/determination must occur within 60 calendar days of the request. This is a significant change as previously it was interpreted to mean 60 school days. Parental consent is also required for evaluations and prior to the start of special education services.

No single assessment or measurement tool may now be used to determine special education qualification. Assessments and measurements used should be in *language and form* that will give the most accurate picture of the child's abilities.

IDEA 2004's recognized that there exists a disproportionate representation of minorities and bilingual students and that pre-service interventions that are *scientifically based on early reading programs, positive behavioral interventions and support, and early intervening services*) may prevent some of those children from needing special education services.

This understanding has led to a child not being considered to have a disability if he/she has not had appropriate education in math or reading, nor shall a child be considered to have a disability if the reason for his/her delays is that English is a second language.

When determining a specific learning disability, the criteria may or may not use a discrepancy between *achievement and intellectual ability* but whether or not the child responds to scientific research-based intervention. In general, children who may not have been found eligible for special education (via testing) but are known to need services (via functioning, excluding lack of instruction) are still eligible for special education services. This change now allows input for evaluation to include state and local testing, classroom observation, academic achievement, and *related developmental needs,*

Changes in Requirements for IEPs-Individualized Education Plans (IEPS) continue to have multiple sections. One section, *present levels,* now addresses *academic achievement and functional performance.* Annual IEP goals must now address the same areas.

IEP goals should be aligned to state standards, thus short term objectives are not required on every IEP. Students with IEPs must not only participate in regular education programs to the full extent possible, they must show progress in those programs.

This means that goals should be written to reflect academic progress. For students who must participate in alternate assessment, there must be alignment to *alternate achievement standards*. Significant change has been made in the definition of the IEP team as it now includes *not less than 1* teacher from each of the areas of special education and regular education be present.

IDEA 2004 recognized that the amount of required paperwork placed upon teachers of students with disabilities should be reduced if possible, for this reason a pilot program has been developed in which some states will participate using multi-year IEPs. Individual student inclusion in this program will require consent by both the school and the parent.

The definition of *assistive technology devices* was amended to exclude devices that are surgically implanted (i.e., cochlear implants), and clarified that students with assistive technology devices shall not be prevented from having special education services. Assistive technology devices may need to monitored by school personnel, but schools are not responsible for the implantation or replacement of such devices surgically. An example of this would be a cochlear implant.

The definition of *a child with a disability* is the term used for children ages 3-9 with a developmental delay now has been was changed to allow for the inclusion of Tourettes Syndrome.

IDEA 2004 recognized that all states must follow the National Instructional Materials Accessibility Standards which states that students who need materials in a certain form will get those at the same time their non-disabled peers receive their materials. Teacher recognition of this standard is important.

Changes in Requirements for Evaluations-The clock/time allowance between the request for an initial evaluation and the determination if a disability is present may be requested has been changed to state the finding/determination must occur within 60 calendar days of the request. This is a significant change as previously it was interpreted to mean 60 school days. Parental consent is also required for evaluations and prior to the start of special education services.

No single assessment or measurement tool may now be used to determine special education qualification. Assessments and measurements used should be in *language and form* that will give the most accurate picture of the child's abilities.

IDEA 2004's recognized that there exists a disproportionate representation of minorities and bilingual students and that pre-service interventions that are *scientifically based on early reading programs, positive behavioral interventions and support, and early intervening services* may prevent some of those children from needing special education services.

This understanding has led to a child not being considered to have a disability if he/she has not had appropriate education in math or reading, nor shall a child be considered to have a disability if the reason for his/her delays is that English is a second language.

When determining a specific learning disability, the criteria may or may not use a discrepancy between *achievement and intellectual ability* but whether or not the child responds to scientific research-based intervention. In general, children who may not have been found eligible for special education (via testing) but are known to need services (via functioning, excluding lack of instruction) are still eligible for special education services. This change now allows input for evaluation to include state and local testing, classroom observation, academic achievement, and *related developmental needs*,

Changes in Requirements for IEPs-Individualized Education Plans (IEPS) continue to have multiple sections. One section, *present levels,* now addresses *academic achievement and functional performance.* Annual IEP goals must now address the same areas.

IEP goals should be aligned to state standards, thus short term objectives are not required on every IEP. Students with IEPs must not only participate in regular education programs to the full extent possible, they must show progress in those programs.

This means that goals should be written to reflect academic progress. For students who must participate in alternate assessment, there must be alignment to *alternate achievement standards*. Significant change has been made in the definition of the IEP team as it now includes *not less than 1* teacher from each of the areas of special education and regular education be present.

IDEA 2004 recognized that the amount of required paperwork placed upon teachers of students with disabilities should be reduced if possible, for this reason a pilot program has been developed in which some states will participate using multi-year IEPs. Individual student inclusion in this program will require consent by both the school and the parent.

Skill 5.2   Apply effective communication skills with school personnel to support students with emotional impairments.

SUPPORT AND PROFESSIONAL SERVICES

When making eligibility, program, and placement decisions about a student, the special education teacher serves as a member of a multidisciplinary team. Teachers are involved in every aspect regarding the education of individual students; therefore, they need to be knowledgeable not only about teaching and instructional techniques, but also know about support services. These services will need to be coordinated, and teachers must be able to work in a collaborative manner.

The concept of mainstreaming special needs students, that is integrating them with their classmates in as many living and learning environments as possible, caught hold about the time that provisions for the Individuals with Disabilities Education Act (IDEA) were formulated in the early to mid-70s. Even though mainstreaming is not specifically addressed in this legislation, the education of all children and youth with disabilities in their least restrictive environment is mandated. In addition, this important legislation defines special education, identifies related services that may be required if special education is to be effective, and requires the participation of parents and other persons involved in the education of children and youth with disabilities.

Close contact and communication must be established and maintained between the school district staff, each base school, and the various specialists (or consultants) providing ancillary services. These persons often serve special needs students in auxiliary (i.e., providing help) and supplementary (i.e., in addition to) ways. Thus, the principles and methods of special education must be shared with regular educators, and tenets and practices of regular education must be conveyed to special educators. Job roles and unique responsibilities and duties of support specialists like speech/language therapists, physical and occupational therapists, social workers, school psychologists and nurses, and others need to be known by all teachers.

Furthermore, the services which can be provided by community resources, and the support that can be given by parents and professional organizations, must be known to all in order for maximum education for exceptional students to occur. Professional services are offered on a local, state, and national level for most areas of disability. Teachers are able to stay abreast of most current practices and changes by reading professional journals, attending professional conferences, and maintaining membership in professional organizations.

Students-Useful standards have been developed by the Council for Exceptional Children (2003) that outline best practices in communicating and relating to children and their families. For example, CEC guidelines suggest that effective teachers:

- Offer students a safe and supportive learning environment, including clearly expressed and reasonable expectations for behavior.
- Create learning environments that encourage self-advocacy and developmentally appropriate independence.
- Offer learning environments that promote active participation in independent or group activities.

Such an environment is an excellent foundation for building rapport and trust with students, and communicating a teacher's respect for and expectation that they take a measure of responsibility for their educational development. Ideally, mutual trust and respect will afford teachers opportunities to learn of and engage students' ideas, preferences and abilities.

Parents and Families-Families know students better than almost anyone, and are a valuable resource for teachers of exceptional students. Often, an insight or observation from a family member, or his or her reinforcement of school standards or activities, mean the difference between success and frustration in a teacher's work with children.

Suggestions for relationship building and collaboration with parents and families include:

- Using laypersons' terms when communicating with families, and make the communication available in the language of the home.
- Searching out and engage family members' knowledge and skills in providing services, educational and therapeutic, to student.
- Exploring and discussing the concerns of families and helping them find tactics for addressing those concerns.
- Planning collaborative meetings with children and their families, and assisting them to become active contributors to their educational team.
- Ensuring that communications with and about families is confidential and conducted with respect for their privacy.
- Offering parents accurate and professionally presented information about the pedagogical and therapeutic work being done with their child.
- Keeping parents abreast of their rights, of the kinds of practices that might violate them, and of available recourse if needed.
- Acknowledging and respect cultural differences.

Paraprofessionals and General Education Teachers -Paraprofessionals and general education teachers are important collaborators with teachers of exceptional students. Although they may have daily exposure to exceptional students, they may not have the theoretical knowledge or experience to assure their effective interaction with such students. They do bring valuable perspective to, and opportunities for breadth and variety in, an exceptional child's educational experience.

General education teachers also offer curriculum and subject matter expertise and a high level of professional support, while paraprofessionals may provide insights born of their particular familiarity with individual students. CEC suggests that teachers can best collaborate with general education teachers and paraprofessionals by:

- Offering information about the characteristics and needs of children with exceptional learning needs.
- Discussing and brainstorming ways to integrate children with exceptionalities into various settings within the school community.
- Modeling best practices, instructional techniques, accommodations, and coaching others in their use.
- Keeping communication about children with exceptional learning needs and their families confidential.
- Consulting with these colleagues in the assessment of individuals with exceptional learning needs.
- Engaging them in group problem-solving and in developing, executing, and assessing collaborative activities.
- Offer support to paraprofessionals by observing their work with students, and offering feedback and suggestions.

This section will specifically address the working relationship teachers should have with those they work with in their classroom environment. There are six basic steps to having a rewarding collaborative relationship with those whom you share a working environment, whether they are Paraprofessionals, aides or volunteers.

While it is understood that there are many titles to those who may be assisting in your room, this section will summarize their titles as "Classroom Assistant."

1. *Get to know each other*-The best way to start a relationship with anyone is to find time alone to get to know each other. Give your new classroom assistant the utmost respect and look at this as an opportunity to share your talents and learn those of your co-worker. Remember that this is your opportunity to find places you agree and disagree, which can help maintain and build your working relationship. Good working relationships require the knowledge of where each others strengths and weaknesses are. So share what your strengths and weaknesses and listen to theirs. This knowledge may create one of one of the best working relationships you have ever had.

2. *Remember Communication is a two way street*-As a professional educator it is important to remember that you must actively communicate with others. This is especially important with your classroom assistant. Let them see you listening. Pay attention and make sure that your classroom assistant sees that you care what he/she thinks. Encourage them to engage you in conversation by asking for more information. When you ask for clarification of what a student said, you are also displaying interest and active listening. Remember also that asking your classroom assistant for details and insights may help you further meet the needs of your students.

   It is also your responsibility to remove and prevent communication barriers in your working relationship. You are the professional! You must be the one to avoid giving negative criticism or put downs. Do not "read" motivations into the actions of your classroom assistant. Learn about them through communicating openly.

3. *Establish Clear Roles and Responsibilities*-The Access Center for Improving Outcomes of All Students K-8, has defined these roles in the table below.

	Teacher Role	Classroom Assistant Role	Areas of Communication
Instruction	• Plan all instruction, including what your goals/objectives that you expect in your small groups. • Provide instruction in whole-class settings.	• Work with small groups of students on specific tasks, including review or re-teaching of content. • Work with one student at a time to provide intensive instruction or remediation on a concept or skill.	• Teachers provide specific content and guidance about curriculum, students and instructional materials. • Classroom Assistants note student progress and give feedback to teachers.
Curriculum & Lesson Plan Development	• Develop all lesson plans and instructional materials. • Ensure alignment with standards, student needs, and IEPs.	• Provide assistance in development of classroom activities, retrieval of materials, and coordination of activities.	• Mutual review of lesson plan components prior to class. • Teachers provide guidance about specific instructional methods.
Classroom Management	• Develop and guide class-wide management plans for behavior and classroom structures. • Develop and monitor individual behavior management plans.	• Assist with the implementation of class-wide and individual behavior management plans. • Monitor hallways, study hall, & other activities outside normal class.	• Teachers provide guidance about specific behavior management strategies & student characteristics. • Classroom Assistants note student progress & activities and give feedback to teachers

("Working Together: Teacher-Paraeducator Collaboration" The Access Center for Improving Outcomes of All Students K-8, http://www.k8accesscenter.org/documents/RESOURCELIST3-1.doc)

While the table is nice and understandable by both parties, it is often helpful to write out what roles and expectations you have for the classroom assistant together in a contract type fashion.

Plan Together-Planning together lets your paraprofesional know you consider them valuable and provides a timeline of expectations that will aide both of you in your classroom delivery to your students. This also gives the impression to your students that you are on the same page and that you both know what is going to happen next.

Show a united front-It is essential to let your students know that both adults in the room deserve the same amount of respect. Have a plan in place on how you should address negative behaviors individually, and together. DO NOT make a statement in front of your students that your classroom assistant is wrong. Take time to address issues you may have regarding class time privately, not in front of the class.

Reevaluate your relationship-Feedback is wonderful! Stop every now and then and discuss how you are working as a team. Be willing to listen to suggestions. Taking this time may be your opportunity to improve your working relationship.

Additional Reading:
"Creating a Classroom Team"
http://www.aft.org/pubsreports/psrp/classroom_team.pdf

"Working Together: Teacher-Paraeducator Collaboration" The Access Center for Improving Outcomes of All Students K-8,
http://www.k8accesscenter.org/documents/RESOURCELIST3-1.doc

Related Service Providers and Administrators-Related service providers and administrators offer specialized skills and abilities that are critical to a exceptional education teacher's ability to advocate for his or her student and meet a school's legal obligations to the student and his or her family.

Related service providers—like speech, occupational and language therapists, psychologists, and physicians—offer expertise and resources unparalleled in meeting a child's developmental needs. Administrators are often experts in the resources available at the school and local education agency levels, the culture and politics of a school system, and can be powerful partners in meeting the needs of exceptional education teachers and students.

A teacher's most effective approach to collaborating with these professional includes:

- Confirming mutual understanding of the accepted goals and objectives of the student with exceptional learning needs as documented in his or her IEP.
- Soliciting input about ways to support related service goals in classroom settings.
- Understanding the needs and motivations of each and acting in support whenever possible.
- Facilitating respectful and beneficial relationships between families and professionals.
- Regularly and accurately communicating observations and data about the child's progress or challenges.

Skill 5.3 **Demonstrate knowledge of factors involved in professional and ethical practice in the education of students with emotional impairments.**

The special educator is expected to demonstrate ethical practice in all areas of his or her teaching responsibilities.

With regards to interaction with students, teaching and discipline practices should reflect practices that are respectful of the student as a person. Researched-based methods should be employed that will provide measurable outcomes.

The ethics of special education goes beyond methods to materials. With students of a variety of age and/or ability levels and often limited funding, appropriate materials can become difficult to obtain. If possible, students should be included in the head count for ordering general education materials.

When alternative materials are needed, it is important to secure those through special education funding sources in the school. Teaching materials that are copyrighted may not be photocopied unless they are specifically intended for such use as printed on the book. The same is true for musical materials that have a copyright. If materials are intended for reproduction it will be stated.

Information technology brings a world of information to the special educator and student's classroom. Careful consideration should be given, however, to the validity of the information before it is incorporated into practice or curricular material. Reputable sources for education practices will have connection to recognized organizations for special educators such as the Council for Exceptional Children or to teacher training programs.

Likewise, students should be guided in the finding and use of valid sites for research and learning. It is important to teach the philosophy that not everything on the internet is true.

Ethical practice in communication is an additional expectation of all educators but especially of those teaching students with disabilities. Confidentiality is crucial. Specific information regarding a student's disability and IEP (Individualized Education Plan) should be discussed only with the team of professionals working with the student and his family. When an exchange of information is needed with another school district, physician, therapist, or other professional outside of the school district, it is necessary to get written permission from the student's parent. Often, forms for such are available from the school district.

Skill 5.4   Demonstrate knowledge of strategies for communicating with and providing information to the families of students with emotional impairments.

The role of the special education teacher is to advocate for the most appropriate education for her students and to guide them in discovering new knowledge and developing new skills to the best of their potential. According to IDEA 2004 (Individual's with Disabilities Education Act) she/he is to prepare them for future, purposeful work in the society with the possibility of post-secondary education or training.

Although each special educator is also a person with a set of experiences, opinions and beliefs, it is important the she/he remain unbiased and positive in her/his professional role with students, parents, administration and the community. Differences in culture, religion, gender, or sexual orientation should not influence the teacher's approach to instruction, student goals or expectations, or advocacy.

In order to remain unbiased, the special educator should avail herself/himself of opportunities to learn about various cultures, religions, genders, and sexual orientations. This can be accomplished through reading, classroom awareness activities as appropriate, and teacher in-service.

Reading to increase awareness and acceptance of cultural differences may be done through professional, adult literature as well as through books to be read with the class.

Cultural activities in the classroom are especially well-received as foods, dress, and games are easily added to curriculum and often address learning standards.

The special educator is charged with academic, social, communicative, and independent skills instruction. Education or influence in other areas is not appropriate.

When the special educator remains unbiased, she/he is better able to meet the needs of the students and not react to additional factors. The students and their families are also more open to school-related suggestions.

The teacher's reaction to differences with students and their families models the commonly taught character education trait of respect. When the teacher demonstrates respect for all individuals in the program, it is likely that respect will also be practiced by students, parents, and administration.

STRATEGIES FOR ASSISTING PARENTS/GUARDIANS IN BECOMING ACTIVE PARTICIPANTS IN THE EDUCATIONAL TEAM

The best resource a teacher has in reaching a student is having contact with his/her parents/guardians. Good teaching recognizes this fact and seeks to strengthen this bound through communication.

The first contact a teacher has with parents should be before the school year starts. While the teacher may be required to send a letter out stating the required supplies for the class, this does not count as an initial contact.

Parents are used to hearing that their child has done something bad/wrong when they receive a phone call from a teacher. Parents should be contacted whenever possible to give positive feedback. When you call John's mother and say, "John got an A on the test today," you have just encouraged the parent to maintain open communication lines with you. Try to give 3 positive calls for every negative call you must give.

Parent-Teacher Conferences are scheduled at regular intervals throughout the school year. These provide excellent opportunities to discuss their children's progress, what they are learning and how it may relate to your future plans for their academic growth. It is not unusual for the parent or teacher to ask for a conference outside of the scheduled Parent-Teacher Conference days. These meetings should be looked at as opportunities to provide assistance to that student's success.

Modern technology has opened two more venues for communicating with parents. School/ Classroom websites are written with the intent of sharing regularly with parents/guardians. Many teachers now post their plans for the marking period and provide extra-credit/homework from these websites. Email is now one of the major modes of communication in the world today. Most parents now have email accounts and are more than willing to give you their email address to be kept appraised of their child's academic progress.

Special events also provide opportunities for parental contact. Poetry readings, science fairs, ice-cream socials, etc. are examples of such events.

The discovery at birth or initial diagnosis of a child's disabling condition(s) has a strong impact upon the family unit. Though reactions are unique to individuals, the first emotion generally felt by a parent of a child with disabilities is shock, followed by disbelief, guilt, rejection, shame, denial, and helplessness. As parents finally accept the realization of their child's condition, many report feelings of anxiety or fearfulness about their personal ability to care for and rear exceptional child. Many parents will doctor shop, hoping to find answers, while others will reject of deny information given them by health care professionals.

Skill 5.5   Analyze procedures for communicating with and promoting self-advocacy in students with emotional impairments.

See skill 1.4 for information on self-advocacy

Sample Test

1. **One technique that has proven especially effective in reducing self-stimulation and repetitive movements in autistic or severely retarded children is:**

A. Shaping.
B. Overcorrection.
C. Fading.
D. Response cost.

2. **In math class, Mary talked out without raising her hand. Her teacher gave her a warning and asked her to state the rule for being recognized to speak. However, Mary was soon talking out again and lost a point from her daily point sheet. This is an example of:**

A. Shaping.
B. Overcorrection.
C. Fading.
D. Response cost.

3. **Which body language would not likely be interpreted as a sign of defensiveness, aggression, or hostility?**

A. Pointing.
B. Direct eye contact.
C. Hands on hips.
D. Arms crossed.

4. **The minimum number of IEP meetings required per year is:**

A. As many as necessary.
B. One.
C. Two.
D. Three.

5. **Satisfaction of the LRE requirement means that:**

A. A school is providing the best services it can offer there.
B. The school is providing the best services the district has to offer.
C. The student is being educated in the least restrictive setting that meets his or her needs.
D. The student is being educated with the fewest special education services necessary.

6. **A review of a student's eligibility for an exceptional student program must be done:**

A. At least once every 3 years.
B. At least once a year.
C. Only if a major change occurs in academic or behavioral performance.
D. When a student transfers to a new school.

7. Crisis intervention methods are above all concerned with:

A. Safety and well-being of the staff and students.
B. Stopping the inappropriate behavior.
C. preventing the behavior from occurring again.
D. The student learning that outbursts are inappropriate.

8. Ricky, a third grade student, runs out of the classroom and onto the roof of the school. He paces around the roof, looks around to see who is watching, and laughs at the people on the ground. He appears to be in control of his behavior. What should the teacher do?

A. Go back inside and leave him up there until he decides he is ready to come down.
B. Climb up to get Ricky so he doesn't fall off and get hurt.
C. Notify the crisis teacher and arrange to have someone monitor Ricky.
D. Call the police.

9. Judy, a fourth grader, is often looking around the room or out of the window. She does not disturb anyone, but has to ask for directions to be repeated and does not finish her work. Her teacher decides to reinforce Judy when she is on task. This would be an example of which method of reinforcement?

A. Fading.
B. DRO.
C. DRI.
D. Shaping.

10. An appropriate time out for a ten-year-old would be:

A. Ten minutes.
B. Twenty minutes.
C. No more than one-half hour.
D. Whatever time it takes for the disruptive behavior to stop.

11. During the science lesson Rudy makes remarks from time to time but his classmates are not attending to them. The teacher reinforces the students who are raising their hand to speak, but ignores Rudy. The teacher reinforces Rudy when he raises his hand. This technique is an example of:

A. Fading.
B. Response Cost.
C. Extinction.
D. Differential reinforcement of incompatible behavior.

12. Mike was caught marking graffiti on the walls of the bathroom. His consequence was to clean all the walls of the bathroom. This type of overcorrection would be:

A. Response cost.
B. Restitution.
C. Positive practice.
D. Negative practice.

13. Which of these would probably not be a result of implementing an extinction strategy?

A. Maladaptive behavior gets worse before it gets better.
B. Maladaptive behavior stops, then starts up again for a brief time.
C. Aggression may occur for a brief period following implementation of extinction.
D. The length of time and patience involved to implement the strategy might tempt the teacher to give up.

14. Withholding or removing a stimulus that reinforces a maladaptive behavior is:

A. Extinction.
B. Overcorrection.
C. Punishment.
D. Reinforcing an incompatible Behavior.

15. Which of these would not be used to strengthen a desired behavior?

A. Contingency contracting.
B. Tokens.
C. Chaining.
D. Overcorrection.

16. If the arrangement in a fixed-ratio schedule of reinforcement is 3, when will the student receive the reinforcer?

A. After every third correct response.
B. After every third correct response in a row.
C. After the third correct response in the time interval of the behavior sample.
D. After the third correct response even if the undesired behavior occurs in between correct responses.

17. Wesley is having trouble ignoring distractions. At first you have him seated at a carrel which is located in a corner of the room. He does well so, you eventually move him out of the carrel for increasing portions of the day. Eventually he is able to sit in a seat with the rest of his classmates. This is an example of:

A. Shaping.
B. Extinction.
C. Fading.
D. Chaining.

18. Laura is beginning to raise her hand first instead of talking out. An effective schedule of reinforcement would be:

A. Continuous.
B. Variable.
C. Intermittent.
D. Fixed.

19. As Laura continues to raise her hand to speak, the teacher would want to change this schedule of reinforcement on order to wean her from reinforcement:

A. Continuous.
B. Variable.
C. Intermittent.
D. Fixed.

20. Laura has demonstrated that she has mastered the goal of raising her hand to speak, reinforcement during the maintenance phase should be:

A. Continuous.
B. Variable.
C. Intermittent.
D. Fixed.

21. An integral part of ecological interventions are consequences that:

A. Are natural and logical.
B. Include extinction and overcorrection.
C. Are immediate and consistent.
D. Involve fading and shaping.

22. Examples of behaviors that are appropriate to be measured for their duration, include all EXCEPT:

A. Thumb-sucking.
B. Hitting.
C. Temper tantrums.
D. Maintaining eye contact.

23. Examples of behaviors that are appropriate to be monitored by measuring frequency include all EXCEPT:

A. Teasing.
B. Talking out.
C. Being on time for class.
D. Daydreaming.

24. Criteria for choosing behaviors to measure by frequency include all but those that:

A. Have an observable beginning.
B. Last a long time.
C. Last a short time.
D. Occur often.

25. Criteria for choosing behaviors to measure by duration include all but those that:

A. Last a short time.
B. Last a long time.
C. Have no readily observable beginning or end.
D. Do not happen often.

26. Data on quiet behaviors (e.g., nail biting or daydreaming) are best measured using a:

A. Interval or time sample.
B. Continuous sample.
C. Variable sample.
D. Fixed-ratio sample.

27. Mr. Jones wants to design an intervention for reducing Jason's sarcastic remarks. He wants to find out who or what is reinforcing Jason's remarks, so he records data on Jason's behavior as well as the attending behavior of his peers. This is an example of collecting data on:

A.   Reciprocal behaviors.
B.   Multiple behaviors for single subjects.
C.   Single behaviors for multiple Subjects.
D.   Qualitative data on Jason.

28. Ms. Beekman has a class of students who frequently talk out. She wishes to begin interventions with the students who are talking out the most. She monitors the talking behavior of the entire class for 1 minute samples every half hour. This is an example of collecting data on:

A.   Multiple behaviors for single subjects.
B.   Reciprocal behaviors.
C.   Single behaviors for multiple subjects.
D.   Continuous behaviors for fixed intervals.

29.   Mark got a B on his social studies test. Mr. Wilner praised him for his good grade but he replies, "I was lucky this time. It must have been an easy test." Mark's statement is an example of:

A.   External locus of control.
B.   Internal locus of control.
C.   Rationalization of his performance.
D.   Modesty.

30. Mr. Smith is on a field trip with a group of high school EH students. On the way they stop at a fast food restaurant for lunch, and Warren and Raul get into a disagreement. After some heated words, Warren stalks out of the restaurant and refuses to return to the group. He leaves the parking lot, continues walking away from the group, and ignores Mr. Smith's directions to come back. What would be the best course of action for Mr. Smith?

A.   Leave the group with the class aide and follow Warren to try to talk him into coming back.
B.   Wait a little while and see if Warren cools off and returns .
C.   Telephone the school and let the crisis teacher notify the police in accordance with school policy.
D.   Call the police himself.

31. Which is the least effective of reinforcers in programs for mildly to moderately handicapped learners?

A. Tokens.
B. Social.
C. Food.
D. Activity.

32. Tyrone likes to throw paper towards the trash can instead of getting up to throw it away. After several attempts of positive interventions, Tyrone has to serve a detention and continue to throw balls of paper at the trash can for the entire detention period. This would be an example of:

A.   Negative practice.
B.   Overcorrection.
C.   Extinction.
D.   Response cost.

33. A student may have great difficulty in meeting a target goal if the teacher has not first considered:

A.   If the student has external or internal locus of control.
B.   If the student is motivated to attain the goal.
C.   If the student has the essential prerequisite skills to perform the goal.
D.   If the student has had previous success or failure meeting the goal in other classes.

34. The Premack principle of increasing the performance of a less-preferred activity by immediately following it with a highly-preferred activity is the basis of:

A.   Response cost.
B.   Token systems.
C   Contingency contracting.
D.   Self-recording management.

35. Mr. Brown finds that his chosen consequence does not seem to be having the desired effect of reducing the target misbehavior. Which of these would LEAST LIKELY account for Mr. Brown's lack of success with the consequence?

A.   The consequence was aversive in Mr. Brown's opinion, but not the students.
B.   The students were not developmentally ready to understand the connection between the behavior and the consequence.
C.   Mr. Brown was inconsistent in applying the consequence.
D.   The intervention had not previously been shown to be effective in studies.

36. Teaching techniques that stimulate active participation and understanding in the mathematics class include all but which of the following?

A. Having students copy computation facts for a set number of times.
B. Asking students to find the error in an algorithm.
C. Giving immediate feedback to students.
D. Having students chart their progress.

37. Justin, a second grader, is reinforced if he is on task at the end of each 10-minute block of time that the teacher observes him. This is an example of what type of reinforcement schedule?

A. Continuous.
B. Fixed-interval.
C. Fixed ratio.
D. Variable ratio.

38. Addressing a student's maladaptive behavior right away with a "time out" should be reserved for situations where:

A. The student has engaged in the behavior continuously throughout the day.
B. Harm might come to the student or others.
C. Lesser interventions have not been effective.
D. The student displayed the behavior the day before.

39. At the beginning of the school year, Annette had a problem with being late to class. Her teacher reinforced her each time she was in her seat when the bell rang. In October, her teacher decided to reward her every other day when she was not tardy to class. The reinforcement schedule appropriate for making the transition to maintenance phase would be:

A. Continuous.
B. Fixed interval.
C. Variable ratio.
D. Fixed ratio.

40. By November, Annette's teacher is satisfied with her record of being on time and decides to change the schedule of reinforcement. The best type of reinforcement schedule for maintenance of behavior is:

A Continuous.
B. Fixed interval.
C. Variable ratio.
D. Fixed ratio.

41. Which of these groups is not comprehensively covered by IDEA?

A. Gifted and talented.
B. Mentally retarded.
C. Specific learning disabilities.
D. Speech and language impaired.

42. Organizing ideas by use of a web or outline is an example of which writing activity?

A.   Revision.
B.   Drafting.
C.   Prewriting.
D.   Final draft.

43. When a teacher is choosing behaviors to modify, the issue of social validity must be considered. Social validity refers to:

A.   The need for the behavior to be performed in public.
B.   Whether the new behavior will be considered significant by those who deal with the child.
C.   Whether there will be opportunities to practice the new behavior in public.
D.   Society's standards of behavior.

44. Dena, a second grader, is a messy eater who leaves her lunch are messy as well. Dena's teacher models correct use of eating utensils and napkins for her. As Dena approximates the target behavior of eating neatly and leaving her area clean, she receives praise and a token. Finally, Dena reaches her target behavior goal and redeems her tokens. Dena's teacher used the strategy of:

A.   Chaining.
B.   Extinction.
C.   Overcorrection.
D.   Shaping.

45. Educators who advocate educating all children in their neighborhood classrooms and schools, propose the end of labeling and segregation of special needs students in special classes, and call for the delivery of special supports and services directly in the classroom may be said to support the:

A.   Full service model.
B.   Regular education initiative.
C.   Full inclusion model.
D.   Mainstream model.

46. In Ellis's ABC model, maladaptive behavior in response to a situation results from:

A.   Antecedent events.
B.   Stimulus events.
C.   Thinking about the consequences.
D.   Irrational beliefs about the event.

47. Section 504 differs from the scope of IDEA because its main focus is on:

A.   Prohibition of discrimination on the basis of disability.
B.   A basis for additional support services and accommodations in a special education setting.
C.   Procedural rights and safeguards for the individual.
D.   Federal funding for educational Services.

48. Public Law-457 amended the IDEA to make provisions for:

A. Education services for "uneducable" children.
B. Education al services for children in jail settings.
C. Procedural rights and safeguards for the individual.
D. Federal funding for educational Services.

49. A holistic approach to stress management should include all of the following EXCEPT:

A. Teaching a variety of coping methods.
B. Cognitive modification of feelings.
C. Teaching the flight or fight response.
D. Cognitive modification of behaviors.

50. Marisol has been mainstreamed into a ninth grade language arts class. Although her behavior is satisfactory and she likes the class, Marisol's reading level is about two years below grade level. The class has been assigned to read "Great Expectations" and write a report. What intervention would be LEAST successful in helping Marisol complete this assignment?

A. Having Marisol listen to a taped recording while following the story in the regular text.
B. Giving her a modified version of the story.
C. Telling her a modified version of the story.
D. Showing a film to the entire class and comparing and contrasting it to the book.

51. Fractions may be thought of in each of these ways EXCEPT:

A. Part of a whole.
B. Part of a parent set.
C. Ratio.
D. An exponent.

52. Many special education students may have trouble with the skills necessary to be successful in algebra and geometry for all but one of these reasons:

A. Prior instruction focused on computation rather than understanding.
B Unwillingness to problem solve.
C. Lack of instruction in prerequisite skills.
D. Large amount of new vocabulary.

53. Which of these processes is NOT directly related to the meaningful development of number concepts in young children:

A. Describing.
B. Classifying.
C. Grouping.
D. Ordering.

54. Mr. Ward wants to assess Jennifer's problem-solving skills in mathematics. Which question would not address her use of strategies?

A. Does Jennifer check for mistakes in computation?
B. Does Jennifer use trial and error to solve problems?
C. Does Jennifer have an alternative strategy if the first one fails?
D. Does Jennifer become easily frustrated if she doesn't immediately get an answer?

55. Ryan is working on a report about dogs. He uses scissors and tape to cut and rearrange sections and paragraphs, then photocopies the paper so he can continue writing. Ryan is in which stage of the writing process?

A. Final Draft.
B. Prewriting.
C. Revision.
D. Drafting.

56. Talking into a tape reorder is an example of which writing activity?

A. Prewriting.
B. Drafting.
C. Final draft.
D. Revision.

57. Publishing a class newsletter, looking through catalogues and filling out order forms and playing the role of secretaries and executives are activities designed to teach:

A. Expressive writing.
B. Transactional writing.
C. Poetic writing.
D. Creative writing.

58. Under the provisions of IDEA, the student is entitled to all of these EXCEPT:

A. Placement in the best Environment.
B. Placement in the least restrictive Environment.
C. provision of educational needs at no cost.
D. Provision of individualized, appropriate educational program.

59. Teacher modeling, student-teacher dialogues, and peer interactions are part of which teaching technique designed to provide support during the initial phases of instruction?

A. Reciprocal teaching.
B. Scaffolding.
C. Peer tutoring.
D. Cooperative learning.

60. Modeling of a behavior by an adult who verbalizes the thinking process, overt self-instruction, and covert self-instruction are components of:

A. Rational-Emotive therapy.
B. Reality therapy.
C. Cognitive behavior modification.
D. Reciprocal teaching.

61. Standards of accuracy for a student's spelling should be based on the student's:

A. Grade level spelling list.
B. Present reading book level.
C. Level of spelling development.
D. Performance on an informal assessment.

62. Which of these techniques is least effective in helping children correct spelling problems?

A. The teacher models the correct spelling in a context.
B. Student sees the incorrect and the correct spelling together in order to visualize the correct spelling.
C. Positive reinforcement as the child tests the rules and tries to approximate the correct spelling.
D. Copying the correct word 5 times.

63. The single most important activity for eventual reading success of young children is:

A. Giving them books.
B. Watching animated stories.
C. Reading aloud to them.
D. Talking about pictures in books.

64. Skilled readers use all but which one of these knowledge sources to construct meanings beyond the literal text:

A. Text knowledge.
B. Syntactic knowledge.
C. Morphological knowledge.
D. Semantic knowledge.

65. The cooperative nature of Glasser's Reality Therapy in which the problem-solving approach is used to correct misbehavior is best signified by:

A. Minimal punishment.
B. Its similar approach to methods that teach students how to deal with academic mistakes.
C. Students' promises to use the alternative behavior plan to help them reach their goals.
D. Procedure sheets used during conflict situations.

66. Diaphragmatic breathing, progressive relaxation training, and exercises are examples of which type of stress coping skills?

A. Rational-emotive.
B. Cognitive-psychological.
C. Somatic-physiological.
D. Stress inoculation.

67. The stress that we experience when we win a race or accomplish a difficult task is called:

A. Stressor.
B. Stresses.
C. Eustress.
D. Distress.

68. Jane is so intimidated by a classmate's teasing that she breaks down in tears and cannot stand up for herself. The feelings she is experiencing is:

A. Stressors.
B. Stresses.
C. Eustress.
D. Distress.

69. The movement towards serving as many children with disabilities as possible in the regular classroom with supports and services is known as:

A. Full service model.
B. Regular education initiative.
C. Full Inclusion model.
D. Mainstream model.

70. Which of the following is NOT a feature of effective classroom rules?

A. They are about 4 to 6 in number.
B. They are negatively stated.
C. Consequences for infraction are consistent and immediate.
D. They can be tailored to individual classroom goals and teaching styles.

71. A suggested amount of time for large-group instruction lesson for a sixth or seventh grade group would be:

A. 5 to 40 minutes.
B. 5 to 50 minutes.
C. 5 to 30 minutes.
D. 5 to 15 minutes.

72. Sam is working to earn half an hour of basketball time with his favorite P E teacher. At the end of each half-hour Sam marks his point sheet with an X if he reached his goal of no call-outs. When he has received 25 marks, he will receive his basketball free time. This behavior management strategy is an example of:

A. Self-recording.
B. Self-evaluation.
C. Self-reinforcement.
D. Self-regulation.

73. Mark has been working on his target goal of completing his mathematics class work. Each day he records on a scale of 0 to 3 how well he has done his work and his teacher provides feedback. This self-management technique is an example of:

A. Self-recording.
B. Self-reinforcement.
C. Self-regulation.
D. Self-evaluation.

74. When Barbara reached her target goal, she chose her reinforcer and softly said to herself, "I worked hard and I deserve this reward." This self-management technique is an example of:

A. Self-reinforcement.
B. Self-recording.
C. Self-regulation.
D. Self-evaluation.

75. Grading should be based on all of the following EXCEPT:

A. Clearly defined mastery of course objectives.
B. A variety of evaluation methods.
C. Performance of the student in relation to other students.
D. Assigning points for activities and basing grades on a point total.

76. The following words describe an IEP objective EXCEPT:

A. Specific.
B. Observable.
C. Measurable.
D. Criterion-referenced.

77. Teacher feedback, task completion, and a sense of pride over mastery or accomplishment of a skill are examples of:

A. Extrinsic reinforcers.
B. Behavior modifiers.
C. Intrinsic reinforces.
D. Positive feedback.

78. Social approval, token reinforcers, and rewards such as pencils or stickers are examples of:

A. Extrinsic reinforcers.
B. Behavior modifiers.
C. Intrinsic reinforcers.
D. Positive feedback.

79. Aggression, escape, and avoidance are unpleasant side effects which can be avoided by using:

A.   Time out.
B.   Response cost.
C.   Overcorrection.
D.   Negative practice.

80. Josie forgot that it was school picture day and did not dress up for the pictures. In the media center, Josie notices some girls in the line waiting to have their pictures taken. They appear to be looking over at her and whispering. Josie feels certain that they are making fun of the way her hair and clothes look and gets so upset that she leaves the line and hides out in the bathroom. Josie did not think to ask when the makeup day for pictures would be. According to Ellis's ABC Model, Jodie's source of stress is:

A.   Her forgetting to dress appropriately for picture day.
B.   The girls in the library who appear to be whispering about her.
C.   Her belief that they are making fun of her appearance.
D.   The girls' insensitive behavior.

81. Token systems are popular for all of these advantages EXCEPT:

A.   The number needed for rewards may be adjusted as needed.
B.   Rewards are easy to maintain.
C.   They are effective for students who generally do not respond to social reinforcers.
D.   Tokens reinforce the relationship of desirable behavior and reinforcement.

82. Which would not be an advantage of using a criterion-referenced test?

A.   Information about an individual's ability level is too specific for the purposes of the assessment.
B.   It can pinpoint exact areas of weaknesses and strengths.
C.   You can design them yourself.
D.   You do not get comparative Information.

83. Which is NOT an example of a standard score?

A.   T Score.
B.   Z Score.
C.   Standard deviation.
D.   Stanine.

84. The most direct method of obtaining assessment data and perhaps the most objective is:

A.   Testing.
B.   Self-recording.
C.   Observation.
D.   Experimenting.

85. The basic tools necessary to observe and record behavior include all BUT:

A.   Cameras.
B.   Timers.
C.   Counters.
D.   Graphs or charts.

86. Which of these characteristics is NOT included in the P.L. 94-142 definition of emotional disturbance:

A.   General pervasive mood of unhappiness or depression.
B.   Social maladjustment manifested in a number of settings.
C.   Tendency to develop physical symptoms, pains, or fear associated with school or personal problems.
D.   Inability to learn which is not attributed to intellectual, sensory, or health factors.

87. Of the various factors that contribute to delinquency and antisocial behavior, which has been found to be the weakest?

A.   Criminal behavior and/or alcoholism in the father.
B.   Lax mother and punishing father.
C.   Socioeconomic disadvantage.
D.   Long history of broken home or marital discord among parents.

88. Poor moral development, lack of empathy, and behavioral excesses such as aggression are the most obvious characteristics of which behavioral disorder?

A.   Autism.
B.   ADD-H.
C.   Conduct disorder.
D.   Pervasive development disorder.

89. School refusal, obsessive-compulsive disorders, psychosis, and separation anxiety are also frequently accompanied by:

A.   Conduct disorder.
B.   ADD-H.
C.   Depression.
D.   Autism.

90. Signs of depression do not typically include:

A.   Hyperactivity.
B.   Changes in sleep patterns.
C.   Recurring thoughts of death or suicide.
D.   Significant changes in weight or appetite.

91. Children who are characterized by impulsivity, generally:

A.   Do not feel sorry for their actions.
B.   Blame others for their actions.
C.   Do not weigh alternatives before acting.
D.   Do not out grow their problem.

92. Which of these is listed as only a minor scale on the Behavior Problem Checklist?

A. Motor Excess.
B. Conduct Disorder.
C. Socialized Aggression.
D. Anxiety Withdrawal.

93. The extent that a test measure what it claims to measure is called:

A. Reliability.
B. Validity.
C. Factor analysis.
D. Chi square.

94. Which is not a goal of collaborative consultation?

A. Prevent learning and behavior problems with mainstreamed students.
B. Coordinate the instructional programs between mainstream and ESE classes,
C. Facilitate solutions to learning and behavior problems.
D. Function as an ESE service model.

95. An important goal of collaborative consultation is:

A. Mainstream as many ESE students as possible.
B. Guidance on how to handle ESE students from the ESE teacher.
C. Mutual empowerment of both the mainstream and the ESE teacher.
D. Document progress of mainstreamed students.

96. Knowledge of evaluation strategies, program interventions, and types of data are examples of which variable for a successful consultation program?

A. People.
B. Process.
C. Procedural implementation.
D. Academic preparation.

97. Skills as an administrator, and background in client, consulter, and consultation skills are examples of which variable in a successful consultation program?

A. People.
B. Process.
C. Procedural implementation.
D. Academic preparation.

98. The ability to identify problems, generate solutions, and knowledge of theoretical perspectives of consultation are examples of which variable in a successful consultation program?

A. People.
B. Process.
C. Procedural implementation.
D. Academic preparation.

99. A serious hindrance to successful mainstreaming is:

A. Lack of adapted materials.
B. Lack of funding.
C. Lack of communication among teachers.
D. Lack of support from administration.

100. Which of the following statements was not offered as a rationale for the REI?

A. Special education students are not usually identified until their learning problems have become severe.
B. Lack of funding will mean that support for the special needs children will not be available in the regular classroom.
C. Putting children in segregated special education placements is stigmatizing.
D. There are students with learning or behavior problems who do not meet special education requirements but who still need special services.

101. The key to success for the exceptional student placed in a regular classroom is:

A. Access to the special aids and materials.
B. Support from the ESE teacher.
C. Modifications in the curriculum.
D The mainstream teacher's belief that the student will profit from the placement.

102. Lack of regular follow-up, difficulty in transporting materials, and lack of consistent support for students who need more assistance are disadvantages of which type of service model?

A. Regular classroom.
B. Consultant with regular teacher.
C. Itinerant.
D. Resource room.

103. Ability to supply specific instructional materials, programs, and methods, and to influence environmental learning variables are advantages of which service model for exceptional students?

A. Regular classroom.
B. Consultant teacher.
C. Itinerant teacher.
D. Resource room.

104. An emphasis on instructional remediation and individualized instruction in problem areas, and a focus on mainstreaming students are characteristics of which model of service delivery?

A. Regular classroom.
B. Consultant teacher.
C. Itinerant teacher.
D. Resource room.

105. Which of these would not be considered a valid attempt to contact a parent for an IEP meeting?

A. Telephone.
B. Copy of correspondence.
C. Message left on an answering machine.
D. Record of home visits.

106. A best practice for evaluation student performance and progress on IEP is:

A. Formal assessment.
B. Curriculum based assessment.
C. Criterion based assessment.
D. Norm-referenced evaluation.

107. Guidelines for an Individualized Family Service Plan (IFSP) would be described in which legislation?

A. PL 94-142
B. PL 99-457
C. PL 101-476
D. ADA

108. In a positive classroom environment, errors are viewed as:

A. Symptoms of deficiencies.
B. Lack of attention or ability.
C. A natural part of the learning process.
D. The result of going too fast.

109. Recess, attending school social or sporting events, and eating lunch with peers are examples of:

A. Privileges.
B. Allowances.
C. Rights.
D. Entitlements.

110. Free time, shopping at the school store, and candy are examples of:

A. Privileges.
B. Allowances.
C. Rights.
D. Entitlements.

111. Eating lunch, access to a bathroom, and privacy are examples of:

A. Privileges.
B. Allowances.
C. Rights.
D. Entitlements.

112. Cheryl is a 15-year-old student receiving educational services in a full-time EH classroom. The date for her IEP review will take place two months before her 16th birthday. According to the requirements of IDEA, what must ADDITIONALLY be included in this review?

A. Graduation plan.
B. Individualized transition plan.
C. Individualized family service plan.
D. Transportation planning.

113. Hector is a 10th grader in a program for the severely emotionally handicapped. After a classmate taunted him about his mother, Hector threw a desk at the other boy and attacked him. As a crisis intervention team attempted to break up the fight, one teacher hurt his knee. The other boy received a concussion. Hector now faces disciplinary measures. How long can he be suspended without the suspension constituting a "change of placement"?

A. 5 days.
B. 10 days.
C. 10 - 30 days.
D. 60 days.

114. The concept that a handicapped student cannot be expelled for misconduct which is a manifestation of the handicap itself is not limited to students which was labeled "seriously emotionally disturbed." Which reason does NOT explain this concept?

A.   Emphasis on individualized evaluation.
B.   Consideration of the problems and needs of handicapped students.
C.   Right to a free and appropriate public education.
D.   Putting these students out of school will just leave them on the streets to commit crimes.

115. An effective classroom behavior management plan includes all but which of the following?

A.   Transition procedures for changing activities.
B.   Clear consequences for rule infractions.
C.   Concise teacher expectations for student behavior.
D.   Copies of lesson plans.

116. Statements like "Darrien is lazy," are not helpful in describing his behavior for all but which of these reasons?

A.   There is no way to determine if any change occurs from the information given.
B.   The student and not the behavior becomes labeled.
C.   Darrien's behavior will manifest itself clearly enough without any written description.
D.   Constructs are open to various interpretations among the people who are asked to define them.

117. Mercie often is not in her seat when the bell rings. She may be found at the pencil sharpener, throwing paper away, or fumbling through her notebook. Which of these descriptions of her behavior can be described as a "pinpoint"?

A.   Is tardy a lot.
B.   Is out of seat.
C.   Is not in seat when late bell rings.
D.   Is disorganized.

118. When choosing behaviors for change, the teacher should ask if there is any evidence that the behavior is presently or potentially harmful to the student or others. This is an example of which test?

A.   Fair-Pair.
B.   "Stranger" test.
C.   Premack principle.
D.   "So-What" Test.

119.Ms. Taylor takes her students to a special gymnastics presentation that the P.E. coach has arranged in the gym. She has a rule against talk-outs and reminds the students that they will lose 5 points on their daily point sheet for talking out. The students get a chance to perform some of the simple stunts. They all easily go through the movements except for Sam, who is known as the class klutz. Sam does not give up, and finally completes the stunts. His classmates cheer him on with comments like "Way to go!" their teacher, however, reminds them that they broke the no talking rule and will lose the points. What mistake was made here?

A. The students forgot the no-talking rule.
B. The teacher considered talk-outs to be maladaptive in all school settings.
C. The other students could have distracted Sam with talk-outs and caused him to get hurt.
D. The teacher should have let the P. E. coach handle the discipline in the gym.

120. Which of the following should be avoided when writing objectives for social behavior?

A. Nonspecific adverbs.
B. Behaviors stated as verbs.
C. Criteria for acceptable performance.
D. Conditions where the behavior is expected to be performed.

121. Criteria for choosing behaviors that are in the most need of change involve all but the following:

A. Observations across settings to rule out certain interventions.
B. Pinpointing the behavior that is the poorest fit in the child's environment.
C. the teacher's concern about what is the most important behavior to target.
D. Analysis of the environmental reinforcers.

122. Ms. Wright is planning an analysis of Audrey's out-of-seat behavior. Her initial data would be called:

A. Pre-referral phase.
B. Intervention phase.
C. Baseline phase.
D. Observation phase.

123. To reinforce Audrey each time she is on-task and in her seat, Ms. Wright decides to deliver specific praise and stickers which Audrey may collect and redeem for a reward. The data collected during the time Ms. Wright is using this intervention is called:

A. Referral phase.
B. Intervention phase.
C. Baseline phase.
D. Observation phase.

124. Indirect requests and attempts to influence or control others through one's use of language is an example of:

A. Morphology.
B. Syntax.
C. Pragmatics.
D. Semantics.

125. Kenny, a fourth grader, has trouble comprehending analogies, using comparative, spatial, and temporal words, and multiple meanings. Language interventions for Kenny would focus on:

A. Morphology.
B. Syntax.
C. Pragmatics.
D. Semantics.

126. Celia, who is in fourth grade, asked, "Where are my ball?" She also has trouble with passive sentences. Language interventions for Celia would target:

A. Morphology.
B. Syntax.
C. Pragmatics.
D. Semantics.

127. Scott is in middle school, but still says statements like "I gotted new high-tops yesterday," and, "I saw three mans in the front office." Language interventions for Scott would target:

A. Morphology.
B. Syntax.
C. Pragmatics.
D. Semantics.

128. Which is not indicative of a handwriting problem?

A. Errors persist over time.
B. Little improvement on simple handwriting tasks.
C. Fatigue after writing for a short time.
D. Occasional letter reversals, word omissions, and poor spacing.

129. All of these are effective in teaching written expression EXCEPT:

A. Exposure to various styles and direct instruction in those styles.
B. Immediate feedback from the teacher with all mistakes clearly marked.
C. Goal setting and peer evaluation of written products according to a set criteria.
D. Incorporating writing with other academic subjects.

130. Mr. Mendez is assessing his student's written expression. Which of these is not a component of written expression?

A. Vocabulary.
B. Morphology.
C. Content.
D. Sentence structure.

131. Ms. Tolbert is teaching spelling to her students. The approach stresses phoneme-grapheme relationships within parts of words. Spelling rules, generalizations, and patterns are taught. A typical spelling list for her third graders might include light, bright, night, fright, and slight. Which approach is Ms. Tolbert using?

A. Rule-based instruction.
B. Fernald method.
C. Gillingham method.
D. Test-Study-Test.

132. At the beginning of the year, Mr. Johnson wants to gain an understanding of his class' social structure in order to help him assess social skills and related problems. The technique that would best help Mr. Johnson accomplish this is:

A. Personal interviews with each student.
B. Parent rating form.
C. Sociometric techniques.
D. Self-reports.

133. In assessing a group's social structure, asking a student to list the classmates whom he or she would choose to be his or her best friend, and preferred play partners is an example of:

A. Peer nomination.
B. Peer rating.
C. Peer assessment.
D. Sociogram.

134. Naming classmates who fit certain behavioral descriptions such as smart, disruptive, or quiet, is an example of which type of sociometric assessment?

A. Peer nomination.
B. Peer rating.
C. Peer assessment.
D. Sociogram.

135. Mr. Johnson asks his students to score each of their classmates in areas such as who they would prefer to play with and work with. A likert-type scale with nonbehavioral criteria is used. This is an example of:

A. Peer nomination.
B. Peer rating.
C. Peer assessment.
D. Sociogram.

136. Which of these explanations would not likely account for the lack of a clear definition of behavior disorders?

A. Problems with measurement.
B. Cultural and/or social influences and views of what is acceptable.
C. The numerous types of manifestations of behavior disorders.
D. Differing theories that use their own terminology and definitions.

137. Ryan is 3, and her temper tantrums last for an hour. Bryan is 8, and he does not stay on task for more than 10 minutes without teacher prompts. These behavior differ form normal children in terms of their:

A. Rate.
B. Topography.
C. Duration.
D. Magnitude.

138. All children cry, hit, fight, and play alone at different times. Children with behavior disorders will perform these behaviors at a higher than normal:

A. Rate.
B. Topography.
C. Duration.
D. Magnitude.

139. The exhibition of two or more types of problem behaviors across different areas of functioning is known as:

A. Multiple maladaptive behaviors.
B. Clustering.
C. Social maladjustment.
D. Conduct disorder.

140. Children with behavior disorders often do not exhibit stimulus control. This means that they have not learned:

A. The right things to do.
B. Where and when certain behaviors are appropriate.
C. Right from wrong.
D. Listening skills.

141. Social withdrawal, anxiety, depression, shyness, and guilt are indicative of:

A. Conduct disorder.
B. Personality disorders.
C. Immaturity.
D. Socialized aggression.

142. Short attention span, daydreaming, clumsiness, and preference for younger playmates are associated with:

A. Conduct disorder.
B. Personality disorders.
C. Immaturity.
D. Socialized aggression.

143. Truancy, gang membership, and feeling of pride in belonging to a delinquent subculture are indicative of:

A.   Conduct disorder.
B.   Personality disorders.
C.   Immaturity.
D.   Socialized aggression.

144. Temper tantrums, disruption of class, disobedience, and bossiness are associated with:

A.   Conduct disorder.
B.   Personality disorders.
C.   Immaturity.
D.   Socialized aggression.

145. Which of these is not true for most children with behavior disorders?

A.   Many score in the "slow learner" or "mildly retarded" range on IQ tests.
B.   They are frequently behind their classmates in terms of academic achievement.
C.   They are bright, but bored with their surroundings.
D.   A large amount of time is spent in nonproductive, nonacademic behaviors.

146. Echolalia, repetitive stereotype actions, and a severe disorder of thinking and communication are indicative of:

A.   Psychosis.
B.   Schizophrenia.
C.   Autism.
D.   Paranoia.

147. Teaching children functional skills that will be useful in their home life and neighborhoods is the basis of:

A.   Curriculum-based instruction.
B.   Community-based instruction.
C.   Transition planning.
D.   Functional curriculum.

148.Disabilities caused by fetal alcohol syndrome are many times higher for which ethnic group?

A.   Native Americans.
B.   Asian Americans.
C.   Hispanic Americans.
D.   African Americans.

149. Which of these would be the least effective measure of behavioral disorders?

A.   Projective test.
B.   Ecological assessment.
C.   Standardized test.
D.   Psychodynamic analysis.

150. Which behavioral disorder is difficult to diagnose in children because the symptoms are manifested quite differently than in adults?

A. Anorexia.
B. Schizophrenia.
C. Paranoia.
D. Depression.

Answer Key

1. B	45. C	89. C	133. A
2. D	46. D	90. A	134. C
3. B	47. A	91. C	135. A
4. B	48. C	92. A	136. C
5. D	49. C	93. B	137. C
6. A	50. C	94. D	138. A
7. A	51. D	95. C	139. B
8. C	52. A	96. B	140. B
9. C	53. C	97. A	141. B
10. A	54. D	98. C	142. C
11. C	55. C	99. C	143. D
12. C	56. C	100. B	144. A
13. B	57. B	101. D	145. C
14. A	58. A	102. C	146. C
15. D	59. B	103. B	147. B
16. B	60. C	104. D	148. A
17. A	61. C	105. C	149. C
18. A	62. D	106. B	150. D
19. D	63. C	107. B	
20. B	64. C	108. C	
21. A	65. C	109. D	
22. B	66. C	110. A	
23. D	67. C	111. C	
24. B	68. D	112. B	
25. A	69. C	113. B	
26. A	70. B	114. D	
27. A	71. C	115. D	
28. C	72. A	116. C	
29. A	73. D	117. C	
30. C	74. A	118. D	
31. C	75. C	119. D	
32. A	76. D	120. A	
33. C	77. C	121. C	
34. C	78. A	122. C	
35. D	79. B	123. B	
36. A	80. C	124. C	
37. B	81. B	125. D	
38. B	82. D	126. B	
39. B	83. C	127. A	
40. C	84. C	128. D	
41. C	85. A	129. B	
42. C	86. B	130. B	
43. D	87. C	131. A	
44. A	88. C	132. C	

Sample Questions with Rationale

1. One technique that has proven especially affective in reducing self-stimulation and repetitive movements in autistic or severely retarded children is:
   a. Shaping
   b. Overcorrection
   c. Fading
   d. Response Cost

A Shaping: To change a person's behavior gradually using rewards as the person comes closer to the desired behavior, or punishment for moving away from it.
B Overcorrection: a form of punishment, e.g., cleaning of a marked surface.
C Fading: gradual lessening of a reward or punishment.
D Response cost a form of punishment, e.g., loss of privileges

b. is correct.
Rationale: All behavior is learned

2. In math class, Mary talked out without raising her hand. Her teacher gave her a warning and asked her to state the rule for being recognized to speak. However, Mary was soon talking again, and lost a point from her daily point sheet. This is an example of:
   a. Shaping
   b. Overcorrection
   c. Fading
   d. Response cost

d. is correct.
Rationale: Mary lost a point in response to the undesirable behavior.

3. Which body language would not likely be interpreted as a sign of defensiveness, aggression, or hostility?
   a. Pointing
   b. Direct eye contact
   c. Hands on hips
   d. Arms

b. is correct.
Rationale: In our culture, A, C, and D are considered nonverbal acts of defiance. Direct eye contact is not considered an act of defiance.

4. The minimum number of IEP meetings required per year is:
   a. as many as necessary
   b. one
   c. two
   d. three

b. is correct.
Rationale: P. L. 99-457 (1986) grants an annual IEP

5. Satisfaction of the LRE requirement means:
   a. The school is providing the best services it can offer
   b. The school is providing the best services the district has to offer
   c. The student is being educated with the fewest special education services necessary
   d. The student is being educated in the least restrictive setting that meets his or her needs

d. is correct.
Rationale: The legislation mandates **LRE** Least Restrictive Environment

6. A review of a student's eligibility for an exceptional student program must be done:
   a. At least once every three years
   b. At least once a year
   c. Only if a major change occurs in academic or behavioral performance
   d. When a student transfers to a new school

a. is correct.
Rationale: P. L. 95-56 1978, (Gifted and Talented Children's Act)

7. Crisis intervention methods are above all concerned with:
   a. Safety and well-being of the staff and students
   b. Stopping the inappropriate behavior
   c. Preventing the behavior from occurring again
   d. The student learning that out bursts are inappropriate

a. is correct.
Rationale: It encompasses B, C, and D.

8. Ricky, a third grade student, runs out of the classroom and onto the roof of the school. He paces around the roof, looks around to see who is watching, and laughs at the person standing on the ground. He appears to be in control of his behavior. What should the teacher do?
   a. Go back inside and leave him up there until he decides he is ready to come down
   b. Climb up to get Ricky so he does not fall off and get hurt
   c. Notify the crisis teacher and arrange to have someone monitor Ricky
   d. Call the police

c. is correct.
Rationale: The teacher cannot be responsible for both Ricky and his or her class. He must pass the responsibility to the appropriate person.

9. Judy, a fourth grader, is often looking around the room or out the window. She does not disturb anyone, but has to ask for directions to be repeated and does not finish her work. Her teacher decides to reinforce Judy when she is on task. Which method of reinforcement is she using?
   a. Fading
   b. DRO
   c. DRI
   d. Shaping

c. is correct.
Rationale: This is an example of Direct Reinforcement (Individual)

10. An appropriate time out for a ten-year old would be:
    a. Ten minutes
    b. Twenty minutes
    c. No more than one half-hour
    d. Whatever time it takes for the disruptive behavior to stop

a. is correct.
Rationale: An appropriate time-out is no more than 10 minutes.

11. During the science lesson Rudy makes remarks from time to time, but his classmates are not attending to them. the teacher reinforces the students who are raising their hand to speak, but ignores Rudy. The teacher reinforces Rudy when he raises his hand. This technique is an example of:
    a. Fading
    b. Response cost
    c. Extinction
    d. Differential reinforcement of incompatible behavior

c. is correct.
Rationale: By ignoring the behavior, the teacher hopes it will become extinct.

12. Mike was caught marking up the walls of the bathroom with graffiti. His consequence was to clean all the walls of the bathroom. This type of overcorrection would be:
    a. Response cost
    b. Restitution
    c. Positive practice
    d. Negative practice

c. is correct.
Rationale: This is a positive form of over correction in which the student is learning another skill.

13. Which of these would probably not be a result of implementing an extinction strategy?
    a. Maladaptive behavior gets worse before it gets better
    b. Maladaptive behavior stops, then starts up again for a brief time
    c. Aggression may occur for a brief period following implementation of extinction
    d. The length of time and patience involved to implement the strategy might tempt the teacher to give up

b. is correct.
Rationale: The student responds in A, B, and C. In B, he ignores the teacher's action.

14. Withholding or removing a stimulus that reinforces a maladaptive behavior is:
    a. Extinction
    b. Overcorrection
    c. Punishment
    d. Reinforcing an incompatible behavior

a. is correct.
Rationale: There is no stimulus involved in this strategy.

15. Which of these would not be used to strengthen a desired behavior?
    a. Contingency contracting
    b. Tokens
    c. Chaining
    d. Overcorrection

d. is correct.
Rationale: A, B, and C are all used to strengthen a desired behavior. D is punishment.

16. If the arrangement in a fixed-ratio schedule of reinforcement is 3, when will the student receive the reinforcer?
    a. After every third correct response
    b. After every third correct response in a row
    c. After the third correct response in the time interval of the behavior sample
    d. After the third correct response even if the undesired behavior occurs in be between correct responses

b. is correct.
Rationale: This is the only one that follows a pattern. A fixed ratio is a pattern.

17. Wesley is having difficulty ignoring distractions. At first you have him seated at a carrel which is located in a corner of the room. He does well, so you eventually move him out of the carrel for increasing portions of the day. Eventually, he is able to sit in a seat with the rest of his classmates. This is an example of:
    a. Shaping
    b. Extinction
    c. Fading
    d. Chaining

a. is correct.
Rationale: The teacher is <u>shaping</u> a desired behavior.

18. Laura is beginning to raise her hand first instead of talking out. An effective schedule of reinforcement should be:
    a. Continuous
    b. Variable
    c. Intermittent
    d. Fixed

a. is correct.
Rationale: The pattern of reinforcement should not be variable, intermittent or fixed. It should be continuous.

19. As Laura continues to raise her hand to speak, the teacher would want to change to this schedule of reinforcement in order to wean her from the reinforcement:
    a. Continuous
    b. Variable
    c. Intermittent
    d. Fixed

d. is correct.
Rationale: The pattern should be in a fixed ratio.

20. Laura has demonstrated that she has mastered the goal of raising her hand to speak; reinforcement during the maintenance phase should be:
    a. Continuous
    b. Variable
    c. Intermittent
    d. Fixed

b. is correct.
Rationale: Reinforcement should be intermittent, as the behavior should occur infrequently.

21. An integral part of ecological interventions are consequences that:
    a. Are natural and logical
    b. Include extinction and overcorrection
    c. Care immediate and consistent
    d. Involve fading and shaping

a. is correct.
Rationale: The student must understand both the behavior and the consequence. The consequence should fit the infraction.

22. Examples of behaviors that are appropriate to be monitored by measuring frequency include all EXCEPT:
    a. Thumb sucking
    b. Hitting
    c. Temper tantrums
    d. Maintaining eye contact

b. is correct.
Rationale: Hitting takes place in an instant. This should be measured by frequency.

23. Examples of behaviors that are appropriate to be monitored by measuring frequency include all EXCEPT:
    a. Teasing
    b. Talking out
    c. Being on time for class
    d. Daydreaming

d. is correct.
Rationale: Daydreaming cannot be measured by frequency. It should be measured by duration.

24. Criteria for choosing behaviors to measure by frequency include all but those that:
    a. Have an observable beginning
    b. Last a long time
    c. Last a short time
    d. Occur often

b. is correct.
Rationale: We use frequency to measure behaviors that do not last a long time.

25. Criteria for choosing behaviors to measure by duration include all but those that:
    a. Last a short time
    b. Last a long time
    c. Have no readily observable beginning or end
    d. Don't happen often

a. is correct.
Rationale: We use duration to measure behavior that do not last a short time.

26. Data on quiet behaviors e.g., nailbiting or daydreaming, are best measured using a (an):
    a. Interval or time sample
    b. Continuous sample
    c. Variable sample
    d. Fixed-ratio sample

a. is correct.
Rationale: An interval or time sample is best to measure the duration of the behavior.

27. Mr. Jones wants to design an intervention for reducing Jason's sarcastic remarks. He wants to find out who or what is reinforcing Jason's remarks, so he records data on Jason's behavior as well as the attending behavior of his peers. This is an example of collecting data on:
   a. Reciprocal behaviors
   b. Multiple behaviors for single subjects
   c. Single behaviors for multiple subjects
   d. Qualitative data on Jason

a. is correct.
Rationale: Jason's peers' behaviors are in response to Jason's disruptive behaviors.

28. Ms Beekman has a class of students who frequently talk out. She wishes to begin interventions with the students who are talking out the most. She monitors the talking behavior of the entire class for 1-minute samples every half-hour. this is an example of collecting data on:
   a. Multiple behavior for single subjects
   b. Reciprocal behaviors
   c. Single behaviors for multiple subjects
   d. Continuous behaviors for fixed intervals

c. is correct.
Rationale: Talking out is the only behavior being observed.

29. Mark got a B on his social studies test. Mr. Wilner praised him for his good grade but he replies, "I was lucky this time. It must have been an easy test." Mark's statement is an example of:
   a. External locus of control
   b. Internal locus of control
   c. Rationalization of his performance
   d. Modesty

a. is correct.
Rationale: Locus of control refers to the way a person perceives the relation between his or her efforts and the outcome of an event. A person who has an external orientation anticipates no relation between his or her efforts and the outcome of an event.

30. Mr. Smith is on a field trip with a group of high school EH students. On the way, they stop at a fast-food restaurant for lunch, and Warren and Raul get into an argument. After some heated words, Warren stalks out of the restaurant and refuses to return to the group. He leaves the parking lot, continues walking away from the group, and ignores Mr. Smith's directions to come back. What would be the best course of action for Mr. Smith?
    a. Leave the group with the class aide and follow Warren to try to talk him into coming back.
    b. Wait a little while and see if Warren cools off and returns.
    c. Telephone the school and let the crisis teacher notify the police in accordance with school policy.
    d. Call the police himself.

c. is correct.
Rationale: Mr. Smith is still responsible for his class. This is his only option.

31. Which is the least effective of reinforcers in programs for mildly to moderately handicapped learners?
    a. Tokens
    b. Social
    c. Food
    d. Activity

c. is correct.
Rationale: Food is the least effective reinforcer for most handicapped children. Tokens, social interaction or activity is more desirable. Food may have reached satiation.

32. Tyrone likes to throw paper towards the trashcan instead of getting up to throw it away. After several attempts at positive interventions, Tyrone has to serve a detention and continue to throw balls of paper at the trashcan for the entire detention period. This would be an example of:
    a. Negative practice
    b. Overcorrection
    c. Extinction
    d. Response cost

a. is correct.
Rationale: Tyrone has to continue to practice the negative behavior.

33. A student may have great difficulty in meeting a target goal if the teacher has not first considered:
    a. If the student has external or internal locus of control.
    b. If the student is motivated to attain the goal.
    c. If the student has the essential prerequisite skills to perform the goal.
    d. If the student has had previous success or failure meeting the goal in other classes.

c. is correct.
Rationale: Prerequisite skills are essential in both setting goals and attaining goals.

34. The Premack Principle of increasing the performance of a less-preferred activity by immediately following it with a highly preferred activity is the basis of:
    a. response cost
    b. token systems
    c. contingency contracting
    d. self-recording management

c. is correct.
Rationale: The student eagerly completes the less desirable activity, to obtain the reward of the more desirable activity, in an unwritten contract.

35. Mr. Brown finds that his chosen consequence does not seem to be having the desired effect of reducing the target misbehavior. Which of these would LEAST LIKELY account for Mr. Brown's lack of success with the consequence?
    a. The consequence was aversive in Mr. Brown's opinion but not the students'.
    b. The students were not developmentally ready to understand the connection.
    c. Mr. Brown was inconsistent in applying the consequence.
    d. The intervention had not previously been shown to be effective in studies.

d. is correct.
Rationale: A, B, and C, might work if applied in the classroom, but research, it is the least of Mr. Brown's options.

36. Teaching techniques that stimulate active participation and understanding in the mathematics class include all but which of the following?
    a. Having students copy computation facts for a set number of times.
    b. Asking students to find the error in an algorithm.
    c. Giving immediate feedback to students.
    d. Having students chart their progress.

a. is correct.
Rationale: Copying does not stimulate participation or understanding.

37. Justin, a second grader, is reinforced if he is on task at the end of each 10-minute block of time that the teacher observes him. This is an example of what type of schedule?
    a. Continuous
    b. Fixed interval
    c. Fixed-ratio
    d. Variable ratio

b. is correct.
Rationale: 10 minutes is a fixed interval of time.

38. Addressing a student's maladaptive behavior right away with a "time out" should be reserved for situations where:
    a. The student has engaged in the behavior continuously throughout the day.
    b. Harm might come to the student or others.
    c. Lesser interventions have not been effective.
    d. The student displayed the behavior the day before.

b. is correct.
Rationale: The best intervention is to move the student away from the harmful environment.

39. At the beginning of the school year, Annette had a problem with being late for class. Her teacher reinforced here each time she was in her seat when the bell rang. In October, her teacher decided to reward her every other day when she was not tardy to class. The reinforcement schedule appropriate for making the transition to maintenance phase would be:
   a. Continuous
   b. Fixed interval
   c. Variable ratio
   d. Fixed ratio

b. is correct.
Rationale: Every other day is a fixed interval of time.

40. By November, Annette's teacher is satisfied with her record of being on time and decides to change the schedule of reinforcement. The best type of reinforcement schedule for maintenance or behavior is:
   a. Continuous
   b. Fixed interval
   c. Variable ratio
   d. Fixed ratio

c. is correct.
Rationale: The behavior will occur infrequently. Variable Ratio is the best schedule.

41. Which of these groups is not comprehensively covered by IDEA?
   a. Gifted and talented
   b. Mentally retarded
   c. Specific learning disabilities
   d. Speech and language impaired

c. is correct.
Rationale: IDEA: Individuals with Disabilities Education Act 101-476 (1990) did not cover all exceptional children. The Gifted and Talented Children's Act, P. L. 95-56 was passed in 1978.

42. Organizing ideas by use of a web or outline is an example of which writing activity?
    a. Revision
    b. Drafting
    c. Prewriting
    d. Final draft

c. is correct.
Rationale: Organizing ideas come before Drafting, Final Draft and Revision.

43. When a teacher is choosing behaviors to modify, the issue of social validity must be considered. Social validity refers to:
    a. The need for the behavior to be performed in public.
    b. Whether the new behavior will be considered significant by those who deal with the child.
    c. Whether there will be opportunities to practice the new behavior in public.
    d. Society's standards of behavior.

d. is correct.
Rationale: Validity has to do with the appropriateness of the behavior. Is it age appropriate? Is it culturally appropriate?

44. Dena, a second grader, is a messy eater who leaves her lunch area messy as well. Dena's teacher models correct use of eating utensils, and napkins for her. As Dena approximates the target behavior of neatly and leaving her area clean, she receives praise and a token. Finally, Dena reaches her target behavior goal and redeems her tokens. Dena's teacher used the strategy of:
    a. Chaining
    b. Extinction
    c. Overcorrection
    d. Shaping

a. is correct.
Rationale: Chaining is a procedure in which individual responses are reinforced when occurring in sequence to form a complex behavior. Shaping, however, targets single behaviors.

45. Educators who advocate educating all children in their neighborhood classrooms and schools, propose the end of labeling and segregation of special needs students in special classes, and call for the delivery of special supports and services directly in the classroom may be said to support the:
    a. Full service model
    b. Regular education initiative
    c. Full inclusion model
    d. Mainstream model

c. is correct.
Rationale: All students must be included in the regular classroom.

46. In Ellis' ABC model, maladaptive behavior in response to a situation results from:
    a. Antecedent events
    b. Stimulus events
    c. Thinking about the consequences
    d. Irrational beliefs about the event

d. is correct.
Rationale: All behavior is learned. This behavior is different from the norm. It is different because of something the child has experienced or learned.

47. Section 504 differs from the scope of IDEA because its main focus is on:
    a. Prohibition of discrimination on the basis of disability.
    b. A basis for additional support services and accommodations in a special education setting.
    c. Procedural rights and safeguards for the individual.
    d. Federal funding for educational services.

a. is correct.
Rationale: Section 504 prohibits discrimination on the basis of disability.

48. Public Law 99-457 amended the EHA to make provisions for:
    a. Education services for "uneducable" children
    b. Education services for children in jail settings
    c. Special education benefits for children birth to five years
    d. Education services for medically fragile children

c. is correct.
Rationale: P.L. 99-457 amended EHA to provide Special Education programs for children 3-5 years, with most states offering outreach programs to identify children with special needs from birth to age 3.

49. A holistic approach to stress management should include all of the following EXCEPT:
    a. Teaching a variety of coping methods
    b. Cognitive modification of feelings
    c. Teaching the fight or flight response
    d. Cognitive modification of behaviors

c. is correct.
Rationale: A, B, and D are coping interventions. C is not.

50. Marisol has been mainstreamed into a ninth grade language arts class. Although her behavior is satisfactory and she likes the class, Marisol's reading level is about two years below grade level. The class has been assigned to read "Great Expectations" and write a report. What intervention would be LEAST successful in helping Marisol complete this assignment?
    a. Having Marisol listen to a taped recording while following the story in the regular text.
    b. Giving her a modified version of the story.
    c. Telling her to choose a different book that she can read.
    d. Showing a film to the entire class and comparing and contrasting it with the book.

c. is correct.
Rationale: A, B, and D, are positive interventions. C is not an intervention.

51. Fractions may be thought of in each of these ways EXCEPT:
    a. Part of a whole
    b. Part of a parent set
    c. Ratio
    d. An exponent

d. is correct.
Rationale: An exponent can never be a fraction

52. Many special education students may have trouble with the skills necessary to be successful in algebra and geometry for all but one of these reasons:
    a. Prior instruction focused on computation rather than understanding
    b. Unwillingness to problem solve
    c. Lack of instruction in prerequisite skills
    d. Large amount of new vocabulary

a. is correct.
Rationale: In order to build skills in math, students must be able to understand math concepts.

53. Which of these processes is NOT directly related to the meaningful development of number concepts in younger children?
    a. Describing
    b. Classifying
    c. Grouping
    d. Ordering

c. is correct.
Rationale: Grouping does not involve the meaningful development of number concepts.

54. Mr. Ward wants to assess Jennifer's problem-solving skills in mathematics. Which question would not address her use of strategies?
    a. Does Jennifer check for mistakes in computation?
    b. Does Jennifer use trial and error to solve problems?
    c. Does Jennifer have an alternative strategy if the first one fails?
    d. Does Jennifer become easily frustrated if she doesn't get an answer immediately?

d. is correct.
Rationale: A, B, and C, are problem-solving skills Jennifer needs to develop.

55. Ryan is working on a report about dogs. He uses scissors and tape to cut and rearrange sections and paragraphs, then photocopies the paper so he can continue writing. In which stage of the writing process is Ryan?
    a. Final draft
    b. Prewriting
    c. Revision
    d. Drafting

c. is correct.
Rationale: Ryan is Revising and reordering before final editing.

56. Talking into a tape recorder is an example of which writing activity?
    a. Prewriting
    b. Drafting
    c. Final Draft
    d. Revision

c. is correct.
Rationale: Ryan is preparing his final draft.

57. publishing a class newsletter, looking through catalogues, and filling out order forms and playing the role of secretaries are activities designed to teach:
    a. Expressive writing
    b. Transactional writing
    c. Poetic writing
    d. Creative writing

b. is correct.
Rationale: Transactional writing includes expository writing, descriptive writing and persuasive writing. It does not include any of the other three types of writing listed.

58. Under the provisions of IDEA, the student is entitled to all of these EXCEPT:
    a. Placement in the best environment
    b. Placement in the least restrictive environment
    c. Provision of educational needs at no cost
    d. Provision of individualized, appropriate educational program

a. is correct.
Rationale: IDEA mandates a least restrictive environment, an IEP, (individual education plan) and a free public education.

59. Teacher modeling, student-teacher dialogues, and peer interactions are part of which teaching technique designed to provide support during the initial stages of instruction?
    a. Reciprocal teaching
    b. Scaffolding
    c. Peer tutoring
    d. Cooperative learning

b. is correct.
Rationale: Scaffolding provides support.

60. Modeling of a behavior by an adult who verbalizes the thinking process, overt self-instruction, and covert self-instruction are components of:
    a. Rational-emotive therapy
    b. Reality therapy
    c. Cognitive behavior modification
    d. Reciprocal teaching

c. is correct.
Rationale: Neither A, B, nor D, involves modification or change of behavior.

61. Standards of accuracy for a student's spelling should be based on the student's:
    a. Grade level spelling list
    b. Present reading book level
    c. Level of spelling development
    d. Performance on an informal assessment

c. is correct.
Rationale: Spelling instruction should include words misspelt in daily writing, generalizing spelling knowledge and mastering objectives in progressive stages of development.

62. Which of these techniques is least effective in helping children correct spelling problems?
    a. The teacher models the correct spelling in a context
    b. Student sees the incorrect and the correct spelling together in order to visualize the correct spelling
    c. Positive reinforcement as the child tests the rules and tries to approximate the correct spelling
    d. Copying the correct word five times

d. is correct.
Rationale: Copying the word is least effective.

63. The single most important activity for eventual reading success of young children is:
   a. Giving them books
   b. Watching animated stories
   c. Reading aloud to them
   d. Talking about pictures in books

C. is correct.
Rationale: Reading aloud exposes them to language.

64. Skilled readers use all but which one of these knowledge sources to construct meanings beyond the literal text:
   a. Text knowledge
   b. Syntactic knowledge
   c. Morphological knowledge
   d. Semantic knowledge

c. is correct.
Rationale: The student is already skilled so morphological knowledge is already in place.

65. The cooperative nature of Glasser's Reality Therapy, in which problem-solving approach is used to correct misbehavior, is best signified by:
   a. Minimal punishment
   b. It's similar approach to methods that teach students how to deal with academic mistakes
   c. Student's promises to use the alternative behavior plan to help them reach their goals
   d. Procedure sheets used during conflict situations

c. is correct.
Rationale: Glasser's Reality Therapy makes use of an alternative behavior plan, a form of group therapy.

66. Diaphragmatic breathing, progressive relaxation training, and exercises are examples of which type of stress coping skills?
    a. Rational-emotive
    b. Cognitive-psychological
    c. Somatic-physiological
    d. Stress inoculation

C. is correct.
Rationale: When we analyze the expression, somatic-physiological, we find, somatic: relating to the body physiological: relating to nature and natural phenomena.

67. The stress that we experience when we win a race or experience a difficult task is called:
    a. Stressor
    b. Stresses
    c. Eustress
    d. Distress

c. is correct.
Rationale: Eustress is a sort of elation, or release of anxiety. It is the opposite of distress.

68. Jane is so intimidated by a classmate's teasing that she breaks down in tears and cannot stand up for herself.
    a. Stressors
    b. Stresses
    c. Eustress
    d. Distress

d. is correct.
Rationale: Jane is in a state of distress.

69. The movement towards serving as many children with disabilities as possible in the regular classroom with supports and services is known as:
    a. Full service model
    b. Regular education initiative
    c. Full inclusion model
    d. Mainstream model

c. is correct.
Rationale: It is the movement to include all students in the regular classroom.

70. Which of the following is NOT a feature of effective classroom rules?
    a. They are about 4to 6 in number
    b. They are negatively stated
    c. Consequences are consistent and immediate
    d. They can be tailored to individual teaching goals and teaching styles

b. is correct.
Rationale: Rules should be positively stated and they should follow the other three features listed.

71. A suggested amount of time for large-group instruction lesson for a sixth or seventh grade group would be:
    a. 5 to 40 minutes
    b. 5 to 20 minutes
    c. 5 to 30 minutes
    d. 5 to 15 minutes

c. is correct.
Rationale: The recommended time for large group instruction is 5 - 15 minutes for grades 1-5 and 5 – 40 minutes for grades 8-12.

72. Sam is working to earn half an hour of basketball time with his favorite PE teacher. At the end of each half-hour, Sam marks his point sheet with an X, if he reached his goal of no call-outs. When he has received 25 marks, he will receive his basketball free time. This behavior management strategy is an example of:
    a. Self-recording
    b. Self-evaluation
    c. Self-reinforcement
    d. Self-regulation

Self-Management-This is an important part of social skills training, especially for older students preparing for employment. Components for self-management include:

1. *self-monitoring:* choosing behaviors and alternatives and monitoring those actions.
2. *self-evaluation:* deciding the effectiveness of the behavior in solving the problem.
3. *self-reinforcement:* telling oneself that one is capable of achieving success.

a. is correct.
Rationale: Sam is recording his behavior.

73. Mark has been working on his target goal of completing his mathematics class work. Each day he records on a scale of 0 to 3 how well he has done his work and his teacher provides feedback. This self-management technique is an example of:
    a. Self-recording
    b. Self reinforcement
    c. Self-regulation
    d. Self-evaluation

d. is correct.
Rationale: Sam is evaluating his behavior, not merely recording it.

74. When Barbara reached her target goal, she chose her reinforcer and said softly to herself, "I worked hard and I deserve this reward". This self-management technique is an example of:
    a. Self-reinforcement
    b. Self recording
    c. Self-regulation
    d. Self-evaluation

a. is correct.
Rationale: Barbara is reinforcing her behavior.

75. Grading should be based on all of the following EXCEPT:
    a. Clearly defined mastery of course objectives
    b. A variety of evaluation methods
    c. Performance of the student in relation to other students
    d. Assigning points for activities and basing grades on a point total

c. is correct.
Rationale: Grading should never be based on the comparison of performance of other students. It should always be based on the student's mastery of course objectives, the methods of evaluation and the grading rubric (how points are assigned).

76. The following words describe an IEP objective EXCEPT:
a. Specific
b. Observable
c. Measurable
d. Criterion-referenced

d. is correct.
Rationale: An Individual Education Plan should be specific, observable, and measurable.

77. Teacher feedback, task completion, and a sense of pride over mastery or accomplishment of a skill are examples of:
a. Extrinsic reinforcers
b. Behavior modifiers
c. Intrinsic reinforcers
d. Positive feedback

Motivation may be achieved through intrinsic reinforcers or extrinsic reinforcers. Intrinsic rieinforcers are usually intangible and extrinsic reinforcers are usually tangible rewards and from an external source.

c. is correct.
Rationale: These are intangibles.

78. Social approval, token reinforcers, and rewards such as pencils or stickers are examples of:
a. Extrinsic reinforcers
b. Behavior modifiers
c. Intrinsic reinforcers
d. Positive feedback reinforcers

a. is correct.
Rationale: These are rewards from external sources

79. Aggression, escape and avoidance are unpleasant side effects, which can be avoided by using:
a. Time-out
b. Response cost
c. Overcorrection
d. Negative practice

b. is correct.
Rationale: In response cost, students know that there will be consequences for these undesirable behaviors.

80. Josie forgot that it was school picture day and did not dress up for the pictures. In the media center, Josie notices some girls in the line waiting to have their pictures taken. They appear to be looking over at her and whispering. Josie feels certain that they are making fun of the way her hair and clothes look and gets so upset that she leaves the line and hides out in the bathroom. Josie did not think of asking when the make-up day for pictures would be. According to Ellis' ABC model, Josie's source of stress is:
   a. Her forgetting to dress appropriately for picture day
   b. The girls in the library who appear to be whispering about her
   c. Her belief that they are making fun of her appearance
   d. The girls' insensitive behavior

c. is correct.
Rationale: Josie is responding to her belief.

81. Token systems are popular for all of these advantages EXCEPT:
   a. The number needed for rewards may be adjusted as needed
   b. Rewards are easy to maintain
   c. They are effective for students who generally do not respond to social reinforcers
   d. Tokens reinforce the relationship between desirable behavior and reinforcement

b. is correct.
Rationale: The ease of maintenance is not a valid reason for developing a token system.

82. Which would not be an advantage of using a criterion-referenced test?
    a. Information about an individual's ability level is too specific for the purposes of the assessment
    b. It can pinpoint exact areas of weaknesses and strengths
    c. You can design them yourself
    d. You do not get comparative information

d. is correct.
Rationale: Criterion-referenced tests measure mastery of content rather than performance compared to others. Test items are usually prepared from specific educational objectives and may be teacher-made or commercially prepared. Scores are measured by the percentage of correct items for a skill (e.g., adding and subtracting fractions with like denominators).

83. Which is NOT an example of a standard score?
    T score
    Z score
    Standard deviation
    Stanine

c. is correct.
Rationale: A, B, and D, are all standardized scores. Stanines are whole number scores from 1 to 9, each representing a wide range of raw scores. Standard deviation is **not a score.** It measures how widely scores vary from the mean.

84. The most direct method of obtaining assessment data and perhaps the most objective is:
    a. Testing
    b. Self-recording
    c. Observation
    d. Experimenting

c. is correct.
Rationale: Observation is often better than testing, due to language, culture or other factors.

85. The basic tools necessary to observe and record behavior include all BUT:
    a. Cameras
    b. Timers
    c. Counters
    d. Graphs or charts

a. is correct.
Rationale: The camera gives a snapshot. It does not record behavior.

86. Which of these characteristics is NOT included in the P.L. 94-142 definition of emotional disturbance?
    a. General pervasive mood of unhappiness or depression
    b. Social maladjustment manifested in a number of settings
    c. Tendency to develop physical symptoms, pains, or fear associated with school or personal problems
    d. Inability to learn which is not attributed to intellectual, sensory, or health factors

b. is correct.
Rationale: Social maladjustment is not considered a disability.

87. Of the various factors that contribute to delinquency, and anti-social behavior, which has been found to be the weakest?
    a. Criminal behavior and/or alcoholism in the father
    b. Lax mother and punishing father
    c. Socioeconomic disadvantage
    d. Long history of broken home and marital discord among parents

c. is correct.
Rationale: There are many examples of A, B, and C, where there is socio-economic advantage.

88. Poor moral development, lack of empathy, and behavioral excesses such as aggression are the most obvious characteristics of which behavioral disorder?
    a. Autism
    b. ADD-H
    c. Conduct disorder
    d. Pervasive developmental disorder

c. is correct.
Rationale: A student with conduct disorder or social maladjustment displays behaviors/values that are in conflict with the school, home, or community. The characteristics listed are all behavioral/social.

89. School refusal, obsessive-compulsive disorders, psychosis, and separation anxiety are also frequently accompanied by:
    a. Conduct disorder
    b. ADD-H
    c. depression
    d. autism

c. is correct.
Rationale: These behaviors are usually accompanied by depression in ADD-H.

90. Signs of depression do not typically include:
    a. Hyperactivity
    b. Changes in sleep patterns
    c. Recurring thoughts of death or suicide
    d. Significant changes in weight or appetite

a. is correct.
Rationale: depression is usually characterized by listlessness, brooding, low anxiety, and little activity. Hyperactivity, conversely is over activity.

91. Children who are characterized by impulsivity generally:
    a. Do not feel sorry for their actions
    b. Blame others for their actions
    c. Do not weigh alternatives before acting
    d. Do not outgrow their problem

c. is correct.
Rationale: They act without thinking, so they either cannot think or do not think before they act.

92. Which of these is listed as only a minor scale on the Behavior Problem Checklist?
    a. Motor Excess
    b. Conduct Disorder
    c. Socialized Aggression
    d. Anxiety/Withdrawal

a. is correct.
Rationale: Motor Excess has to do with over activity, or hyperactivity, physical movement. The other three items are disorders, all of which may be characterized by excessive activity.

93. The extent that a test measures what it claims to measure is called:
    a. Reliability
    b. Validity
    c. Factor analysis
    d. Chi Square

b. is correct.
Rationale: The degree to which a test measures what it claims to measure.

94. Which is not a goal of collaborative consultation?
    a. Prevent learning and behavior problems with mainstreamed students
    b. Coordinate the instructional programs between mainstream and ESE classes
    c. Facilitate solutions to learning and behavior problems
    d. Function as an ESE service model

d. is correct.
Rationale: A, B, and C are goals. Functioning as an Exceptional Student Education model is not a goal. Collaborative consultation is necessary for the classification of students with disabilities and provision of services to satisfy their needs.

95. An important goal of collaborative consultation is:
    a. Mainstream as many ESE students as possible
    b. Guidance on how to handle ESE students from the ESE teacher
    c. Mutual empowerment of both the mainstream and the ESE teacher
    d. Document progress of mainstreamed students

C. is correct.
Rationale: Empowerment of these service providers is extremely important.

96. Knowledge of evaluation strategies, program interventions, and types of data are examples of which variable for a successful consultation program?
    a. People
    b. Process
    c. Procedural implementation
    d. Academic preparation

b. is correct.
Rationale: Consultation programs cannot be successful without knowledge of the process.

97. Skills as an administrator and background in client, consulter, and consultation skills are examples of which variable in a successful consultation program?
    a. people
    b. Process
    c. Procedural implementation
    d. Academic preparation

a. is correct.
Rationale: Consultation programs cannot be successful without people skills.

98. The ability to identify problems, generate solutions, and knowledge of theoretical perspectives of consultation are examples of which variable in a successful consultation program?
    a. People
    b. Process
    c. Procedural implementation
    d. Academic preparation

c. is correct.
Rationale: Consultation programs cannot be successful without implementation skills.

99. A serious hindrance to successful mainstreaming is:
    a. Lack of adapted materials
    b. Lack of funding
    c. Lack of communication among teachers
    d. Lack of support from administration

c. is correct.
Rationale: All 4 choices are hindrances but lack of communication and consultation between the service providers is serious.

100. Which of the following statements was not offered as a rationale for REI?
    a. Special education students are not usually identified until their learning problems have become severe
    b. Lack of funding will mean that support for the special needs children will not be available in the regular classroom.
    c. Putting children in segregated special education placements is stigmatizing
    d. There are students with learning or behavior problems who do not meet special education requirements but who still need special services

b. is correct.
Rationale: All except lack of funding were offered in support of Regular Education Intervention or Inclusion.

101. The key to success for the exceptional student placed in a regular classroom is:
    a. Access to the special aids and materials
    b. Support from the ESE teacher
    c. Modification in the curriculum
    d. The mainstream teacher's belief that the student will profit from the placement

d. is correct.
Rationale: Without the regular teacher's belief that the student can benefit, no special accommodations will be provided.

102. Lack of regular follow-up, difficulty in transporting materials, and lack of consistent support for students who need more assistance are disadvantages of which type of service model?
    a. Regular classroom
    b. Consultant with regular teacher
    c. Itinerant
    d. Resource room

c. is correct.
Rationale: The itinerant model, as the name implies, is not regular.

103. Ability to supply specific instructional materials, programs, and methods and to influence environmental learning variables are advantages of which service model for exceptional students?
    a. Regular classroom
    b. Consultant teacher
    c. Itinerant teacher
    d. Resource room

b. is correct.
Rationale: Consultation is usually done by specialists.

104. An emphasis on instructional remediation and individualized instruction in problem areas, and a focus on mainstreaming are characteristics of which model of service delivery?
    a. Regular classroom
    b. Consultant teacher
    c. Itinerant teacher
    d. Resource room

d. is correct.
Rationale: The Resource room is usually a bridge to mainstreaming.

105. Which of these would not be considered a valid attempt to contact a parent for an IEP meeting?
    a. Telephone
    b. Copy of correspondence
    c. Message left on answering machine
    d. Record of home visits

c. is correct.
Rationale: A message left on an answering machine is not direct contact.

106. A best practice for evaluating student performance and progress on IEPs is:
    a. Formal assessment
    b. Curriculum based assessment
    c. Criterion based assessment
    d. Norm-referenced evaluation

b. is correct.
Rationale: This is a teacher-prepared test that measures the student's progress, but at the same time shows the teacher whether or not the accommodations are effective.

107. Guidelines for an Individualized Family Service Plan (IFSP) would be described in which legislation?
    a. P.L. 94-142
    b. P. L. 99 – 457
    c. P.L. 101 – 476
    d. ADA

b. is correct.
Rationale: P. L. 99-457, 1986 provides services for children of ages 3-5 and their families; P.L. 101 – 476 is IDEA; P.L. 94 – 142 Education for All Handicapped Children Act, was passed in the Civil Rights era. ADA is the Americans with Disabilities Act.

108. In a positive classroom environment, errors are viewed as:
    a. Symptoms of deficiencies
    b. Lack of attention or ability
    c. A natural part of the learning process
    d. The result of going too fast

c. is correct.
Rationale: We often learn a great deal from our mistakes and shortcomings. It is normal. Where it is not normal, fear develops. This fear of failure, inhibits children from working and achieving. Copying and other types of cheating, results.

109. Recess, attending school social or sporting events, and eating lunch with peers are examples of:
    a. Privileges
    b. Allowances
    c. Rights
    d. Entitlements

d. is correct.
Rationale: These are entitlements. They may be used as consequences.

110. Free time, shopping at the school store, and candy are examples of:
    a. Privileges
    b. Allowances
    c. Rights
    d. Entitlements

a. is correct.
Rationale: These are privileges, or positive consequences.

111. Eating lunch, access to a bathroom, and privacy are examples of:
    a. Privileges
    b. Allowances
    c. Rights
    d. Entitlements

c. is correct.
Rationale: These are rights. They may not be used as consequences.

112. Cheryl is a 15-year old student receiving educational services in a full-time EH classroom. The date for her IEP review is planned for two months before her 16th birthday. According to the requirements of IDEA, what must ADDITIONALLY be included in this review?
    a. Graduation plan
    b. Individualized transition plan
    c. Individualized family service plan
    d. Transportation planning

b. is correct.
Rationale: This is necessary, as the student should be transitioning from school to work.

113. Hector is 10th grader in a program for the severely emotionally handicapped. After a classmate taunted him about his mother, Hector threw a desk at the other boy and attacked him. A crisis intervention team tried to break up the fight, one teacher hurt his knee. The other boy received a concussion. Hector now faces disciplinary measures. How long can he be suspended without the suspension constituting a "change of placement?"
    a. 5 days
    b. 10 days
    c. 10 + 30 days
    d. 60 days

b. is correct.
Rationale: According to ***Honig versus Doe,*** 1988, _Where the student has presented an immediate threat to others, that student may be temporarily suspended for up to 10 school days to give the school and the parents time to review the IEP and discuss possible alternatives to the current placement._

114. The concept that a handicapped student cannot be expelled for misconduct which is a manifestation of the handicap itself, is not limited to students which are labeled "seriously emotionally disturbed". Which reason does not explain this concept?
    a. Emphasis on individualized evaluation
    b. Consideration of the problems and needs of handicapped students
    c. Right to a free and appropriate public education
    d. Putting these students out of school will just leave them on the streets to commit crimes

d. is correct.
Rationale: A, B, and C are tenets of IDEA, and should take place in the least restrictive environment. D does not explain this concept.

115. An effective classroom behavior management plan includes all but which of the following?
     a. Transition procedures for changing activities
     b. Clear consequences for rule infractions
     c. Concise teacher expectations for student behavior
     d. Copies of lesson plans

d. is correct.
Rationale: D is not a part of any behavior management plan. A, B, and C are.

116. Statements like "Darren is lazy" are not helpful in describing his behavior for all but which of these reasons?
     a. There is no way to determine if any change occurs from the information given
     b. The student and not the behavior becomes labeled
     c. Darren's behavior will manifest itself clearly enough without any written description
     d. Constructs are open to various interpretations among the people who are asked to define them

c. is correct.
Rationale: 'Darren is lazy' is a label. It can be interpreted in a variety of ways and there is no way to measure this description for change. A description should be measurable.

117. Often, Marcie is not in her seat when the bell rings. She may be found at the pencil sharpener, throwing paper away, or fumbling through her notebook. Which of these descriptions of her behavior can be described as a pinpoint?
     a. Is tardy a lot
     b. Is out of seat
     c. Is not in seat when late bell rings
     d. Is disorganized

c. is correct.
Rationale: Even though A, B, and D describe the behavior, C is most precise.

118. When choosing behaviors for change, the teacher should ask if there is any evidence that the behavior is presently or potentially harmful to the student or others. This is an example of which test?
    a. Fair-Pair
    b. "Stranger" Test
    c. Premack Principle
    d. "So – What?" Test

D. is correct.

119. Mrs. Taylor takes her students to a special gymnastics presentation that the P.E. coach has arranged in the gym. She has a rule against talk-outs and reminds the students that they will lose 5 points on their daily point sheet for talking out. The students get a chance to perform some of the simple stunts. They all easily go through the movements except for Sam, who is known as the class klutz. Sam does not give up and finally completes the stunts. His classmates cheer him on with comments like "Way to go". Their teacher, however, reminds them that they broke the no talking rule and will lose the points. What mistake was made here?
    a. The students forgot the no talking rule
    b. The teacher considered talk outs to be maladaptive in all school settings
    c. The other students could have distracted Sam with talk-outs and caused him to get hurt
    d. The teacher should have let the P.E. coach handle the discipline in the gym

d. is correct.
Rationale: The gym environment is different from a classroom environment. The gym teacher should have been in control of a possibly hazardous environment.

120. Which of the following should be avoided when writing objectives for social behavior?
    a. Non-specific adverbs
    b. Behaviors stated as verbs
    c. Criteria for acceptable performance
    d. Conditions where the behavior is expected to be performed

a. is correct.
Rationale: Behaviors should be specific. The more clearly the behavior is described, the less the chance for error.

121. Criteria for choosing behaviors that are in the most need of change involve all but the following:
    a. Observations across settings to rule out certain interventions
    b. Pinpointing the behavior that is the poorest fit in the child's environment
    c. The teacher's concern about what is the most important behavior to target
    d. Analysis of the environmental reinforcers

c. is correct.
Rationale: The teacher must take care of the criteria in A, B, and D. Her concerns are of the least importance.

122. Ms. Wright is planning an analysis of Audrey's out of seat behavior. Her initial data would be called:
    a. Pre-referral phase
    b. Intervention phase
    c. Baseline phase
    d. Observation phase

c. is correct.
Rationale: Ms Wright is a teacher. She should begin at the Baseline phase.

123. To reinforce Audrey each time she is on task and in her seat, Ms. Wright delivers specific praise and stickers, which Audrey may collect and redeem for a reward. The data collected during the time Ms. Wright is using this intervention is called:
    a. Referral phase
    b. Intervention phase
    c. Baseline phase
    d. Observation phase

b. is correct.
Rationale: Ms Wright is involved in behavior modification. This is the intervention phase.

124. Indirect requests and attempts to influence or control others through one's use of language is an example of:
    a. Morphology
    b. Syntax
    c. Pragmatics
    d. Semantics

c. is correct.
Rationale: Pragmatics involves the way that language is used to communicate and interact with others. It is often used to control the actions and attitudes of people.

125. Kenny, a fourth grader, has trouble comprehending analogies, using comparative, spatial and temporal words, and multiple meanings. Language interventions for Kenny would focus on:
    a. Morphology
    b. Syntax
    c. Pragmatics
    d. Semantics

d. is correct.
Rationale: Semantics has to do with word meanings. Semantic tests measure receptive and expressive vocabulary skills.

126. Celia, who is in first grade, asked, "Where is my ball"? She also has trouble with passive sentences. Language interventions for Celia would target:
    a. Morphology
    b. Syntax
    c. Pragmatics
    d. Semantics

b. is correct.
Rationale: Syntax refers to the rules for arranging words to make sentences.

127. Scott is in middle school, but still makes statements like "I gotted new high-tops yesterday," and "I saw three mans in the front office." Language interventions fro Scott would target:
    a. Morphology
    b. Syntax
    c. Pragmatics
    d. Semantics

a. is correct.
Rationale: Morphology is the process of combining phonemes into meaningful words.

128. Which is not indicative of a handwriting problem?
    a. Errors persisting over time
    b. Little improvement on simple handwriting tasks
    c. Fatigue after writing for a short time
    d. Occasional letter reversals, word omissions, and poor spacing

d. is correct.
Rationale: A, B, and C are physical, handwriting problems. D, however, is a problem with language development.

129. All of these are effective in teaching written expression EXCEPT:
    a. Exposure to various styles and direct instruction in those styles
    b. Immediate feedback from the teacher with all mistakes clearly marked.
    c. Goal setting and peer evaluation of written products according to set criteria
    d. Incorporating writing with other academic subjects

b. is correct.
Rationale: Teacher feedback is not always necessary. The student can have feedback from his peers, or emotional response, or apply skills learned to other subjects.

130. Mr. Mendez is assessing his students' written expression. Which of these is not a component of written expression?
    a. Vocabulary
    b. Morphology
    c. Content
    d. Sentence structure

b. is correct.
Rationale: Morphology is correct. Vocabulary consists of words, content is made up of ideas, which are expressed in words, and Sentences are constructed from words. Morphemes, however, are not always words. They may be prefixes or suffixes.

131. Ms. Tolbert is teaching spelling to her students. The approach stresses phoneme-grapheme relationships within parts of words. Spelling rules, generalizations, and patterns are taught. A typical spelling list for her third graders might include light, bright, night, fright, and slight. Which approach is Ms. Tolbert using?
    a. Rule-based Instruction
    b. Fernald Method
    c. Gillingham Method
    d. Test-Study -Test

a. is correct.
Rationale: Rule-based Instruction employs a system of rules and generalizations. It may be taught using the linguistic or phonics approach.

132. At the beginning of the year, Mr. Johnson wants to gain an understanding of his class' social structure in order to help him assess social skills and related problems. The technique that would best help Mr. Johnson accomplish this is:
    a. Personal interviews with each student
    b. Parent rating form
    c. Sociometric techniques
    d. Self-reports

c. is correct.
Rationale: The issue of reliability and validity arises with A, B, and D. C is the best technique.
Sociometric Measures: There are three basic formats. (a) peer nominations based on non-behavioral criteria such as preferred playmates, (b) peer ratings in which students rate all of their peers on nonbehavioral criteria such as work preferences, and (c) peer assessments, in which peers are rated with respect to specific behaviors.

133. In assessing a group's social structure, asking a student to list a classmate whom he or she would choose to be his or her best friends, preferred play partners, and preferred work partners is an example of:
    a. Peer nomination
    b. Peer rating
    c. Peer assessment
    d. Sociogram

a. is correct.
Rationale: Students are asked to nominate their peers.

134. Naming classmates who fit certain behavioral descriptions such as smart, disruptive or quiet, is an example of which type of sociometric assessment?
    a. Peer nomination
    b. Peer rating
    c. Peer assessment
    d. Sociogram

c. is correct.
Rationale: Students are asked to assess their peers' behavior.

135. Mr. Johnson asks his students to score each of their classmates in areas such as who they would prefer to play with and work with. A likert-type scale with non-behavioral criteria is used. This is an example of:
    a. Peer nomination
    b. Peer rating
    c. Peer assessment
    d. Sociogram

a. is correct.
Rationale: Students are asked for their preferences on non-behavioral criteria.

136. Which of these explanations would not likely account for the lack of a clear definition of behavior disorders?
    a. Problems with measurement
    b. Cultural and/or social influences and views of what is acceptable
    c. The numerous types of manifestations of behavior disorders
    d. Differing theories that use their own terminology and definitions

c. is correct.
Rationale: A, B, and D, are factors that account for the lack of a clear definition of some behavioral disorders. C is not a factor.

137. Ryan is 3, and her temper tantrums last for an hour. Bryan is 8, and he does not stay on task for more than 10 minutes without teacher prompts. These behaviors differ from normal children in terms of their:
    a. Rate
    b. Topography
    c. Duration
    d. Magnitude

c. is correct.
Rationale: It is not normal for temper tantrums to last an hour. At age eight, a normal student stays on task much longer than ten minutes without teacher prompts.

138. All children cry, hit, fight, and play alone at different times. Children with behavior disorders will perform these behaviors at a higher than normal:
    a. Rate
    b. Topography
    c. Duration
    d. Magnitude

a. is correct.
Rationale: Children with behavior disorders display them at a much higher rate than normal children.

139. The exhibition of two or more types of problem behaviors across different areas of functioning is known as:
    a. Multiple maladaptive behaviors
    b. Clustering
    c. Social maladjustment
    d. Conduct disorder

b. is correct.
Rationale: Children with behavior disorders do display a single behavior. They display a range of behaviors. These behaviors are usually clustered together, hence, clustering.

140. Children with behavior disorders often do not exhibit stimulus control. This means they have not learned:
    a. The right things to do
    b. Where and when certain behaviors are appropriate
    c. Right from wrong
    d. Listening skills

b. is correct.
Rationale: These children respond to stimuli at almost any place and time. They are not able to stop and think or control their responses to stimuli.

141. Social withdrawal, anxiety, depression, shyness, and guilt are indicative of:
    a. Conduct disorder
    b. Personality disorders
    c. Immaturity
    d. Socialized aggression

b. is correct.
Rationale: These are all personality disorders.

142. Short attention span, daydreaming, clumsiness, and preference for younger playmates are associated with:
    a. Conduct disorder
    b. Personality disorders
    c. Immaturity
    d. Socialized aggression

c. is correct.
Rationale: These disorders show immaturity. The student is not acting age appropriately.

143. Truancy, gang membership, and a feeling of pride in belonging to a delinquent subculture are indicative of:
    a. Conduct disorder
    b. Personality disorders
    c. Immaturity
    d. Socialized aggression

D. is correct.
Rationale: The student is acting out by using aggression. This gives him a sense of belonging.

144. Temper tantrums, disruption or disobedience, and bossiness are associated with:
    a. Conduct disorder
    b. Personality disorders
    c. Immaturity
    d. Socialized aggression

a. is correct.
Rationale: These behaviors are designed to attract attention. They are Conduct Disorders.

145. Which of these is not true for most children with behavior disorders?
    a. Many score in the "slow learner"
    b. They are frequently behind classes in academic achievement
    c. They are bright but bored with their surroundings
    d. A large amount of time is spent in nonproductive, nonacademic behaviors

C. is correct.
Rationale: Most children with conduct disorders display the traits found in A, B, and D.

146. Echolalia, repetitive stereotyped actions, and a severe disorder of thinking and communication are indicative of:
    a. Psychosis
    b. Schizophrenia
    c. Autism
    d. Paranoia

c. is correct.
Rationale: The behaviors listed are indicative of autism.

147. Teaching children functional skills that will be useful in their home life and neighborhoods is the basis of:
    a. Curriculum-based instruction
    b. Community-based instruction
    c. Transition planning
    d. Functional curriculum

b. is correct.
Rationale: Teaching functional skills in the wider curriculum is considered community based instruction.

148. Disabilities caused by fetal alcohol syndrome are many times higher for which ethnic group?
    a. Native Americans
    b. Asian Americans
    c. Hispanic Americans
    d. African Americans

a. is correct.
Rationale: There is a very high incidence of this syndrome in Native American children on reservations.

149. Which of these would be the least effective measure of behavioral disorders?
    a. Projective test
    b. Ecological assessment
    c. Standardized test
    d. Psychodynamic analysis

c. is correct.
Rationale: These tests make comparisons, rather than measure skills.

150. Which behavioral disorder is difficult to diagnose in children because the symptoms are manifested quite differently than in adults?
    a. Anorexia
    b. Schizophrenia
    c. Paranoia
    d. Depression

d. is correct.
Rationale: In an adult, it may be displayed as age-appropriate behavior, and go undiagnosed. In a child, it may be displayed as not age appropriate, so it is easier to recognize.

REFERENCES

AGER, C.L. & COLE, C.L. (1991). A review of cognitive-behavioral interventions for children and adolescents with behavioral disorders. Behavioral Disorders. 16(4), 260-275.

AIKEN, L.R. (1985). Psychological Testing and Assessment (5th ed.) Boston: Allyn and Bacon.

ALBERTO, P.A. & TROUTHMAN, A.C. (1990). Applied Behavior Analysis for Teachers: Influencing Students Performance. Columbus, Ohio: Charles E. Merrill.

ALGOZZINE, B. (1990) Behavior Problem Management. Educator's Resource Service. Gaithersburg, MD: Aspen Publishers.

ALGOZZINE, B., RUHL, K., 7 RAMSEY, R. (1991). Behaviorally Disordered? Assessment for Identification and Instruction CED Mini-library. Renson, VA: The Council for Exceptional Children.

AMBRON, S.R. (1981. Child Development (3rd ed.). New York: Holt, Rinehart and Winston.

ANERSON, V., & BLACK, L. (Eds.). (1987, Winter). National news: U.S. Department of Education releases special report (Editorial). GLRS Journal [Georgia Learning Resources System].

ANGUILI, r. (1987, Winter). The 1986 Amendment to the Education of the Handicapped Act. Confederation [A quarterly publication of the Georgia Federation Council for Exceptional Children].

ASHLOCK, R.B. (1976). Error Patterns in Computation: A Semi-programmed Approach (2nd ed.). Columbus, Ohio: Charles E. Merrill.

ASSOCIATION OF RETARDED CITIZENS OF GEORGIA (1987). 1986-87 Government Report. College Park, GA: Author.

AUSUBEL, D.P. & SULLIVAN, E.V. (1970) Theory and Problems of Child Development. New York: Grune & Stratton.

BANKS, J.A., & McGee Banks, C.A. (1993). Multicultural Education (2nd ed.). Boston: Allyn and Bacon.

BARRETT, T.C. (Ed.). (1967). The Evaluation of Children's Reading Achievement. In Perspectives in Reading No. 8. Newark, Delaware: International Reading Association.

BARTOLI, J.S. (1989). An ecological response to Cole's interactivity alternative. Journal of Learning Disabilities, 22(5). 292-297.

BASILE-JACKSON, J. The Exceptional Child in the Regular Classroom. Augusta, GA: East Georgia Center, Georgia Learning Resources System.

BAUER, A.M., & SHEA, T.M. (1989). Teaching Exceptional Students in Your Classroom. Boston: Allyn and Bacon.

BENTLEY, E.L. Jr. (1980). Questioning Skills [Videocassette & manual series]. Northbrook, IL. Hubbard Scientific Company. (Project STRETCH [Strategies to Train Regular Educators to Teach Children with Handicaps]. Module 1. ISBN 0-8331-1906-0).

BERDINE, W.H. & BLACKHURST, A.E. (1985). An Introduction to Special Education. (2nd ed.) Boston: Little, Brown and Company.

BLAKE, K. (1976). The Mentally Retarded: An Educational Pschology. Englewood Cliff, NJ: Prentice-Hall.

BOHLINE, D.S. (1985). Intellectual and Affective Characteristics of Attention Deficit Disordered Children. Journal of Learning Disabilities. 18 (10). 604-608.

BOONE, R. (1983). Legislation and litigation. In R.E. Schmid, & L. Negata (Eds.). Contemporary Issues in Special Education. New York: McGraw Hill.

BRANTLINGER, E.A., & GUSKIN, S.L. (1988). Implications of social and cultural differences for special education. In Meten, E.L. Vergason, G.A., & Whelan, R.J. Effective Instructional Strategies for Exceptional Children. Denver, CO: Love Publishing.

BREWTON, B. (1990). Preliminary identification of the socially maladjusted. In Georgia Psycho-educational Network, Monograph #1. An Educational Perspective On: Emotional Disturbance and Social Maladjustment. Atlanta, GA Psychoeducational Network.

BROLIN, D.E. & KOKASKA, C.J. (1979). Career Education for Handicapped Children Approach. Renton, VA: The Council for Exceptional Children.

BROLIN, D.E. (Ed). (1989) Life Centered Career Education: A Competency Based Approach. Reston, VA: The Council for Exceptional Children.

BROWN, J.W., LEWIS, R.B., & HARCLEROAD, F.F. (1983). AV instruction: Technology, Media, and Methods (6TH ED.). New York: McGraw-Hill.

BRYAN, T.H., & BRYAN, J.H. (1986). Understanding Learning Disabilities (3rd ed.). Palo Alto, CA: Mayfield.

BRYEN, D.N. (1982). Inquiries Into Child Language. Boston: Allyn & Bacon.

BUCHER, B.D. (1987). Winning Them Over. New York: Times Books.

BUSH, W.L., & WAUGH, K.W. (1982). Diagnosing Learning Problems (3rd ed.) Columbus, OH: Charles E. Merrill.

CAMPBELL, P. (1986). Special Needs Report [Newsletter]. 1(1). 1-3.

CARBO, M., & DUNN, K. (1986). Teaching Students to Read Through Their Individual Learning Styles. Englewood Cliffs, NJ. Prentice Hall.

CARTWRIGHT, G.P. & CARTWRIGHT, C.A., & WARD, M.E. (1984). Educating Special Learners (2nd ed.). Belmont, CA: Wadsworth.

CEJKA, J.M. (Consultant), & NEEDHAM, F. (Senior Editor). (1976). Approaches to Mainstreaming. [Filmstrip and cassette kit, units 1 & 2]. Boston: Teaching Resources Corporation. (Catalog Nos. 09-210 & 09-220).

CHALFANT, J. C. (1985). Identifying Learning Disabled Students: A Summary of the National Task Force Report. Learning Disabilities Focus. 1, 9-20.

CHARLES, C.M. (1976). Individualizing Instructions. St Louis: The C.V. Mosby Company.

CHRISPEELS, J.H. (1991). District Leadership in Parent Involvement - Policies and Actions in Sand Diego. Phi Delta Kappa, 71, 367-371.

CLARIZIO, H.F. (1987). Differentiating Characteristics. In Georgia Psychoeducational Network, Monograph #1, An educational Perspective on: Emotional Disturbance and Social Maladjustment. Atlanta, GA Psychoeducational Network.

CLARIZIO, H.F. & MCCOY, G.F. (1983) Behavior Disorders in Children (3rd ed.). New York: Harper & Row.]

COLES, G.S. (1989). Excerpts from The Learning Mystique: A Critical Look at Disabilities. Journal of Learning Disabilities. 22 (5). 267-278.

COLLINS, E. (1980). Grouping and Special Students. [Videocassette & manual series]. Northbrook, IL: Hubbard Scientific Company. (Project STRETCH [Strategies to Train Regular Educators to Teach Children with Handicaps], Module 17, ISBN 0- 8331-1922-2).

CRAIG, E., & CRAIG, L. (1990). Reading In the Content Areas [Videocassette & manual series]. Northbrook, IL: Hubbard Scientific Company. (Project STRETCH [Strategies to Train Regular Educators to Teach Children with Handicaps].Module 13, ISBN 0-8331-1918-4).

COMPTON, C., (1984). A Guide to 75 Tests for Special Education. Belmont, CA., Pitman Learning.

COUNCIL FOR EXCEPTIONAL CHILDREN. (1976). Introducing P.L. 94-142. [Filmstrip-cassette kit manual]. Reston, VA: Author.

COUNCIL FOR EXCEPTIONAL CHILDREN. (1987). The Council for Exceptional Children's Fall 1987. Catalog of Products and Services. Renton, VA: Author.

COUNCIL FOR EXCEPTIONAL CHILDREN DELEGATE ASSEMBLY. (1983). Council for Exceptional Children Code of Ethics (Adopted April 1983). Reston, VA: Author.

CZAJKA, J.L. (1984). Digest of Data on Person With Disabilities (Mathematics Policy Research, Inc.). Washington, D.C.: U.S. Government Printing Office.

DELL, H.D. (1972). Individualizing Instruction: Materials and Classroom Procedures. Chicago: Science Research Associates.

DEMONBREUN, C., & MORRIS, J. Classroom Management [Videocassette & Manual series]. Northbrook, IL: Hubbard Scientific Company. Project STRETCH (Strategies to Train Regular Educators to Teach Children with Handicaps]. Module 5, ISBN 0-8331-1910-9).

DEPARTMENT OF EDUCATION. Education for the Handicapped Law Reports. Supplement 45 (1981), p. 102: 52. Washington, D.C.: U.S. Government Printing Office.

DEPARTMENT OF HEALTH, EDUCATION AND WELFARE, OFFICE OF EDUCATION. (1977, August 23). Education of Handicapped Children. Federal Register, 42, (163).

DIANA VS. STATE BOARD OF EDUCATION, Civil No. 70-37 R.F.P. (N.D.Cal. January, 1970).

DIGANGI, S.A., PERRYMAN, P., & RUTHERFORD, R.B., Jr. (1990). Juvenile Offenders in the 90's A Descriptive Analysis. Perceptions, 25(4), 5-8.

DIVISION OF EDUCATIONAL SERVICES, SPECIAL EDUCATION PROGRAMS (1986). Fifteenth Annual Report to Congress on Implementation of the Education of the Handicapped Act. Washington, D.C.: U.S. Government Printing Office.

DOYLE, B.A. (1978). Math Readiness Skills. Paper presented at National Association of School Psychologists, New York. K.J. (1978). Teaching Students Through Their Individual Learning Styles.

DUNN, R.S., & DUNN, K.J. (1978). Teaching Students Through Their Individual Learning Styles: A Practical Approach. Reston, VA: Reston.

EPSTEIN, M.H., PATTON, J.R., POLLOWAY, E.A., & FOLEY, R. (1989). Mild retardation: Student characteristics and services. Education and Training of the Mentally Retarded, 24, 7-16.

EKWALL, E.E., & SHANKER, J.L. 1983). Diagnosis and Remediation of the Disabled Reader (2nd ed.) Boston: Allyn and Bacon.

FIRTH, E.E. & REYNOLDS, I. (1983). Slide tape shows: A creative activity for the gifted students. Teaching Exceptional Children. 15(3), 151-153.
FRYMIER, J., & GANSNEDER, B. (1989). The Phi Delta Kappa Study of Students at Risk. Phi Delta Kappa. 71(2) 142-146.

FUCHS, D., & DENO, S.L. 1992). Effects of curriculum within curriculum-based measurement. Exceptional Children 58 (232-242).

FUCHS, D., & FUCHS, L.S. (1989). Effects of examiner familiarity on Black, Caucasian, and Hispanic Children. A Meta-Analysis. Exceptional Children. 55, 303-308.

FUCHS, L.S., & SHINN, M.R. (1989). Writing CBM IEP objectives. In M.R. Shinn, Curriculum-based Measurement: Assessing Special Students. New York: Guilford Press.

GAGE, N.L. (1990). Dealing With the Dropout Problems? Phi Delta Kappa. 72(4), 280-285.

GALLAGHER, P.A. (1988). Teaching Students with Behavior Disorders: Techniques and Activities for Classroom Instruction (2nd ed.). Denver, CO: Love Publishing.

GEARHEART, B.R. (1980). Special Education for the 80s. St. Louis, MO: The C.V. Cosby Company.

GEARHART, B.R. & WEISHAHN, M.W. (1986). The Handicapped Student in the Regular Classroom (2nd ed.). St Louis, MO: The C.V. Mosby Company.

GEARHART, B.R. (1985). <u>Learning Disabilities: Educational Strategies</u> (4th ed.). St. Louis: Times Mirror/ Mosby College of Publishing.

GEORGIA DEPARTMENT OF EDUCATION, PROGRAM FOR EXCEPTIONAL CHILDREN. (1986). <u>Mild Mentally Handicapped</u> (Vol. II), Atlanta, GA: Office of Instructional Services, Division of Special Programs, and Program for Exceptional Children. Resource Manuals for Program for Exceptional Children.

GEORGIA DEPARTMENT OF HUMAN RESOURCES, DIVISION OF REHABILITATION SERVICES. (1987, February). Request for Proposal [Memorandum]. Atlanta, GA: Author.

GEORGIA PSYCHOEDUCATIONAL NETWORK (1990). <u>An Educational Perspective on: Emotional Disturbance and Social Maladjustment.</u> Monograph #1. Atlanta, GA Psychoeducational Network.

GEREN, K. (1979). <u>Complete Special Education Handbook.</u> West Nyack, NY: Parker.

GILLET, P.K. (1988). Career Development. Robinson, G.A., Patton, J.R., Polloway, E.A., & Sargent, L.R. (eds.). <u>Best Practices in Mild Mental Disabilities.</u> Reston, VA: The Division on Mental Retardation of the Council for Exceptional Children.

GLEASON, J.B. (1993). <u>The Development of Language</u> (3rd ed.). New York: Macmillan Publishing.

GOOD, T.L., & BROPHY, J.E. (1978). <u>Looking into Classrooms</u> (2nd Ed.). New York: Harper & Row.

HALL, M.A. (1979). Language-Centered Reading: Premises and Recommendations. <u>Language Arts, 56</u> 664-670.

HALLLAHAN, D.P. & KAUFFMAN, J.M. (1988). <u>Exceptional Children: Introduction to Special Education.</u> (4th Ed.). Englewood Cliffs, NJ; Prentice-Hall.

HALLAHAN, D.P. & KAUFFMAN, J.M. (1994). <u>Exceptional Children: Introduction to Special Education</u> 6th ed.). Boston: Allyn and Bacon.

HAMMILL, D.D., & BARTEL, N.R. (1982). <u>Teaching Children With Learning and Behavior Problems</u> (3rd ed.). Boston: Allyn and Bacon.

HAMMILL, D.D., & BARTEL, N.R. (1986). <u>Teaching Students with Learning and Behavior Problems</u> (4th ed.). Boston and Bacon.

HAMILL, D.D., & BROWN, L. & BRYANT, B. (1989) A Consumer's Guide to Tests in Print. Austin, TX: Pro-Ed.

HANEY, J.B. & ULLMER, E.J. ((1970). Educational Media and the Teacher. Dubuque, IA: Wm. C. Brown Company.

HARDMAN, M.L., DREW, C.J., EGAN, M.W., & WOLF, B. (1984). Human Exceptionality: Society, School, and Family. Boston: Allyn and Bacon.

HARDMAN, M.L., DREW, C.J., EGAN, M.W., & WORLF, B. (1990). Human Exceptionality (3rd ed.). Boston: Allyn and Bacon.

HARGROVE, L.J., & POTEET, J.A. (1984). Assessment in Special Education. Englewood Cliffs, NJ: Prentice-Hall.

HARING, N.G., & BATEMAN, B. (1977). Teaching the Learning Disabled Child. Englewood Cliffs, NJ: Prentice-Hall.

HARRIS, K.R., & PRESSLEY, M. (1991). The Nature of Cognitive Strategy Instruction: Interactive strategy instruction. Exceptional Children, 57, 392-401.

HART, T., & CADORA, M.J. (1980). The Exceptional Child: Label the Behavior [Videocassette & manual series], Northbrook, IL: Hubbard Scientific Company. (Project STRETCH [Strategies to Train Regular Educators to Teach Children with Handicaps], Module 12, ISBN 0-8331-1917-6). HART, V. (1981) Mainstreaming Children with Special Needs. New York: Longman.

HENLEY, M., RAMSEY,R.S., & ALGOZZINE, B. (1993). Characteristics of and Strategies for Teaching Students with Mild Disabilities. Boston: Allyn and Bacon.

HEWETT, F.M., & FORNESS, S.R. (1984). Education of Exceptional Learners. (3rd ed.). Boston: Allyn and Bacon.

HOWE, C.E. (1981) Administration of Special Education. Denver: Love.

HUMAN SERVICES RESEARCH INSTITUTE (1985). Summary of Data on Handicapped Children and Youth. (Digest). Washington, D.C.: U.S. Government Printing Office.

JOHNSON, D.W. (1972) Reaching Out: Interpersonal Effectiveness and Self-Actualization. Englewood Cliffs, NJ: Prentice-Hall.

JOHNSON, D.W. (1978) Human Relations and Your Career: A Guide to Interpersonal Skills. Englewood Cliffs, NJ: Prentice-Hall.

JOHNSON, D.W., & JOHNSON, R.T. (1990). Social Skills for Successful Group Work. Educational Leadership. 47 (4) 29-33.

JOHNSON, S.W., & MORASKY, R.L. Learning Disabilities (2nd ed.) Boston: Allyn and Bacon.

JONES, F.H. (1987). Positive Classroom Discipline. New York: McGraw-Hill Book Company.

JONES, V.F., & JONES, L. S. (1986). Comprehensive Classroom Management: Creating Positive Learning Environments. (2nd ed.). Boston: Allyn and Bacon.

JONES, V.F. & JONES, L.S. (1981). Responsible Classroom Discipline: Creating Positive Learning Environments and Solving Problems. Boston: Allyn and Bacon.

KAUFFMAN, J.M. (1981) Characteristics of Children's Behavior Disorders. (2nd ed.). Columbus, OH: Charles E. Merrill.

KAUFFMAN, J.M. (1989). Characteristics of Behavior Disorders of Children and Youth. (4th ed.). Columbus, OH: Merrill Publishing.

KEM, M., & NELSON, M. (1983). Strategies for Managing Behavior Problems in the Classroom. Columbus, OH: Charles E. Merrill.

KERR, M.M., & NELSON, M. (1983) Strategies for Managing Behavior Problems in the Classroom. Columbus, OH: Charles E. Merrill.

KIRK, S.A., & GALLAGHER, J.J. (1986). Educating Exceptional Children (5th ed.). Boston: Houghton Mifflin.

KOHFELDT, J. (1976). Blueprints for construction. Focus on Exceptional Children. 8 (5), 1-14.

KOKASKA, C.J., & BROLIN, D.E. (1985). Career Education for Handicapped Individuals (2nd ed.). Columbus, OH: Charles E. Merrill.

LAMBIE, R.A. (1980). A systematic approach for changing materials, instruction, and assignments to meet individual needs. Focus on Exceptional Children, 13(1), 1-12.

LARSON, S.C., & POPLIN, M.S. (1980). Methods for Educating the Handicapped: An Individualized Education Program Approach. Boston: Allyn and Bacon.

LERNER, J. (1976) Children with Learning Disabilities. (2nd ed.). Boston: Houghton Mifflin.

LERNER, J. (1989). Learning Disabilities,: Theories, Diagnosis and Teaching Strategies (3rd ed.). Boston: Houghton Mifflin.

LEVENKRON, S. (1991). Obsessive-Compulsive Disorders. New York: Warner Books.

LEWIS, R.B., & DOORLAG, D.H. (1991). Teaching Special Students in the Mainstream. (3rd ed.). New York: Merrill.

LINDSLEY, O. R. (1990). Precision Teaching: By Teachers for Children. Teaching Exceptional Children, 22. (3), 10-15.

LINDDBERG, L., & SWEDLOW, R. (1985). Young Children Exploring and Learning. Boston: Allyn and Bacon.

LONG, N.J., MORSE, W.C., & NEWMAN, R.G. (1980). Conflict in the Classroom: The Education of Emotionally Disturbed Children. Belmont, CA: Wadsworth.

LOSEN, S.M., & LOSEN, J.G. (1985). The Special Education Team. Boston: Allyn and Bacon.

LOVITT, T.C. (1989). Introduction to Learning Disabilities. Boston: Allyn and Bacon.

LUND, N.J. * DUCHAN, J.F. (1988)/ Assessing Children's Language in Naturalist Contexts. Englewood Cliffs, NJ: Prentice Hall

MALE, M. (1994) Technology for Inclusion: Meeting the Special Needs of all Children. (2nd ed.). Boston: Allyn and Bacon.

MANDELBAUM, L.H. (1989). Reading. In G.A. Robinson, J.R., Patton, E.A., Polloway, & L.R. Sargent (eds.). Best Practices in Mild Mental Retardation. Reston, VA: The Division of Mental Retardation, Council for Exceptional Children.

MANNIX. D. (1993). Social Skills for Special Children. West Nyack, NY: The Center for Applied Research in Education.

MARSHALL, ET AL, VS. GEORGIA U.S. District court for the Southern District of Georgia. C.V. 482-233. June 28, 1984.

MARSHALL, E.K., KURTZ, P.D., & ASSOCIATES. Interpersonal Helping Skills. San Francisco, CA: Jossey-Bass Publications.

MARSTON, D.B. (1989) A curriculum-based measurement approach to assessing academic performance: What it is and why do it. In M. Shinn (Ed.). Curriculum-Based Measurement: Assessing Special Children. New York: Guilford Press.

MCDOWELL, R.L., ADAMSON, G.W., & WOOD, F.H. (1982). Teaching Emotionally Disturbed Children. Boston: Little, Brown and Company. MCGINNIS, E., GOLDSTEIN, A.P. (1990). Skill Streaming in Early

Childhood: Teaching Prosocial Skills to the Preschool and Kindergarten Child. Champaign, IL: Research Press.

MCLOUGHLIN, J.A., & LEWIS, R.B. (1986). Assessing Special Students (3rd ed.). Columbus, OH: Charles E. Merrill.

MERCER, C.D. (1987). Students with Learning Disabilities. (3rd. ed.). Merrill Publishing.

MERCER, C.D., & MERCER, A.R. (1985). Teaching Children with Learning Problems (2nd ed.). Columbus, OH: Charles E. Merrill.

MEYEN, E.L., VERGASON, G.A., & WHELAN, R.J. (Eds.). (1988). Effective Instructional Strategies for Exceptional Children. Denver, CO: Love Publishing.

MILLER, L.K. (1980). Principles of Everyday Behavior Analysis (2nd ed.). Monterey, CA: Brooks/Cole Publishing Company. MILLS VS. THE BOARD OF EDUCATON OF THE DISTRICT OF COLUMBIA, 348F. Supp. 866 (D.C. 1972).

MOPSICK, S.L. & AGARD, J.A. (Eds.) (1980). Cambridge, MA: Abbott Associates.

MORRIS, C.G. (1985). Psychology: An Introduction (5th ed.). Englewood Cliffs, NJ: Prentice-Hall.

MORRIS, J. (1980). Behavior Modification. [Videocassette and manual series]. Northbrook, IL: Hubbard Scientific Company. (Project STRETCH [Strategies to Train Regular Educators to Teach Children with Handicaps,] Module 16, Metropolitan Cooperative Educational Service Agency.). MORRIS, J. & DEMONBREUN, C. (1980). Learning Styles [Videocassettes & Manual series]. Northbrook, IL: Hubbard Scientific Company. (Project STRETCH [Strategies to Train Regular Educators to Teach Children with Handicaps], Module 15, ISBN 0-8331-1920-6).

MORRIS, R.J. (1985). Behavior Modification with Exceptional Children: Principles and Practices. Glenview, IL: Scott, Foresman and Company.

MORSINK, C.V. (1984). Teaching Special Needs Students in Regular Classrooms. Boston: Little, Brown and Company.

MORSINK, C.V., THOMAS, C.C., & CORREA, V.L. (1991). Interactive Teaming, Consultation and Collaboration in Special Programs. New York: MacMillan Publishing.

MULLSEWHITE, C.R. (1986). Adaptive Play for Special Needs Children: Strategies to Enhance Communication and Learning. San Diego: College Hill Press.

NORTH CENTRAL GEORGIA LEARNING RESOURCES SYSTEM/CHILD SERVE. (1985). Strategies Handbook for Classroom Teachers. Ellijay, GA.

PATTON, J.R., CRONIN, M.E., POLLOWAY, E.A., HUTCHINSON, D., & ROBINSON, G.A. (1988). Curricular considerations: A life skills orientation. In Robinson, G.A., Patton, J.R., Polloway, E.A., & Sargent, L.R. (Eds.). Best Practices in Mental Disabilities. Des Moines, IA: Iowa Department of Education, Bureau of Special Education.

PATTON, J.R., KAUGGMAN, J.M., BLACKBOURN, J.M., & BROWN, B.G. (1991). Exceptional Children in Focus (5th ed.). New York: MacMillan.

PAUL, J.L. (Ed.). (1981). Understanding and Working with parents of Children with Special Needs. New York: Holt, Rinehart and Winston.

PAUL, J.L. & EPANCHIN, B.C. (1991). Educating Emotionally Disturbed Children and Youth: Theories and Practices for Teachers. (2nd ed.). New York: MacMillan. PENNSYLVANIA ASSOCIATION FOR RETARDED CHILDREN VS. COMMONWEALTH OF PENNSYLVANIA, 334 F. Supp. 1257 (E.D., PA., 1971), 343 F. Supp. 279 (L.D. PA., 19972).

PHILLIPS, V., & MCCULLOUGH, L. (1990). Consultation based programming: Instituting the Collaborative Work Ethic. Exceptional Children. 56 (4), 291-304.

PODEMSKI, R.S., PRICE, B.K., SMITH, T.E.C., & MARSH, G.E., IL (1984). Comprehensive Administration of Special Education. Rockville, MD: Aspen Systems Corporation.

POLLOWAY, E.A., & PATTON, J.R. (1989). Strategies for Teaching Learners with Special Needs. (5th ed.). New York: Merrill.

POLLOWAY, E.A., PATTON, J.R., PAYNE, J.S., & PAYNE, R.A. 1989). Strategies for Teaching Learners with Special Needs, 4th ed.). Columbus, OH: Merrill Publishing.

PUGACH, M.C., & JOHNSON, L.J. (1989a). The challenge of implementing collaboration between general and special education. Exceptional Children, 56 (3), 232-235.

PUGACH, M.C., & JOHNSON, L.J. (1989b). Pre-referral interventions: Progress, Problems, and Challenges. Exceptional Children, 56 (3), 217-226.

RADABAUGH, M.T., & YUKISH, J.F. (1982). Curriculum and Methods for the Mildly Handicapped. Boston: Allyn and Bacon.

RAMSEY, R.S. (1981). Perceptions of disturbed and disturbing behavioral characteristics by school personnel. (Doctoral Dissertation, University of Florida) Dissertation Abstracts International, 42(49), DA8203709.

RAMSEY, R.S. (1986). Taking the practicum beyond the public school door. Journal of Adolescence. 21(83), 547-552.

RAMSEY, R.S., (1988). Preparatory Guide for Special Education Teacher competency Tests. Boston: Allyn and Bacon, Inc.

RAMSEY, R.S., DIXON, M.J., & SMITH, G.G.B. (1986) Eyes on the Special Education: Professional Knowledge Teacher Competency Test. Albany, GA: Southwest Georgia Learning Resources System Center.

RAMSEY R.W., & RAMSEY, R.S. (1978). Educating the emotionally handicapped child   in the public school setting. Journal of Adolescence. 13(52), 537-541.

REINHEART, H.R. (1980). Children I Conflict: Educational Strategies for the Emotionally Disturbed and Behaviorally Disordered. (2nd ed.). St Louis, MO: The C.V. Mosby Company.

ROBINSON, G.A., PATTON, J.R., POLLOWAY, E.A., & SARGENT, L.R. (Eds.). (1989a). Best Practices in Mental Disabilities. Des Moines, IA Iowa Department   of Education, Bureau of Special Education.

ROBINSON, G.A., PATTON, J.R., POLLOWAY, E.A., & SARGENT, L.R. (Eds.). (1989b). Best Practices in Mental Disabilities. Renton, VA: The Division on Mental Retardation of the Council for Exceptional Children.

ROTHSTEIN, L.F. (1995). Special education Law (2nd ed.). New York: Longman Publishers.

SABATINO, D.A., SABATION, A.C., & MANN, L. (1983). Management: A Handbook of Tactics, Strategies, and Programs. Aspen Systems Corporation.

SALVIA, J., & YSSELDYKE, J.E. (1985). Assessment in Special Education (3rd. ed.). Boston: Houghton Mifflin.

SALVIA J., & YSSELDYKE, J.E. (1991). Assessment (5th ed.). Boston: Houghton Mifflin.

SALVIA, J. & YSSELDYKE, J.E. (1995) Assessment (6th ed.). Boston: Houghton Mifflin.

SATTLER, J.M. (1982). Assessment of Children's Intelligence and Special Abilities (2nd ed.). Boston: Allyn and Bacon.

SCHLOSS, P.J., HARRIMAN, N., & PFIEFER, K. (in press). Application of a sequential prompt reduction technique to the independent composition performance of behaviorally disordered youth. Behavioral Disorders.

SCHLOSS, P.J.., & SEDLAK, R.A.(1986). Instructional Methods for Students with Learning and Behavior Problems. Boston: Allyn and Bacon.

SCHMUCK, R.A., & SCHMUCK, P.A. (1971). Group Processes in the Classroom. Dubuque, IA: William C. Brown Company.

SCHUBERT, D.G. (1978). Your teaching - the tape recorder. Reading Improvement, 15(1), 78-80.

SCHULZ, J.B., CARPENTER, C.D., & TURNBULL, A.P. (1991). Mainstreaming Exceptional Students: A Guide for Classroom Teachers. Boston: Allyn and Bacon.

SEMMEL, M.I., ABERNATHY, T.V., BUTERA G., & LESAR, S. (1991). Teacher perception of the regular education initiative. Exceptional Children, 58 (1), 3-23.

SHEA, T.M., & BAUER, A.M. (1985). Parents and Teachers of Exceptional Students: A Handbook for Involvement. Boston: Allyn and Bacon.

SIMEONSSON, R.J. (1986). Psychological and Development Assessment of Special Children. Boston: Allyn and Bacon.

SMITH, C.R. (1991). Learning Disabilities: The Interaction of Learner, Task, and Setting. Boston: Little, Brown, and Company.

SMITH, D.D., & LUCKASSON, R. (1992). Introduction to Special Education: Teaching in an Age of Challenge. Boston: Allyn and Bacon.

SMITH, J.E., & PATTON, J.M. (1989). A Resource Module on Adverse Causes of Mild Mental Retardation. (Prepared for the President's Committee on Mental Retardation).

SMITH, T.E.C., FINN, D.M., & DOWDY, C.A. (1993). Teaching Students With Mild Disabilities. Fort Worth, TX: Harcourt Brace Jovanovich College Publishers.

SMITH-DAVIS, J. (1989a April). A National Perspective on Special Education. Keynote presentation at the GLRS/College/University Forum, Macon, GA.

STEPHENS, T.M. (1976). Directive Teaching of Children with Learning and Behavioral Disorders. Columbus, OH Charles E. Merrill.

STERNBURG, R.J. (1990). Thinking Styles: Key to Understanding Performance. Phi Delta Kappa, 71(5), 366-371.

SULZER, B., & MAYER, G.R. (1972). Behavior Modification Procedures for School Personnel. Hinsdale, IL: Dryden.

TATEYAMA-SNIEZEK, K.M. (1990.) Cooperative Learning: Does it improve the academic achievement of students with handicaps? Exceptional Children, 57(2), 426-427.

THIAGARAJAN, S. (1976). Designing instructional games for handicapped learners. Focus on Exceptional Children. 7(9), 1-11.

THOMAS, O. (1980). Individualized Instruction [Videocassette & manual series]. Northbrook, IL: Hubbard Scientific Company. (Project STRETCH [Strategies to Train Regular Educators to Teach Children with Handicaps]. Module 14, ISBN 0- 8331-1919-2).

THOMAS, O. (1980). Spelling [Videocassette & manual series]. (Project STRETCH [Strategies to Train Regular Educators to Teach Children with Handicaps]. Module 10, ISBN 0-83311915-X).

THORNTON, C.A., TUCKER, B.F., DOSSEY, J.A., & BAZIK, E.F. (1983). Teaching Mathematics to Children with Special Needs. Menlo Park, CA: Addison-Wesley.

TURKEL, S.R., & PODEL, D.M. (1984). Computer-assisted learning for mildly handicapped students. Teaching Exceptional Children. 16(4), 258-262.

TURNBULL, A.P., STRICKLAND, B.B., & BRANTLEY, J.C. (1978). Developing Individualized Education Programs. Columbus, OH: Charles E. Merrill.

U.S. DEPARTMENT OF EDUCATION. (1993). To Assure the Free Appropriate Public Education of all Children with Disabilities. (Fifteenth annual report to Congress on the Implementation of The Individuals with Disabilities Education Act.). Washington, D.C.

WALKER, J.E., & SHEA, T.M. (1991). Behavior Management: A Practical Approach for Educators. New York: MacMillan.

WALLACE, G., & KAUFFMAN, J.M. (1978). Teaching Children with Learning Problems. Columbus, OH: Charles E. Merrill.

WEHMAN, P., & MCLAUGHLIN, P.J. (1981). Program Development in Special Education. New York: McGraw-Hill.

WEINTRAUB, F.J. (1987, March). [Interview].

WESSON, C.L. (1991). Curriculum-based measurement and two models of follow-up consultation. Exceptional Children. 57(3), 246-256.

WEST, R.P., YOUNG, K.R., & SPOONER, F. (1990). Precision Teaching: An Introduction. Teaching Exceptional Children. 22(3), 4-9.

WHEELER, J. (1987). Transitioning Persons with Moderate and Severe Disabilities from School to Adulthood: What Makes it Work? Materials Development Center, School of Education, and Human Services. University of Wisconsin-Stout.

WHITING, J., & AULTMAN, L. (1990). Workshop for Parents. (Workshop materials). Albany, GA: Southwest Georgia Learning Resources System Center.

WIEDERHOLT, J.L., HAMMILL, D.D., & BROWN, V.L. (1983). The Resource Room Teacher: A Guide to Effective Practices (2nd ed.). Boston: Allyn and Bacon.

WIIG, E.H., & SEMEL, E.M. (1984). Language Assessment and Intervention for the Learning Disabled. (2nd ed.). Columbus, OH: Charles E. Merrill.

WOLFGANG, C.H., & GLICKMAN, C.D.(1986). Solving Discipline Problems: Strategies for Classroom Teachers (2nd ed.). Boston: Allyn and Bacon.

YSSELKYKE, J.E., ALGOZZINE, B., (1990). Introduction to Special Education (2nd ed.). Boston: Houghton Mifflin.

YSSELDYKE, J.E., ALGOZZINE, B., & THURLOW, M.L. (1992). Critical Issues in Special Education (2nd ed.). Boston: Houghton Mifflin Company.

YSSEDLYKE, J.E., THURLOW, M.L., WOTRUBA, J.W., NANIA, PA.A (1990). Instructional arrangements: Perceptions From General Education. Teaching Exceptional Children, 22(4), 4-8.

ZARGONA, N., VAUGHN, S., 7 MCINTOSH, R. (1991). Social Skills Interventions and children with behavior problems: A review. <u>Behavior Disorders, 16</u>(4), 260-275.

ZIGMOND, N., & BAKER, J. (1990). Mainstream experiences for learning disabled students (Project Meld): Preliminary report. <u>Exceptional Children, 57</u>(2), 176-185.

ZIRPOLI, T.J., & MELLOY, K.J. (1993). <u>Behavior Management.</u> New York: Merrill.

XAMonline, INC. 21 Orient Ave. Melrose, MA 02176

Toll Free number 800-509-4128

TO ORDER Fax 781-662-9268 OR www.XAMonline.com

MICHIGAN TEST FOR TEACHER EXAMINATION - MTTC - 2007

PO#   Store/School:

Address 1:

Address 2 (Ship to other):

City, State Zip

Credit card number_____-_____-_____-_____   expiration_____

EMAIL _____

PHONE   **FAX**

13# ISBN 2007	TITLE	Qty	Retail	Total
978-1-58197-968-8	MTTC Basic Skills 96			
978-1-58197-954-1	MTTC Biology 17			
978-1-58197-955-8	MTTC Chemistry 18			
978-1-58197-957-2	MTTC Earth-Space Science 20			
978-1-58197-966-4	MTTC Elementary Education 83			
978-1-58197-967-1	MTTC Elementary Education 83 Sample Questions			
978-1-58197-950-3	MTTC English 02			
978-1-58197-961-9	MTTC Family and Consumer Sciences 40			
978-1-58197-959-6	MTTC French Sample Test 23			
978-1-58197-965-7	MTTC Guidance Counselor 51			
978-1-58197-964-0	MTTC Humanities& Fine Arts 53, 54			
978-1-58197-972-5	MTTC Integrated Science (Secondary) 94			
978-1-58197-973-2	MTTC Emotionally Impaired 59			
978-1-58197-953-4	MTTC Learning Disabled 63			
978-1-58197-963-3	MTTC Library Media 48			
978-1-58197-958-9	MTTC Mathematics (Secondary) 22			
978-1-58197-962-6	MTTC Physical Education 44			
978-1-58197-956-5	MTTC Physics Sample Test 19			
978-1-58197-952-7	MTTC Political Science 10			
978-1-58197-951-0	MTTC Reading 05			
978-1-58197-960-2	MTTC Spanish 28			
978-158197-970-1	MTTC Social Studies 84			
			SUBTOTAL	
FOR PRODUCT PRICES GO TO **WWW.XAMONLINE.COM**			**Ship**	$8.25
			TOTAL	

LaVergne, TN USA
30 April 2010
181090LV00001B/25/A